The Saint of Kathmandu

THE SAINT OF KATHMANDU

and Other Tales of the

Sacred in Distant Lands

SARAH LEVINE

BEACON PRESS
Boston

Beacon Press
Boston, Massachusetts
www.beacon.org

Beacon Press books are published under the auspices of
the Unitarian Universalist Association of Congregations.

Printed in the United States of America
24 23 22 21   8 7 6 5 4 3 2

This book is printed on acid-free paper that meets the uncoated
paper ANSI/NISO specifications for permanence as revised in 1992.

Text design and composition by Susan E. Kelly
at Wilsted & Taylor Publishing Services

Library of Congress Cataloging-in-Publication Data

LeVine, Sarah
    The Saint of Kathmandu : and other tales of the sacred in distant
lands / Sarah LeVine.
      p. cm.
    ISBN 978-0-8070-1313-7 (PBK.)
    1. Women—Religious life. 2. Religions. I. Title.
    BL625.7.L48 2008
    203—dc22   2007045465

Jacket art

Top left: Young pilgrims dressed in Aztec costume on procession
through the cathedral square on a festival day. San Juan de Los Lagos,
Mexico, 1994. Photo by Anna Winger

Top center: Members of the Bori spirit possession cult in trance.
Northern Nigeria, 1969. Photo by Sarah LeVine

Top right: A Muslim chief's wives with the senior wife's five-year-old
ward. Northern Nigeria, 1969. Photo by Sarah LeVine

Bottom: Nepalese nuns circumambulating the tree under which the
Buddha was born. Lumbini, Nepal, 1998. Photo by Sarah LeVine

Back cover: Looking toward Lake Victoria, western Kenya, 1976.
Photo by Sarah LeVine

This book is for Nina Murray,
and in memory of Judy Gardner,
with affection and gratitude.

Contents

Preface

As an anthropologist, I ask a lot of questions; and I get asked a lot of questions too. In November 2006, I spent a whole day in the house of Jayalakshmi, a South Indian village woman belonging to a low Hindu caste. I chatted with her, her husband, her mother-in-law, and her five best friends, watched her children play, quarrel, and make peace, asked everyone questions, wrote many pages of notes, nodded off in the afternoon heat, woke up again, and asked more questions. When evening came, I closed my notebook and said to Jayalakshmi, "I've been grilling you. Now it's your turn to grill me," which she was delighted to do.

"How did you get married?" was her first question, and when I explained that no, my parents didn't arrange my marriage, I chose my husband myself, she frowned. "So you had a love marriage. That can happen here too, unfortunately. If a Muslim boy and a girl from our community fall in love, they cannot marry properly so then they elope, and when the girl comes to her husband's house empty-handed her in-laws call her an infidel and treat her badly."

I said that even though my parents hadn't arranged my marriage, I'd had a very nice wedding. I added that though I hadn't brought them a dowry, my in-laws had treated me well. But Jayalakshmi's expression showed that she didn't believe me.

"Do you and your husband own the house you live in, or do you rent, just as we do?" was her second question. When I replied that we owned our house, quick as a whip she said, "If you're rich, why don't you wear more gold?" Picking up my left hand, she examined my wedding ring, which had cost ten dollars in a cut-rate jewelry store almost forty years ago. "It's too narrow!" With a disdainful glance at my faded Gap pants and hand-loomed Guatemalan shirt, she added, "And why aren't you better dressed?"

"What is your religion?" was her next question.

Whenever I've been asked this, which over the years has happened rather often, I've felt I should come clean and say, "Though I was brought up as an Anglican, there's a lot about the Church of England that I don't agree with." But usually I leave aside the complications, and this time I did too. "I'm a Christian," I said.

I wasn't the first Christian Jayalakshmi had come across—some of her neighbors attended the new Pentecostal church on the far side of the sweepers' ward, beyond where the sweepers, who belonged to the lowest untouchable caste, lived—but she wanted to know more about me and this husband I'd chosen myself. "Is your husband also Christian?"

"In fact he has no religion. He doesn't believe that God exists."

"How is that possible?" Jayalakshmi looked baffled. I was about to explain that he'd grown up in a family of militant atheists and that his relatives, at least those I'd met, appeared to be quite happy, balanced, and moral people; but thinking better of it, I merely shrugged.

"In your country, are there many like your husband?"

"Perhaps not all *that* many," I said, whereupon, reassured, Jayalakshmi started asking me about my children, where they lived, and what they did for a living—a far less perplexing topic than whether or not God exists.

In the 1960s, when I started out as an anthropologist, most of my teachers in the ivory towers where I'd been spending my youth had watched consumerism rise exponentially and church congregations dwindle, and declared that industrialized, bureaucratized, increasingly well-educated Americans were heading in the same direction as rapidly secularizing Europeans. The United States, which, at the beginning of the twentieth century had been organized by notions of God and the sacred, was now ruled, so the theory went, by the power and exigencies of technology. Old ways of understanding and behaving had been rendered obsolete. The sacred canopy had been torn to shreds. As Europe had gone, so was the United States going; and so, as it modernized and *rationalized,* the rest of the world would go.

But the theory has been proved wrong. Though today a new cohort of scientists is once again seeking to demonstrate—just as their intellectual forefathers did a century ago—that religious faith is irrational and belief in God is a delusion, outside Europe, for myriad historical and cultural reasons, most of the world, including the United States, continues to be as furiously religious as ever.

I decided to tell these stories from my many years of fieldwork around the world soon after 9/11, when I realized that many of my sophisticated friends—most of whom, like my husband, were rationalists—found Islamic beliefs and practices just as baffling as I had more than thirty years earlier, when I'd lived in a Muslim community in West Africa. In the days after 9/11, I keenly remembered how, despite my efforts to be an "objective" social scientist, I'd had great difficulty, given my ignorance and largely unexamined prejudices, in developing sympathy for Islam as I encountered it "on the ground." This has sometimes been the case with the religions of other people, including Hindus, Buddhists, and Christians of various persuasions, among whom, in subsequent decades, I've lived and carried out research.

My research has mainly been about how usually poor and often illiterate parents in sub-Saharan Africa, Latin America, and South Asia raise their children, and what Americans might learn from them. My focus has always been on family life: what parents want for their children, how modern schooling helps women take better care of their own and their families' health, and how children are socialized at home and in the community. Under pressure to accomplish as much of my "official" (i.e., funded) assignment as possible in yet another new language, and in what was always too short a time, I have learned about the local religion somewhat haphazardly.

In the narratives that follow, I hope to show how, more by chance than design, I came to make sense of the religious beliefs and practices of a few people to whom I became close in some of the countries where I have worked. With a few notable exceptions, the social science literature hasn't been much help. Most of what I've gleaned has come from hanging out in homes and in churches and temples during religious festivals, from asking patient people what are, in their view, simple-minded questions, and from serendipitous observation. Since my work has been largely with women, more often than not it has been from women that I have learned how religious faith sustains in the face of uncertainties and sorrow, and how it can provide a measure of freedom in societies in which the only escape from male control may be to turn one's back on family life altogether by becoming a courtesan, a labor migrant, or a saint.

As a people, Americans may be as religious as they were forty years ago; but many would hesitate to apply that adjective to themselves. Rather, they are more likely to describe themselves as "spiritual," a word that only came into popular use in the 1960s. As, increasingly, people rejected the moral authority of hierarchy, doctrine, and religious history, mainline Protestantism, together with Catholicism and Judaism, found itself in crisis. But though at midcentury the sacred canopy lay in shreds, the sacred has not only survived, it has thrived. Conceptions of it today center less on the authority of scripture than on personal experience and transformation. Religious affiliation is no longer a matter of birth or upbringing, it is an individual decision; and whatever the decision, it needn't be binding. In our postmodern world, there are no universal truths, only personal perspectives —which tend to shift. The United States has become a nation of seekers in search of the right "fit"; and what fits right depends on direct experience of the sacred revealed in myriad forms: Jesus Christ; the Higher Power of the New Age; Allah; Krishna; or the ancestor spirits of Native Americans. Or the sacred may even be formless, empty, as it is in Zen.

Wherever I've worked in the world, I've found that, just as in America, personal experience of the sacred—more than orthodox belief and time-hallowed practice—helps one through hard times. In Nigeria I watched Muslim fundamentalists seeking cures for their afflictions become possessed by pagan spirits, a practice their imams vociferously condemned; in Mexico, I became aware that the Virgin Mary was the constant companion of my pragmatic, plain-speaking landlady; in Kenya I saw my fundamentalist Christian friends seek the help of their ancestor spirits, in whom—officially—they no longer believed. In Nepal and northern India I traveled with prosperous Theravada Buddhists who meditated to still their passions and to intensify their identification with the Buddha, who, millennia ago, had stilled *his* passions and attained enlightenment; and in Hong Kong I watched thirty thousand Filipina maids, long separated from family and friends, become suffused with the Holy Spirit —having just received the Eucharist in a mass conducted by a cardinal. Lastly, in New England I sat in meditation with Zen Buddhists raised as Catholics, Jews, Quakers, Presbyterians, Episcopalians, and Southern Baptists as they experienced the Buddha within.

The context and chronology of my explorations are true to life; but some of the characters in these stories are pastiches, events have sometimes been condensed, and many of the place names and almost all the personal names have been changed. Some conversations are lifted from my journals; many are reconstituted from memory; a few are fiction. My focus is always on my characters' need for religious faith and the uses they make of it, and on my own attempts to understand what I have gleaned about their experience.

BORI

Spirit Possession in a Muslim Town

"Sit, please." Alhajia Rabi indicated a rickety chair with a ripped vinyl seat. "I am busy now, but later we will talk."

As the only purveyor of western medicine in Kaura, a Nigerian town one hundred miles south of the Sahara Desert, the Alhajia treated patients in a squat, iron-roofed, green-shuttered dispensary on a lane behind the Magaji's mud-walled palace. The Magaji, chief of Kaura, had instructed his messenger to bring me to her. "The Alhajia and I used to work together," he'd told me. Before the eldest son of his father's elder brother had been deposed by the provincial governor for egregious corruption and he'd been appointed in his place, the Magaji had been a nurse.

"While I treated gents, she treated ladies," he'd explained to me. "Of course my appointment as chief necessitated my resignation. The Ministry of Health has promised a replacement but none has been forthcoming so far. Thus my former room in the dispensary is padlocked, and for medical attention our Kaura gents must travel to the clinic in faraway Funtua. As the road there is long and full of potholes, for sick people it is a horrible journey. They scream and even beg for death to take them. In fact, meeting death on the way is not infrequent. But our ladies and our children, too, are fortunate." Alhajia Rabi in her white uniform—crisp head tie, long-sleeved blouse, toe-length wrapper—had remained at her post. "She attended the school established by the old emir of Zaria, and later, also in Zaria, she took midwifery training. So she knows English. Somewhat, at least." As the nephew and grandson of chiefs, he himself had found favor with the British colonial government, which had sent him for training to Hillingdon Hospital, Uxbridge, England. Twenty-five years after he returned, his English remained fluent, authoritative, and tinged with a Home Counties accent. "You will find that Alhajia Rabi knows how to speak with white people. I have confidence, Madam, that she will inform you fully about the ladies and the children of this place." As an afterthought, he'd added, "She is a good Muslim also. Twice she has made the hajj." (Hence her title, "Alhajia," reserved for women who had made the pilgimage to Mecca.)

Seated at a broad table this Tuesday morning, Alhajia Rabi gazed intently at the women whom her "boy" Musa summoned one by one to present their complaints. Many held small children in their arms or had infants tied to their backs. Since the Alhajia and I occupied the dispensary's only chairs, the women were required to stand. After listening for two minutes maximum, the Alhajia would rise magisterially. If, as an aid to the diagnostic procedure, a physical examination seemed warranted, she would usher her patient behind the grubby blue curtain that closed off the rear of the room—or, in the case of a child, have the mother lay him on the table, whereupon, as she explained to me, the procedure was to pull up shirt, pull down shorts, and place ear to chest and then to stomach. But often she proceeded immediately to treatment. A glass-fronted cabinet behind her contained six large jars variously marked in black capitals: COUGH, WEAKNESS, DIARRHEA, VOMIT, FEVER, ACHE. Shaking out a handful of tablets, she'd dump them into a sheet of paper torn from a school exercise book and, while deftly folding them into a packet, would bark instructions. Sometimes, in addition to prescribing tablets, she swabbed gentian violet on gashes and insect bites, squeezed thick curls of ointment onto squares of paper, or proffered acid yellow tonic. If the patient hadn't had the foresight to bring her own bottle, the Alhajia would sell her, for a penny, one of the empties lined up on top of the cabinet, throwing in a rag, to be used as a stopper, for the price. One in roughly fifteen patients merited a penicillin injection.

When I arrived at the dispensary, the line of swathed women shielding themselves with black umbrellas from the West African sun, already fierce at nine o'clock in the morning, had wound away down the lane. But given the Alhajia's streamlined approach to clinical practice, by eleven o'clock the line had evaporated and the few remaining women, heads still covered but umbrellas folded, were squatting inside the building on the earthen floor. When, by eleven-twenty, the last had been attended to, the Alhajia produced a key from inside her wrapper, locked the cabinet, and turned to me. With narrowed eyes, she asked suspiciously, "Well, Madam, what is it that you want?"

"I have come to learn how mothers in Kaura bring up their children."

"Are there no women in your own place who could teach you these things?"

"They would teach me how Americans bring up their children, and I want to know how *Kaura* mothers do it."

The Alhajia looked at me in skeptical silence. "How many children have you got?" she asked.

"I don't have any."

"None at all? Why is that?"

"I've been too busy studying..."

"How old are you?"

"Twenty-eight."

"So old! Then why do you still study?"

Ignoring her implied "when you should be having children," I plunged on. "The Magaji told me you're a child health expert, and that you know all the women in Kaura. Most important, that they trust you," I added, hoping to beguile her. The Magaji had also informed me that in this Muslim town in which all females between the ages of twelve and fifty were married and *kulle* (in purdah—confined to the house, to protect their purity and the honor of their families), Alhajia Rabi, alone among respectable women, was free to walk the streets by day and learn everybody's business.

Kicking off wedge-heeled slippers, the Alhajia stretched out her legs and as, head down, she mopped her face and neck with a corner of the salmon-colored towel on which she'd examined her child patients, she studied her own small hennaed feet. Though her forehead was lined, when she pushed back her head tie, I saw that her elaborately braided hair was black. As I had found to be the case with most people in Kaura, it was difficult to tell her age. "Without me, the ladies here would hardly survive." With a complacent burp, she added, "Do you wish to talk to them?"

"Yes, that's the general idea."

"But how? You make too many mistakes in our language."

A grammar book, pocket dictionary, and several months of lessons from an ex–Peace Corps volunteer in the States had only equipped me with "kitchen" Hausa, the lingua franca of the area; this meant I could just about deal with our servant, a skinny fellow named Ali, and the children who came to our door selling onions, okra, and guinea-fowl eggs. "Perhaps you could teach me to speak your language better," I suggested.

"Where will I find time for teaching? Every day, so many ladies and children are coming..." The Alhajia sighed deeply. "And when they are too sick to come or they are giving birth I must run to help in the compounds. Many nights, I have no sleep at all." But suddenly she brightened. "My idea," she exclaimed, jabbing her forehead with an index finger. "You will help me! You will keep the records!"

It emerged that though the health ministry required records, she had largely neglected to keep them. From a drawer in her examining table she produced a tattered ledger, a wooden ruler, and a stubby blue pencil. My task would be to draw columns and list in them every patient's name, diagnosis, and medicine prescribed. I should arrive at eight o'clock each morning and on days when she didn't have too many patients she would help me hone my conversational skills.

"First time in Nigeria?" she asked as she replaced ledger, ruler, and pencil stub.

"Second time. My first, I was a teacher in the East."

She looked at me doubtfully. "In Iboland? Those people are Christians, not Muslims," she added, her implication being "Why would you want to go there?" which was pretty much what my parents had said when, as—in their view—a still dangerously impulsive twenty-one-year-old just out of university, I'd announced I'd joined a volunteer organization which was sending me to Nigeria to teach "whatever you know that they think might be useful." (This turned out to be European history, Latin, and elementary French.)

"Yes," I said. "Hausaland's a lot different." For one thing, in Iboland women aren't in purdah, I said under my breath.

The following morning we wrestled with vocabulary for female body parts, which, together with some useful phrases, I wrote in my spiral notebook. But the morning after that, as soon as the last patient had departed, the Alhajia indicated that to remain in the dispensary after her day's work was done was not to her taste. I could also study in her house, she observed. And so, with Musa taking up the rear, we proceeded through the center of Kaura, our progress slowed by the Alhajia's frequent stops to chat with shopkeepers, cloth peddlers, herders returning from market to their cattle camps in the bush, children selling kola nuts from round tin trays, and the occasional leprous beggar. Outside the iron-studded gates of the Magaji's palace turbaned men dozed beneath dusty-leafed neem trees and caparisoned horses, tethered to the trees, flicked at flies with lazy tails. The Magaji was not "on seat" (in his office, attending to business), Alhajia Rabi informed me. "Gone to settle a case in Giwa where there are camel thieves." Wrinkling her nose disdainfully, she added, "And when he is absent his people only sleep."

Just as we were passing, the noon call to prayer issued from the white minaret of the town's main mosque, across the road from the palace. Men stirred, sat up, stretched, adjusted turbans, reached for kettles, performed ablutions. That done, they rolled out mats and knelt, facing east, for their devotions. Meanwhile, from the yard of the primary school next door a stream of jostling barefoot boys in embroidered caps and long khaki shirts poured out into the road. Their cries and high-pitched chatter almost drowned out the muezzin's call. A small phalanx of girls in blue frocks and neat white head ties followed decorously behind them.

Momentarily trapped by the tide of schoolchildren, three young women in bright silks, eyes outlined in kohl, heads boldly uncovered, stood in the middle of the road. Holding hands, they laughed at the children, at one another, at life in general. They looked inordinately cheerful. As we drew close, they greeted the Alhajia, who, with a curt nod, swept by. *"Karuwai,"* she muttered distastefully and abruptly turned off the road into a narrow lane.

"What are *karuwai?*"

"They have run away from their husbands."

"Why are they out in the street at midday? Are they prostitutes?"

"Surely you saw their dresses?"

"They were very colorful..."

"Colorful *and* costly! Prostitutes you see in the lorry park. They are old and ugly and wear cheap dresses. *Karuwai* are young and pretty. Instead of going with any man who brings three shillings, each has only one or two rich friends."

"So would you call them courtesans?"

The Alhajia's brow furrowed. "That word I do not know."

In the entrance hall of the compound where the Alhajia rented rooms we came upon a small boy and girl fighting over a pink plastic doll. (Black dolls had not yet been seen in Kaura; in fact the peddlers who went house to house selling head ties, water bottles, rubber sandals, and soap had only recently added pink dolls to their wares.) The boy jumped backwards, doll clasped tightly to his chest, and the girl raced up to the Alhajia, grabbed a fistful of her wrapper and unleashed a piercing wail; whereupon, with a snort of irritation, the Alhajia darted forward and snatched the doll from the boy's grasp. Then, scooping the little girl into her arms and beckoning to me to follow, she strode across the compound to her own quarters.

We entered a room which, shuttered since morning, was mercifully cool. Setting the child on the earthen floor, the Alhajia presented her to me. "Her name is Laraba," she told me. "When my friend Rakia gave birth, I said, 'When you wean this child, you will give her to me!' Rakia is my bond-friend. Bond-friends may deny each other nothing, so how could she refuse my request? After weaning, she sent Laraba to me. Kaura is a better place than Giwa, where Rakia is married. Here Laraba can drink milk and eat meat and green vegetables every day. When it is the season I buy for her papaya." She added proudly, "See how well she grows!" Indeed, in a region where more than half the children died before age five, Laraba, fair-skinned and too cute for her own good, appeared to be bursting with health.

After opening one of the shutters a crack so that a shaft of burning sunlight sliced across the floor, the Alhajia withdrew in order to exchange her nurse's uniform for a dramatically patterned cotton blouse and wrapper. Meanwhile, Musa had been sent to the corner shop for orange Fantas, which we drank from the bottles while seated on tightly woven grass mats. The packet of biscuits that Musa had also bought was pounced upon by Laraba; clutching it closely, she ran outside. "That one will give her husband much trouble," the Alhajia remarked, smiling indulgently.

"You're already thinking about her marriage? She's still so little."

"And soon she will be big! At twelve years, I myself was married, Madam."

But that marriage, it emerged, had been to a previous husband. Her current husband, Mamman, was the emir of Katsina's driver. In the dry season he drove the emir about in a great black pennanted Mercedes Benz, which, in the rainy season, he exchanged for a gray Land Rover. As his duties kept him mostly in Katsina City and the Alhajia's kept her mostly in Kaura, husband and wife met only on the third weekend of the month.

Though on occasion Mamman visited her in Kaura, usually it was the Alhajia who visited him in Katsina, four hours away in the back of a lorry, or, if she was lucky, by bus.

"Who cooks for your husband when you aren't there?"

"His other wives," she replied matter-of-factly. "It is because they are *there* in Katsina City that I am free to work *here*." As for Laraba, "Eight more years and then, like I was, she'll be married."

"But what about school? Will she study?"

"Already she studies. Each afternoon Musa takes her and that boy Suliman, with whom we found her fighting, to study the Koran in the house of Malam Hussein."

"They don't study in the mosque?"

"May females enter the mosque?" the Alhajia shot back. The Alhajia herself had never set foot in a mosque. Mosques were for gents only. But the Koran was a quite different matter. "The Koran is for ladies as well as for gents." As a child she—like several other girls she knew—had committed it to memory in its entirety. "When Laraba marries she too will have it by heart. She will also attend the government school, as I did. Four or five standards [grade levels] will be sufficient. If she studies longer, she will find it difficult to settle in her husband's home."

"Did you find it difficult?"

The Alhajia rolled her eyes heavenward. Then, drinking down the last of her Fanta, she said briskly, "You wish to study the Hausa language, isn't it? So let us speak about the sicknesses of this hot season. First, meningitis." But hardly had my lesson begun than a young woman entered the room. Dark-red wrapper tied high under her armpits, "In God We Trust" marching in orange letters across her buttocks, she seated herself on the mat beside us and urgently engaged the Alhajia. Within moments, she was joined by a second young woman with a baby on her hip. The Alhajia turned to me. "These are daughters of this house, they have come back here because they have trouble with their husbands. Excuse me, please, but I must give them advice."

A roll of drums came from the direction of the town's main

gate. Laraba reappeared and, ignoring her mother's visitors, tucked in her elbows, lowered chin to chest, and began to dance. On several afternoons since our arrival in Kaura my husband and I had heard drumming. We knew that the *bori* cult, in which adepts become possessed by vengeful spirits, was found throughout the region; but when we'd asked our landlord if we were hearing *bori* drums he'd replied evasively. "You Europeans entertain yourselves with music, isn't it?" he'd said. "Well, we do as well." Our neighbor, a Yoruba agricultural officer who had recently transferred to Kaura from his southern homeland, had suggested, "It should be for a wedding." But it wasn't the wedding season.

Now, breaking off her conversation with the troubled young women, the Alhajia remarked to me in English, "Do you hear that?" Disdainfully she added, "The rains will soon come and those *maguzawa* people should go to prepare their fields for planting. But no, they are idle, they only want to play their drums." Grabbing Laraba's plump arm, she ordered the child to stop dancing; but Laraba twisted out of her mother's grasp and skipped off to the compound entrance hall where, away from maternal supervision, she could dance as she liked.

Later, in our newly constructed cinder-block bungalow—in mud-walled Kaura, cinder blocks were a recent innovation—my husband and I lunched on sardine sandwiches washed down with water boiled that morning and still hot. (Our landlord, Alhaji Aziz, who drove a big blue Opel and prided himself on being modern, had fully wired our bungalow; but because the electricity only came on for three hours after sunset, refrigeration was not in the cards.) In our oven of a bedroom, we took our siesta, watched raptly by half a dozen boys and girls lined up outside our window. Certainly, we had curtains; I had sewn them myself on the hand-operated Singer sewing machine I'd bought from a Lebanese merchant in Zaria City. But drawing them was out of the question; with the temperature at midday reaching one hundred and ten degrees Fahrenheit, we treasured every slightest breath of air. When, a couple of hours later, we awoke in pools of sweat, only one boy still stood at the window and, in the road behind him, shadows had grown long. But those idle people near the town gate were still drumming.

Returning from the dispensary one noontime, the Alhajia and I saw the emir's Land Rover parked in the lane and Mamman, a gnarled, graying man in a brass-buttoned uniform, smoking a cigarette in the entrance hall of the compound. On the threshold, the Alhajia tensed for a second before prostrating herself once, twice, three times at his sandaled feet and hurrying off to the kitchen. Normally Musa produced meals unaided but under present circumstances he required close supervision. Within moments we heard a frantic squawking as he chased, caught, and wrung the neck of one of the scrawny chickens that scratched out a living in the yard behind the kitchen. Left alone with Mamman, I attempted to draw him out. I learned that he was on his way back from buying a fan belt for the Mercedes in Zaria City; but since his English—acquired, in the course of his professional duties, from European mechanics—was even more limited than my Hausa, our halting exchange about the weather and the state of the Zaria–Katsina road soon petered out. Laraba dashed in, saw Mamman, and pulled up with a shriek that brought the Alhajia racing from the kitchen. But then, having coached the little girl through the rituals of greeting, she returned to food preparation and Laraba too made off.

Within a few moments Mamman had escaped the awkward silence by slumping in openmouthed slumber against the wall. Head lolling on his right shoulder, he began to snore, and I took out my notebook and tried to memorize vocabulary. Only when the Alhajia, bringing chicken stew and thick corn-flour porridge on a green-rimmed tin plate, knelt before him and spoke to him quietly, did Mamman wake up. She remained kneeling, head bowed in a pose of uncharacteristic submission, while he gobbled his food, cleaned his plate with a last fingerful of porridge, belched loudly, and stood up. After a quick trip to the latrine in the rear of the compound, he climbed back into the emir's dove-gray Land Rover, started it up, and reversed out of the lane.

During the ninety-five minutes he'd spent in her quarters he'd scarcely addressed a word to his wife.

Given the Alhajia's commanding presence, her importance in the town, her two trips to Mecca, her singularity in so many respects, I had expected her to have a more impressive husband. True, Mamman's master was an emir, a king, who lived in a proper palace with towers and castellated battlements and uniformed guards at its great gates, unlike the Magaji, who, even though English speakers called his place a palace, lived in an overgrown house, its sprawl contained by walls of wattle and daub in urgent need of repair. True, Mamman tooled around in two of the most expensive vehicles in Katsina province. But he still looked like a chump. What was the Alhajia doing with such a disappointing fellow? I was unlikely to find out from the lady herself. Though she was a fount of information about other people, when it came to her own affairs, she was nothing if not discreet.

The Alhajia began taking me with her when she went out on house calls and in several compounds I met women who had infants or toddlers. Having noted their names and the names of their husbands and marked where they lived on the rough map I'd drawn of the town, a day or two later I'd set out on my own to try to find them again. Not a drop of rain had fallen since the previous October and now, in late March, the air was so laden with dust that visibility was down to a few hundred yards. Kaura, the countryside around it, Katsina Province, and the entire sub-Saharan region were enveloped in a dense yellowish haze. Mentally, I was as well. I'd attempted to prepare for my encounter with Hausa society by reading about their religion (Wahhabi Islamic fundamentalism, as in Saudi Arabia); social system (rigidly stratified); residential pattern (patrilocal); gender roles (radically unequal); levels of sexually transmitted diseases (exceptionally high); fertility rates (exceptionally low); and child mortality (among the highest on the planet). I'd also struggled through a bewildering translation of the Koran, and since Kaura was the first place in which I'd done field research, my husband, who'd worked in several places previously, had provided me with the following ground rules: Every culture is internally consistent. Therefore:

1. If something doesn't make sense to you, the outsider, it's your job to figure it out from the *insider's* point of view.
2. Cultivate the observing ego. (Supposedly, as someone who'd had seven hundred hours of psychoanalysis, I'd developed some capacity to monitor my thoughts.)
3. If something strikes you as objectionable, keep your opinion to yourself.
4. If you don't understand what people are saying, ask them to repeat what they've said. Ask them to repeat it ten times if necessary. Just keep at it. Everything will come clear eventually.

Eventually. But now that I was actually in Kaura, despite my attempts to follow my husband's rules, I was making precious little sense of what I saw and heard.

Since, aside from the Alhajia, there wasn't a single woman in the district who'd ever been to a western school, I was pretty much on my own with my youth, my inexperience, my broken Hausa, and the absurdity—in the eyes of the locals and, increasingly, in my own as well—of attempting to study the socialization of young children when I'd never had a child myself. But in addition to these obvious handicaps, I sensed a determination on the part of the men with whom I sat in entrance halls, talking about the price of cotton and the civil war being fought far away in the south, that an outsider should only be allowed to see what they thought should be seen; furthermore, their determination was one that the Alhajia, my guide to the Hausa female experience, shared.

In fact my husband and I weren't the only outsiders in Kaura. Fathers Dan, Greg, and Hugo lived at the mission a couple of miles down the Funtua road. Father Dan was from Minnesota,

Father Greg was from Ohio, and Father Hugo was from Michigan. Dominican priests with PhDs in philosophy from Chicago Loyola, all three had been on this particular frontier of Christendom for many years. They were forbidden by the provincial government from proselytizing Muslims, so their quarry were *maguzawa* pagans living far out in the bush. But the government also forbade them to spend the night away from their mission, which meant that at sunrise they'd be off to distant villages to do as much as they could of the Lord's work before sunset, when they had to head back. For all their roaring through trackless wastes on battered motorcycles their converts had been few. Indeed Father Hugo had just about quit trying to make any. He mostly stayed home, and when my husband and I visited him we would find him in his study drinking warm Heinekens and reading Saint Thomas Aquinas, or in the kitchen coaxing ice cream out of a preindustrial ice-cream maker which required hard-to-obtain rock salt. Once or twice we came upon him on the steps of the chapel after saying mass for the benefit of himself and his stooped Ilorin servant, Samuel.

During my stint in Iboland, where the churches were full to overflowing—in sharp contrast with England, where they were almost empty—I'd undergone postadolescent religious confusion ("crisis" would be too noble a concept; disappointment in the Anglican Church seems more apt). Imagining that the Catholic church with its global reach would suit me better, I'd often attended mass. I'd had no trouble following the Latin liturgy (the Second Vatican Council being still in session, the shift to the vernacular hadn't yet occurred), the Irish parish priest was dynamic, and faith and hope shone in the faces of the people who filled his hangarlike church to bursting four or five times each Sunday. However, my slide from devotion to doubt continued. How could I recite the Apostolic creed when I no longer believed in the virgin birth, the resurrection of the body, or the life of the world to come? But my main problem was with the promise of forgiveness of sins through grace. I wished I believed this were possible, but I didn't. I believed my redemption was my own business. If ever attained, it would be through my own efforts, not through grace. In America not long afterwards, Freud—and my husband—persuaded me that religious belief was a psychological defense mechanism against anxiety and, yes, the confusion I myself was experiencing. Doubt congealed into sad unbelief—something akin to mourning. But barred from the Holy Land though I felt myself to be, I was still aware of the seasons as they passed within it: Lent, Palm Sunday, Passion Week, Easter, Ascension Day. In my head, I kept on watching *The Life of Christ* (The Movie), and occasionally I'd slip into an Episcopal church to hear the Good News. But it had been a long time since I'd taken the Eucharist. As my husband and I drank warm beer, ate peppermint ice cream, the specialty of the house, and talked about the civil war with Father Hugo, I did think about joining him and old Samuel in the mission chapel, but I never quite summoned the resolve. Sad unbelief outweighed my longing to be part of an inside group, albeit a group of three people.

My husband who, as a man, was forbidden to set foot in the women's quarters, could not accompany me on my compound visits. But even though I went about the town on my own I was rarely alone, because the lanes swarmed with children. The government school, which was only open in the morning, had just 117 registered students (of whom, as the headmaster had informed me glumly, on any given day fewer than 70 showed up). Even the wealthiest men in the town had little use for western education. Most had made their fortunes without ever setting a foot inside a school; success in business came from the assiduous forging of connections and reciprocal obligations. In their view, sitting in a classroom was an utter waste of time. The Magaji, who aspired to be an enlightened ruler and had despaired of attracting students any other way, had imposed a quota on each household. But many household heads had fulfilled their quotas by enrolling their servants' children rather than their own. They confidently expected that, by and by, their own children would learn the skills required by the marketplace in the marketplace itself. As a result, though virtually all children over age three attended Koranic school for a couple of hours at some point during the day, sons and daughters of good family spent most of their time hawking snack food prepared by their secluded mothers, and providing an instant audience for any excitement that occurred in the streets. For the moment, at least, the under-twelve set had decided that escorting Madam was the most exciting pastime on offer.

By now I was becoming known as the Alhajia's protégée and therefore trustworthy, and some of the merchants—traders in groundnuts and cotton—began inviting me to visit their wives, who, aside from occasional outings to the dispensary, almost never left home in daylight. A servant, appearing at our door with a penciled note ("Come please Madam"), would lead me through the lanes to his master's house, where, in the slow stifling months before the rains, the women were much in need of entertainment. (Even though, given my linguistic inadequacies, conversation was restricted to banalities, my visits rated as entertainment.) The Alhajia kept careful track of these invitations and seemed to find my growing popularity personally gratifying. When she learned that I'd received a summons from the Magaji himself she was especially pleased. "Three wives you will find there—Fatima, Adama, and Hasana. Fatima is my mother's youngest sister's bond-friend. You will greet her for me, please."

At four o'clock the following afternoon, the Magaji's messenger, a lithe young person named Akbar, arrived at our bungalow on his orange bicycle. As he rode around town, he wore a man's long shirt and loose trousers; but, instead of the traditional white cotton, his suit was sewn from loudly patterned cloth usually worn by women within the confines of their own quarters. His outfit—of cotton printed with red-and-green sea urchins on a dark-blue ground—was complemented by kohl-rimmed eyes that were often obscured by a pair of pink-framed wraparound sunglasses, two "golden" bracelets and three necklaces, pointy patent-leather shoes, and a cap tipped flirtatiously over his left ear. As he peddled about his master's business, jangling his bracelets and voluptuously wiggling his rear end, children would call after him, "*Dauda, Dauda,* boy-girl, boy-girl!" an epithet that seemingly upset him not at all.

When I refused his invitation to ride on his crossbar, Akbar sighed melodramatically. "Then I too must walk." He set off up the road and, followed closely by my perennial posse of child escorts, I hurried to catch up.

As we made our way toward the palace, Akbar remarked in English, "Kaura people think you are quite interesting."

"Where did you learn English?" I asked, astonished.

"In school, of course."

"So you studied."

"I am the Magaji's *dan gida,* his son of the house. Not his really son, you understand . . . I think in English you say 'ward.' The Magaji sent me to school in Katsina City to become a government clerk." But, bored and restless, Akbar had dropped out of Standard 7, and instead of becoming a clerk in the provincial capital, he'd returned to Kaura to become the Magaji's messenger.

Just as we reached the palace, where the children fell back and squatted in the shade to await my reappearance in due course, I heard drumming start up in the distance. "What's that about, Akbar?" I asked, but he was absorbed in propping his bicycle against the great entrance door and didn't reply.

In the entrance hall the Magaji's retainers, clients, and sycophants gossiped and dozed. In this heat, even their master's being back on seat wasn't enough to keep most of them awake.

Abubakar Usman Dan Usman, Magajin Kaura, greatgrandson of Usman Dan Fodio, the Fulani chieftain who, in the name of Allah, had swept down from the Sahara in 1804, converted the Hausa people to Islam with fire and the sword, and sent out his many sons to rule his new empire, sat at a fruitwood desk in a high-ceilinged whitewashed office lined with wooden shelves on which dung-colored record books rose in dusty piles. On the wall behind him was a large framed photograph of a lanky young man, in striped tie, tweed jacket, and checked deerstalker's hat, standing in front of the fountain in Trafalgar

Square. In the intervening decades the Magaji had just about doubled his weight.

"How kind of you to come, Madam!" He folded the English-language newspaper he'd been reading and rose to his feet, a massive, white-robed, turbaned figure.

"How kind of you to invite me!"

"It is my great pleasure." He bowed graciously and cut straight to the point. "In fact it has been reported to me that you possess a sewing machine. You have been observed using it in your house. I would like you to teach my wives how to use such a machine."

"There are plenty of tailors in Kaura who are far more expert than I am," I protested.

"That may well be true, Madam, but those tailors cannot instruct my wives. My wives require a lady teacher. Do you see lady tailors in Kaura? No, you do not!" He clapped his hands and Akbar sauntered in with a large wooden box.

"So you've already bought one!"

The Magaji smiled. "Having enquired of your landlord, Aziz, where you purchased yours, I myself sent for one from that very same Zaria shop." He came out from behind his desk. "Now I will take you to my wives."

"May I ask you a question?" He cocked his head expectantly.

"Are those *bori* drums we're hearing?"

He stared at me impassively. "Those drums are indeed of *bori*, Madam. It is the *maguzawa* pagans who play them." His tone was uncharacteristically dry. "They live far out in the bush, but at this season they come to Kaura to trade in the market and after finishing their business they like to play their drums and dance. Often they sing also. They say they are calling to the spirits of the bush. Kaura people are entertained by the singing and dancing of those pagans, but Kaura people are *Muslims*, Madam. We Muslims must pray five times a day, give alms to the poor, fast during the holy month of Ramadan, and make the hajj at least once in our lifetime." His voice rose. "We know there is no God but Allah and Muhammad is his Prophet. As for those bush spirits, we do not concern ourselves with them." He straightened his shoulders and adjusted the deep folds of his outer robe. "Now come!" he commanded and, with a preoccupied look, swept past me.

I followed him through a warren of courtyards into a wide, cool chamber in which three women were waiting. He made the briefest of introductions, ordered Akbar to place the wooden box on the floor in front of his senior wife, Fatima, and then, with the directive "Have a nice time!" and a slight bow, retired, taking Akbar with him.

Fatima, tall and stout, appeared to be in her fifties; Adama and Hasana were both tall also but extremely thin and about thirty years younger. Though all three had the fair complexions so much admired by Hausa people, their plain faces and silk dresses—dull blue, dull pink, and dull green—reminded me of certain upper-class English girls I'd gone to school with: restrained in all things, including the colors of their cashmere twin sets. The women were flanked by female servants and boys and girls of various ages who stared at me, open-mouthed. After a few moments of tense silence, Fatima nodded to a servant, who brought me a stool, and then, with co-wives, servants, and children ranged around us, she began a familiar catechism: Who is your father? How many wives does he have, and how much land? What crops does he grow? What vehicle does he drive? When, as best I could, I had supplied answers, she requested the same information about my brother, uncles, and male first cousins; only then did she ask about my husband. My admission that I was his second wife sparked immediate interest. "Has the first wife been seen in Kaura?"

"No, she hasn't. She and my husband got divorced."

"Where are her children?"

"She didn't have any children."

"Ah." Everyone nodded in concert.

"When she left your husband's house, where did she go?"

"She married another man and lives in Australia."

"Australia?" They hadn't heard of Australia. "Are there Muslims in Australia?"

"There must be some, but not very many."

"And in Australia, has that lady given birth?"

"Yes, she has a son."

Again, everyone nodded. Adama, who looked about my own age, took over the interrogation. "So you are the only wife?"

"In Europe and America, and even in Australia, a man may only have one wife at a time." For the sake of the record, I added, "And a woman may only have one husband."

"If you're alone, then must you cook every day for your husband?"

"Well, yes." Theoretically, Ali did the cooking; but in practice, being used to an open fire, he'd been stymied by our Italian propane gas stove. My efforts to help him rise to this technological challenge having failed, he swept the house, washed and ironed our clothes, and did the dishes. Although he peeled the potatoes, it was I who actually cooked them in the ovenlike hut in the dusty yard behind our cinder-block bungalow.

Now it was Hasana's turn. "Sometimes our husband has discussions with your husband. I have seen them talking in the office. Even though his eyes are weak and he wears glasses, your husband is nice looking. Is this your first marriage?"

"Yes."

"Did your father arrange it?"

"He certainly did not!"

"How many children have you got?"

"None so far."

"Why not?"

"We are using family planning." Family planning? Even though I'd used the Hausa term, they seemed mystified. After I'd attempted, in a few poorly constructed sentences, to explain the objectives and mechanics of birth control, Fatima remarked that such medicine was not available in Kaura. Why should it be? Hausa people liked children very much. They were looking for medicine that would give them not fewer children but as many as possible!

Time, I decided, to reverse roles. I turned to Hasana. "How long have you been married?"

"I came six years ago."

"And which of these children are yours?"

"When I came here I left my son with his father in Funtua."

"So the Magaji is not your first husband?" No, he was not.
"How often do you see your son?"

"Since I came here I have not seen him."

I stared at her, aghast. "In six years! Why not?"

"Because of *kunya*. It is our custom."

Yes, I'd read about *kunya*, the respect that Hausa mothers
and children must have for one another. It dictated that a mother
should never look directly at or speak to her eldest child—and,
in aristocratic families like the Magaji's, to *any* of her children.
It dictated that, as soon as he was weaned, a child must be sent
away to be raised by another woman, sometimes a relative but
just as often someone who'd "asked" for him, just as Alhajia
Rabi had asked her friend Rakia for Laraba. Thereafter mother
and child should avoid each other for the rest of their lives. But
though I'd read about *kunya*, that hadn't prepared me to see
—as I did almost daily—young mothers nursing babies with
averted gaze and steadfastly refusing to respond to an infant's
coos and babbles, or to a toddler's urgent pleas. Alhajia Rabi
lavished love upon Laraba, another woman's child; but what
about Rakia, Laraba's birth mother? Was she forever bereft?

"When my son grows big enough perhaps he may visit me,"
Hasana added softly.

"How big is big enough?"

Hasana shrugged. "His father will decide. When he com-
pletes his schooling, it may be possible."

"Don't you miss him?"

"There are many children here," was her patient answer.

"There are nine," Fatima interjected.

"Which of them are yours?" I asked her.

"None was born in this house. This one," she indicated a
small boy, "is my sister's son and that girl is Adama's brother's
daughter. The rest came here from various houses. Many people
ask us to take their children. It is nice for a child to grow up in
the house of the chief. But we cannot accept all of them, so some

we must refuse. Now," she added firmly, "you must teach us how to use this machine."

A servant lifted off the wooden cover to reveal a model that most probably had made its debut around 1900 in a mail-order catalog in the American Midwest: purplish, with mother-of-pearl inlays, it had a dull silver-colored wheel propelled by a thick band of rubber and a black handle. I doubted that this model was still available anywhere other than in markets ringing the Sahara.

"Would you like to go first?" I asked Fatima.

After the dispensary closed one morning, the Alhajia said she had a few errands to run, so I went with her. As we passed a large compound not far from the market I noticed some brightly dressed young women standing in the entrance. They were calling out greetings to passersby, including, to her obvious discomfort, the Alhajia. With a pained expression she informed me, "That compound is where the *karuwai*, those women you call courtesans, live."

A pretty young girl came running out to us, pushed her face up close to the Alhajia's, and pulled down a lower lid to reveal a badly inflamed eye.

"Come tomorrow!" the Alhajia ordered.

The next morning when the girl showed up at the dispensary, the Alhajia gave her a curl of ointment in a square of newspaper, and in the ledger, I wrote "Yelwa," "conjunctivitis," "ointment." After she left, the Alhajia seemed preoccupied and at the end of the morning she admitted that Yelwa was her eldest brother's daughter. "Four years ago, my brother gave her to an old Alhaji. I told him, No, no, a small girl like that should not be married to an old man! You should give her to somebody nearer to her own age. But my brother is too stubborn. He said, 'That Alhaji is my friend, he sells electric generators in Kano. He has a big house and plenty of money. Yelwa will have a fan in the hot season, he will give her beautiful clothes. He will take her on the hajj, not in a bus but in an airplane, and at Mecca he will buy her silks from India. She will be the treasure of his old age!'

"So they gave Yelwa to that old man, and it was just as I'd predicted—before one year was finished she ran away. But she didn't go back to my brother's house as she should have. I heard she was traveling from one place to another, and then four months ago she came to Kaura, to the *karuwai* quarter. Here, there are plenty of men who like her. Your landlord, Aziz, is one of them. He is rich, he has many lorries, and four wives also. One in Kano, one in Funtua, and two here. Even so, his servant often brings Yelwa to him. He gives her beautiful dresses and jewelry and makeup, and people say he would like to send one of his wives away and bring Yelwa into his house instead. But she herself has told me that though she's happy to have him as her special friend, she has no interest in having him as her husband." The Alhajia sighed sorrowfully. "It is one thing for a woman to stay with the *karuwai* for a short time. Then after she has amused herself, after she has had her rest, she should again marry. But Yelwa says, 'Why should I stay in one house and do as one man tells me and never go out except after the sun has set?' "

It soon became obvious that all three of the Magaji's wives were accomplished seamstresses. They sewed most of their own clothes and those of their foster children, including blouses with set-in French-seamed sleeves and complicated basket-weave collars. Once they'd learned how to fill a spool and thread the needle, they required little further instruction. Although Adama and Hasana seemed to enjoy whirring away on the machine, after a session or two Fatima's interest faded. She preferred to continue sewing by hand, as she had done expertly since childhood. On my third visit, Adama showed me a blouse she had just finished that was much more ambitious than any garment I'd ever attempted. I told her so and then, since I was out of a job as a sewing teacher and there were no mother–infant pairs in the household for me to observe, I excused myself.

"Sit, sit!" they chorused. "Now we know how to use this machine, but you still make too many mistakes in our language. If you come here every day we will correct them and you will rapidly improve."

Since the Alhajia had recently been called away to a review course on "ladies' troubles" (with a focus, she'd informed me, on gonorrhea and syphilis—"Many ladies suffer from those diseases...They catch them from their husbands. I promise you, all the men here are like *dogs!*"), the dispensary was shut for the duration. Ladies seeking medical attention were having to brave the potholes on the Kaura–Funtua road, just like the gents. As I was no longer needed as clinical record keeper, I took to spending my mornings in the Magaji's palace. If he had no other pressing business, Akbar would come to fetch me at nine o'clock. Once or twice I even rode on the crossbar of his bicycle; but mostly we walked up the street together and he told me news in a mixture of Hausa and Standard 7 English. Romance—other people's as much as his own—was what appeared to absorb him. He would have had me believe that the apparent staidness of the town was an illusion, that within one hour of sunset—which, in that latitude occurred with year-round regularity at six p.m.— the deeply shadowed lanes of Kaura came alive with women, properly sequestered wives as well as *karuwai,* on their way to assignations. Furthermore it was he—the boy-girl—whom lovers trusted more than any other to deliver notes and whisper messages. This counterculture—which everyone knew about and which nobody was willing to talk about, at least not to me— throve under cover of darkness. And he was at its epicenter.

If the Magaji spotted me, head spinning with the latest gossip (only partly understood and still undigested), hurrying through the entrance hall to the women's quarters, he would call me into his office to inquire after my husband and how his work was going. He didn't ask how my work was going; but could what I did with his wives honestly be described as *work?*

We would take turns asking one another questions and since there were three of them and only one of me, I got them to let me ask three questions to every one of theirs. Fatima and the Magaji were first cousins; their fathers, long dead, had been brothers. Married when they were ten and thirteen, respectively, they'd been together for over forty years. Adama too, was Fatima's cousin, but on her mother's side, which meant she wasn't considered to be related to the Magaji.

"I brought her in," explained Fatima, "and it was she who brought in Hasana." The two younger women had been friends since childhood, when they'd both hawked sweets through the lanes of Old Zaria City. "It is good for friends to become co-wives. Then there is not so much jealousy. It makes for a peaceful house."

But I learned that, in the years between when he'd married Fatima and when he'd married Adama, the Magaji had had fifteen other wives. "They were unhappy here because they did not have children," Fatima explained. "They went to their homes and afterwards they married other men."

"Do they have children now?"

"Some do." They had had news that Dige, their co-wife who had left most recently, had married a man in Funtua and given birth to twin boys. "Dige was here for five years, we went on the hajj together. It was after that that she left us," said Fatima. "We were sorry not to see her anymore."

"We're still sorry," Adama added.

One morning when Fatima and I were sitting apart from Adama and Hasana, who were at the sewing machine, I mentioned receiving a letter from Alhajia Rabi. "She is doing well in Kaduna and sends her greetings. She says she is the only Hausa woman taking the course. The rest are Yorubas and middle-belt people." As an afterthought, I added, "Do you know any other Hausa woman who works for the government?"

Fatima shrugged. "No, I do not... She is unlucky."

"Unlucky? Why do you say that? She works so hard in the dispensary and everyone respects her."

"But she has had seven husbands. What good luck is there in that?"

"*Seven?*"

"It is the truth." Fatima counted them off on her fingers.

"Her first marriage was in Zaria, near to where she was born. She was the first wife of the eldest son of a rich trader. The second husband, not so rich, was from Zaria also. There, she was the second wife. After that, she moved about to Giwa, Funtua, and other places; and now to Katsina. Already when she married in Giwa she was the fourth wife, the most junior, and it has been so in every other place where she has married since."

It was difficult to imagine imperious Alhajia Rabi being anyone's fourth wife; but then, I only knew what she'd chosen to tell me, about her school days in Zaria, the courses she'd been sent to take, her friendships with the Scottish matron of the Zaria hospital and the Malaysian woman she'd met at Mecca with whom she still exchanged postcards on the Muslim holiday of Id el Fitr—all of which showed her in a fortunate light.

"She has not yet given up hope of conceiving," said Fatima quietly. "She went so many times to hospital in Zaria and Kaduna, and in Kano also. Twice she has made the hajj, paying her own expenses. So much merit has she earned already, and a third hajj she is planning to make, as she told us... And still she goes looking for healers. To Jos, Maiduguri, to the Bornu people... Lately she went up to Maridi in Niger. Yet until now she is disappointed. Will she stay with Sarkin Katsina's driver? We cannot know that... Some women run here and there and everywhere. Until they are old they keep on running from one man to the next."

"But you didn't."

Fatima smiled faintly. "The Magaji and I, even before marriage we were friends. We'd grown up in this house. In this very room we'd played together. We were too much used to each other to go apart. And as for them..." She cocked her head toward Adama and Hasana, intent on their work at the sewing machine. "Yes, they remain here. But Dige and so many others have not..." She added flatly, "It isn't only women who keep running. Men do also. Though since Dige left, there have only been three of us here, our husband could yet bring in a fourth."

But Hasana had a child by her previous husband and Dige had just had twins by her new husband. Don't you see it's the

Magaji's problem, I almost blurted out. *He's* the one who's sterile. I bet that you're all fine. But I bit my tongue. Don't set the cat among the pigeons. Don't raise incendiary issues. Wait till *they* raise them. Then it'll be okay to jump in.

A week or so later, when our servant, Ali, and I were passing the *karuwai* compound on our way home from the market, I spotted Akbar wearing his pink-rimmed sunglasses. He was pedaling toward us through the crowd; but before he saw us he veered off the road and disappeared into the compound. As Ali and I drew level with it, a drum started beating, then a second, and a third. "Here!" I thrust the onions and powdered milk I'd been carrying into Ali's arms and slipped through the clutch of women in the entrance. A veranda ran around three sides of the inner courtyard and on the fourth, facing the entrance, drummers, backed by a bank of musicians with fiddles, gourd rattles, and flutes, were warming up. Some of the men seated expectantly on benches in mud-stained clothes were pagans from villages round about Kaura; several were with wives whose sun-bleached cotton dresses told of a life of toil in the fields. As they weren't Muslims, pagans weren't required to seclude their women; poor peasant farmers, most couldn't have afforded to anyway. Mixed in with them were townspeople—the men in loose gray or blue robes, their wives dressed decorously in Dacron and polyester—and a scattering of Yoruba traders from southern Nigeria in blindingly white robes; a few of the traders were accompanied by handsome wives whose head ties glinted with threads of silver and gold. By the look of things, the wealthier Hausas whose compounds I frequented didn't patronize *bori*.

In the middle of the front row was bold, rebellious Yelwa, Alhajia Rabi's niece and lover of Aziz, my landlord. Seeing me, she eagerly beckoned me to where she sat amidst a bevy of her "sisters." But as I was crossing the courtyard to join her, a broad-shouldered woman stepped out from the veranda and intercepted me. Swathed in dark green and half a head taller than I was, she had an almost military bearing. "So, you have come to *bori!*"

I bowed. "With your permission."

"I have seen you on the road with Rabi. Why did you not come here sooner?" Her tone was of someone used to command.

"I didn't know the place."

"So Rabi did not tell you about us?" The woman smiled ironically. "Well, now that you do know, come as often as you like."

From a room on the far side of the courtyard Akbar appeared carrying a spindly chair that he placed in a narrow strip of shade. He pointed at me and then at the chair and so, having greeting Yelwa, I made my way over.

"The Magajiya is happy to see you," he announced, squatting down beside me.

"The Magajiya? Who is that?"

"The woman who addressed you. Don't you know that we have two chiefs in this town? One gent, one lady. One is chief of Kaura and father to the people, and the other is chief of *bori* and mother to the *karuwai*."

"And you are the favorite of both," I teased.

He shrugged. "Everyone in this compound is my friend."

He laid a hennaed hand on my arm, signaling me to be quiet. The drummers were beating their great ochre-colored gourds with new intensity. Balancing them on their ankles, they raised them from the ground and lowered them again, up, down, up, down, so that the sound rolled out, cut off sharply, and rolled out again in syncopated sequence. Meanwhile the musicians bowed furiously on their single-stringed fiddles and people in the audience ran forward to slap coins and banknotes on the ground in front of them. A row of men squatting to one side watched like hawks as notes and coins accumulated. When the piles of money had reached a height they found acceptable they leapt to their feet and burst into song, just as a man came bounding out from the veranda.

He was shirtless and over his loincloth he wore the skin of an animal—a monkey or a goat—to which were tied long strings of cowrie shells; strips of leather threaded with cowries wound around his ankles and calves almost up to his knees. Twirling around like a top, he leapt high in the air and, landing in the very center of the courtyard, brought out a handful of cowries from under his animal-skin skirt. He threw them to the ground, bent over them, scrutinized them and with a great whoop of delight, gathered them all together and threw them down again.

"That one is a spendthrift, he has lost all his money," Akbar shouted above the din. "It is Dan Galadima, the spirit of gamblers, who is riding him."

Now the musicians were switching to a different rhythm and the praise singers to a different song. Akbar tugged at my hand and I bent low so he could yell in my ear, "They are calling Sarkin Rafi. He is the spirit who drives people mad."

On the other side of the yard, a strikingly handsome young man who had been sitting on a stool, staring at the ground, reared up, kicked over his stool, and, with a great leap, landed within three feet of the orchestra, where he crouched, eyes rolled back, shaking from head to toe. Then, jumping to his feet, he plunged into a wild dance. Round and round he whirled, churning the earth so that people sitting on the front benches covered their mouths and nostrils against the dust. With a shriek, he leapt fully four feet into the air and landed so hard on his buttocks that the ground shook. For a few seconds he sat there, legs outstretched, snorting, snarling, clawing at the earth, which he threw in handfuls over his head and shoulders and smeared across his chest. He renewed his dance a second time and then a third, leaping high and falling with a bone-breaking thump. He sat, pouring sweat, with his tongue hanging loose, chest heaving; the whites of his eyes were huge in his earth-smeared face. Then suddenly he toppled over on his side, rolled like a log across the courtyard, and lay still.

Within moments a new group of praise singers had jumped to their feet, and a woman crouching beside a wooden pillar on the veranda threw off the blanket in which, despite the heat, she had tightly wrapped herself. Two women, barefoot, wrappers hitched high beneath their armpits, ran to her and half-carried, half-dragged her off the veranda and out between the crowded benches. They set her, back slumped, chin on chest, on the square of pounded earth in front of the musicians. For a while she stayed so perfectly still, it seemed she'd fainted. But as the praise singers shouted invocations, she twitched and shuddered and, eyes rolled back, rose to her feet. Gabbling to herself, she began an ungainly dance. When she stumbled her two caretakers were at her side in an instant; they steadied her, whispered to her, and turned her loose to dance again. Abruptly, she dropped to her hands and knees. As the musicians shook their rattles and the praise singers sang with even greater intensity, she dropped to her belly and began crawling across the courtyard. Akbar yelled in my ear, "Danko, the serpent spirit of the rivers, has caught her!" The woman curved first one way, then another, slithering across the courtyard in a snakelike fashion until, rearing up from her waist, she spat at the praise singers. Slithering a few feet further, she reared up again and spat at the drummers. Like Sarkin Rafi, she too was pouring sweat; and, as if she were a horse at the end of a race, foam clung to her lips and her neck and sprayed down across her breasts.

"She is boiling," Akbar shouted, hand cupped to my ear. "See how the sickness boils out of her!"

Now the drumming was slowing, singers were falling silent, musicians were setting down bows, wiping off mouthpieces.

The Magajiya, who, arms akimbo, had been watching the proceedings, turned and walked off to the rear of the compound. Onlookers stood up, stretched, and engaged in conversations. The madman and the gambler got to their feet, dusted themselves off, and crossed from sunlight into shade. The serpent lady was helped back to the veranda, where she drank deeply from a water gourd. After an interval all three would dance again, Akbar told me. He gestured toward a group of ordinary-looking men and women near the compound entrance. "Those people will be taken by the spirits also. They too will dance. Now I will go and buy for us Fanta."

My head was reeling, my coccyx ached vicariously from watching Sarkin Rafi's shattering falls; my face felt as if it too were lathered, my body as if it were smeared with earth and sweat. I told Akbar I was going home, that I needed to recover from the performance.

Only it wasn't a performance, Akbar impressed upon me the next morning when he arrived to escort me to the palace. "When the *bori* are called by rich people to weddings and naming ceremonies it is for entertainment that they dance and jump and shout in languages we cannot understand. Then perhaps they are only playing. But what you saw in the *karuwai* compound—those people were not playing, they were truly possessed."

"I don't *know* what I saw, Akbar." I'd never before seen people crawling on the ground, frothing at the mouth, or leaping in the air and crashing down on their buttocks. Though once, one hot afternoon on the grounds of a midwestern mental hospital I'd observed a mountainous woman in a grubby blouse and baggy pants bent over a flower bed bright with scarlet geraniums from which she was scooping handfuls of earth. My fellow graduate students and I had watched in horror while she ate the earth in great ravenous mouthfuls. The staff psychologist who was showing us around explained that the woman was well known for flushing her Thorazine down the toilet. "The nurses do their best to keep an eye on her but she's crafty... And when she doesn't take her medicine she regresses to the oral stage..." Were those people I'd seen in the *karuwai* compound regressed to the oral stage, I wondered? Or had they fallen off the developmental ladder altogether, into Hades?

Akbar propped his bike against the cinder-block wall, removed and folded his sunglasses, placed them in his shirt pocket, and, followed by half a dozen children, entered our bungalow. Seated on our red vinyl couch with the children sprawled at his feet, he explained that the world was full of angry spirits.

"They can punish me—and even you—though neither of us has done anything to offend them." Restless, vengeful, eternally dissatisfied, Sarkin Rafi, the madman, Dan Galadima, the gambler, Danko, the snake, and scores of other spirits were always on the lookout for human beings to share their torment. "They see innocent people and seize upon them. They command them"—Akbar pointed at me—" 'You will carry me from here to there. And you"—he pointed at one of the children—"will carry me back again!' They make such people crazy, just as they themselves are crazy; or they paralyze their legs, they make all their hair fall out, they cover them with boils, they make men impotent, they make women miscarry and their wombs dry up. It is only by inviting the spirits to come to them, by letting themselves be ridden, by speaking with their voices and behaving just as they do, that those who are afflicted find peace."

At one time the madman we'd seen yesterday had been murderously insane. He'd burned down his own house in Sokoto. He would have decapitated his own son if his brothers hadn't overpowered him in time and chained him to a post. After that they'd taken him to healers all over the region, but none had cured him. Finally, they'd brought him here to the Magajiya of Kaura, who was famous for treating mad people. As a young woman, spirits had taken possession of her also. She'd run away from her husband and wandered with staring eyes through the countryside. In rags, she'd shouted nonsense and muttered to herself. Children would throw stones at her and she'd throw them back, and also the dung of farm animals. But by and by she'd reached Kaura, where the Magajiya of those days had seen her and had compassion. She'd taken the unfortunate young woman into the *karuwai* compound, prepared medicines for her, and, when she was calm enough, taught her how to call to Sarkin Rafi and have him enter her. But whereas once he'd ruled her so completely that for more than twelve months she'd had not one moment of sanity, now he came only when she invited him. He would possess her for a week or a month even and then he'd leave her and again she'd be in her right mind. Once she'd learned how to dance with Sarkin Rafi and, having satisfied him, how to send him away, she hadn't returned to the house where she had married. She'd stayed with the old Magajiya in the *karuwai* quarter. She'd learned to tell which spirit, out of craving and spitefulness, caused stillbirths, which one rashes, which one leprosy. She'd learned to make medicines for these afflictions and for epilepsy, paralysis, barrenness, and impotence. And having learned how to ward off the spirit that afflicted her, she'd taught so many other unlucky people how to ward off the spirits that afflicted *them*. Eventually, after the passing of the old Magajiya, she'd succeeded her as chief of *bori*.

But unfortunately, skilled though she was, she couldn't help everyone who came to her, Akbar said sadly, and even those she helped were never really cured. Once somebody fell victim to a spirit, they could never again be completely free. The Magajiya herself wasn't completely free. From time to time she, like every victim, had to permit her tormenting spirit to "ride" her. Sarkin Rafi and Dan Galadima were particularly demanding; they required evidence of their victims' submission more frequently than most. The madman we'd seen yesterday—leaping and plunging and covering himself with dirt—was obliged to spend every dry season in Kaura with the Magajiya because almost every afternoon Sarkin Rafi called him out to dance. Were he to refuse to obey his master, instead of being able to return quietly to Sokoto when the summer rains began, he'd be in the bush chattering, screaming, throwing stones at goatherds and cattle, a madman once again.

"The gambler, too, spends the dry season with the Magajiya," Akbar continued. "He was the only son of a rich man, he inherited a large farm, two shops, two lorries. But all he thought about was gambling. He would even place bets on the arrival of the rainy season—how many days late, how many days early! When he had lost everything except his house and a single field his uncle brought him here. So long as he stays with the Magajiya, Dan Galadima cannot seriously harm him, and his wives and children have a roof over their heads."

As for the woman whom Danko afflicted, she had married in Funtua and three times given birth there to dead children. After that she didn't conceive again and, as if that weren't hardship enough, she'd started to go blind. A miserable, distraught creature, she'd come to the Magajiya in the cold season, when the harmattan winds whipped down from the desert and in morning frost silvered the dead grass. The Magajiya had placed her in the care of the women who'd been attending to her yesterday. They too were tormented by Danko but they'd learned how to harness him, and they undertook to teach the Funtua woman everything they knew. To begin with, when she heard Danko's music, it meant nothing to her. But after a while, when Danko called out to her, she began to give him heed. She began to answer him, to welcome him, and finally to let him mount and ride her.

"Each time he rode her she would get hotter than the time before. When you saw her yesterday she was sweating like a pig. This is a good sign. It means her affliction is leaving her. But when she's cured she won't go home to her husband. Most of the women stay with the Magajiya, both to help others and for their own well-being. In order to keep their spirit masters satisfied, from time to time they have to let themselves be ridden." With a flirtatious shake of his shoulders, Akbar added, "Besides, why should they go home to be in purdah again? They've tasted *karuwanci*, the free life, and they prefer it!"

As for the audience, some came just for amusement. On special occasions rich people called the *bori* dancers to their houses to perform for their guests; but not many could afford a private performance and so most, if they wanted to see the dancing, came to the *karuwai* compound. "Provided you give a little money to the musicians you can watch all afternoon," said Akbar. "But the truth is most come because they are afflicted in some way or other... by migraine headaches, or yaws, or a weak chest... And many men come because they fear sterility, and many women because they cannot conceive." In the *karuwai* compound they were encouraged by seeing others gradually master the spirits who afflicted them. At times the mere spectacle itself sent onlookers into a trance and should that happen the Magajiya and her assistants were there to guide them and make sure they came to no harm.

"And always, when they return to their normal state, they feel stronger," Akbar concluded.

"Have the wives of the Magaji come?"

Akbar chuckled. "Childless though they are, neither they nor the Magaji have ever come. Nor has your Rabi."

"They don't believe in the spirits?"

"Of course they do, but those Alhajis and Alhajias are big people. They are very pious, very proud. The quarter of the *karuwai* is out of bounds for them. But my master and your landlord Aziz are rich. If they wish, they can invite *bori* people to their compounds. They can meet them secretly. Your Rabi, too." He paused. "Shall we go this afternoon to the Magajiya? I believe she likes you and would welcome you again."

I looked at him, aghast. "You want me to go back *this afternoon?*"

"Why not? Surely you found *bori* interesting. You have asked me so many questions about what you saw, and some I cannot answer. If you go back, you can ask the Magajiya whatever you want."

"Oh sure, I found *bori* interesting..." I looked down at my hands. "I don't think I'm up to seeing it again...not for a while at least. I need to recover..."

"From what do you need to recover?"

"It was an assault on the consciousness," I said in English.

"*Assault on the consciousness.* What does that mean?"

"Seeing those people...well, losing control, scared me, Akbar..." I looked up at him. "I could lose control as well." I could tumble off the ladder, into Hades.

He seemed puzzled. "But the Magajiya would be with you. If something bad happened, she would help you," he said. When I didn't respond he took out his sunglasses and rose to his feet. "Come," he ordered, "they must be asking for you in the palace."

"Wait a moment, Akbar. Tell me why *you* go to *bori?*"

Quick as a whip he replied, "I am called *dan gida,* son of the house. The polite English word for that is *ward.* But a better word is *slave.*"

In some long-ago tribal war, he told me, his ancestor had been taken captive by the Magaji's ancestor and brought back to Kaura, where because his own people had failed to redeem him, he'd lived out his life as a slave. When the British came they abolished slavery, but most slaves, having nowhere else to go or kin to help them, stayed with their masters, on whom they depended, as before, for everything—food, shelter, clothing, the wherewithal for marriage and a decent death.

"I have no home," Akbar said quietly, "so I stay in the Magaji's compound, in the back, near the latrines. The *karuwai* have no homes either, so they stay in the Magajiya's compound. I go to *bori* every afternoon in the dry season because my friends are there."

I arrived at the palace a good deal later than usual, but the Magaji's wives seemed not to have noticed my absence. They had a visitor, an elderly woman named Safia who just the evening before had returned from Mecca after an absence of four years. She had made the journey overland with her husband and youngest son; and, to finance their expedition, the son had spent many months both on the way out and on the way home working as a laborer in the cotton fields of the Sudan while the parents traded cloth in the markets of nearby towns. As a new Alhajia, Safia was making the customary round of visits to dispense blessings and receive congratulations. A small, dark-skinned woman, she was transfused with pride and happiness as she told stories of life along the pilgrim's way. After she left, I learned that whereas, like Safia, Hasana had only made the hajj once, Adama had made it twice and Fatima four times. The first time, almost twenty years earlier, the Magaji had only taken Fatima, as his senior wife, and they had traveled by bus across the breadth of Africa to the seacoast of the Sudan and thence by ferryboat to Jidda. The second time they'd taken a propeller plane from Kano to Khartoum, where they'd spent two days before flying on to Cairo and thence to Mecca. But in the 1960s, at least for the rich—and the Magaji was a rich man—the hajj experience had been transformed by the jet plane. Nowadays it was possible to set off from Kaura in the morning and reach Mecca that same night. They went by car to Kano where, together with several thousand fellow pilgrims, they were transported to Saudi Arabia in a fleet of chartered planes. "When we arrived we were separated," said Adama.

"Men to one side, women to the other," said Hasana.

"For fifteen days we were on our own," said Fatima. "We could please ourselves. No purdah." Why should there be? In their camp there were only women and eunuchs.

"Hasana added, "There were some boy-girls like Akbar also, but should we worry about them? We could leave our quarters whenever we wanted—at midday or at midnight."

"There were women selling foreign foods and we tasted all of them—Arabian food and Indian food, and food from Malacca."

"On the last day we went to the Kabbah. But every other day we went to the shops—at any hour, they would be open and at any hour we could go. In Kaura we can never do so. We must send a servant to buy for us. Although traders sometimes bring their merchandise into the entrance hall, what they offer us is limited. But in Mecca, the choice is limitless and there we could see everything for ourselves. Silks, both light and heavy, gold earrings, jeweled slippers, bracelets, carpets. We each bought one pair of earrings, but the carpets were too expensive. At them we could only look."

"The women we met were friendly. They came from countries I'd never heard of," said Hasana. "But everyone knew a few words of Arabic so we could converse a little."

"And for the rest, we used our hands," said Adama.

They'd had the time of their lives.

"The Magaji makes the hajj every four years," said Fatima. "Next winter we will go and you will come with us! The journey is very quick and comfortable. Only four hours in the plane. You will find the hajj so interesting, you will fill your notebook up completely."

"You, too, will have the time of your life!"

I had visions of Sir Richard Burton, who'd traveled in disguise to Mecca and Medina in 1826. My heart leapt. And sank immediately. "Only Muslims are permitted to visit the holy places. If the Saudis catch me, a Christian..." Or at least a Christian dropout, I said to myself.

"Why would they catch you?" Fatima retorted. "Instead of your language you will speak ours. You will dress as we do. You are the same height as Hasana and your hair and complexion, are they so different?"

It was true that we both had dark-brown wavy hair; and with my deeply tanned face I might conceivably "pass" as a Hausa woman of Taureg ancestry. But I'd have to show my passport, I pointed out, and the cat would be out of the bag. "You will leave your passport in Kaura. The Magaji is permitted four wives and there are only three of us. You will be his fourth wife and he will provide papers for you, just as he does for us," said Fatima decisively.

Adama and Hasana giggled; the children and the servants guffawed.

"My husband wouldn't agree to that," I said.

"No need for him to worry. It is only for the hajj that you will be our co-wife." Fatima added, smiling, "Besides, as I told you, in Mecca wives are separated from their husbands. You'll be safe with us."

"I'm sure I shall." I was thrilled by the prospect. "Thank you, I accept your invitation. There's nothing I want to do more than to go on the hajj with you!"

"Then you must speak to your husband about it and I will speak to ours."

I did broach the subject with my husband but my argument—which was that by venturing where no western woman had yet dared to tread and by writing about it afterwards I stood to make an important scholarly contribution—he rejected it out of hand. "You could be arrested, thrown in jail, held for decades, executed! What sort of contribution would *that* be?"

Clearly, I needed to come up with a better argument. But before I could do so and before Fatima had had a chance to approach the Magaji, who happened to be seven hundred miles away at a meeting in Lagos, my life changed forever.

One afternoon I went to observe the small son of a woman named Mariamu. As I walked into the compound, the little boy came toddling toward me with Mariamu, whom I hadn't seen since the previous observation two weeks earlier, in pursuit. Grabbing her child, she greeted me warmly and then, taking a step back, looked me up and down, an amused expression on her face. "So," she exclaimed, "at last you are pregnant!"

"Oh no, I'm not!"

"But your breasts are swollen. That's the first sign."

"I can't be pregnant," I protested. "We've been using family planning." In addition to which, with night temperatures in late May falling no lower than one hundred degrees, sex had become a once-in-a-rare-while activity.

Mariamu shrugged and, tying her son onto her back, led the way to the inner courtyard where her three co-wives were napping in the shade. Mariamu clapped her hands and one by one they rolled over and sat up. "Look at her," she ordered. "Tell me, what do you see?"

Before the week was out my husband and I made the five-hour round trip to the hospital in Zaria City to consult Dr. Agrawal, who confirmed Mariamu's diagnosis. I was nine weeks pregnant. The last two periods I'd had had been false. "Discharge was due to foetal implantation, not to period. Not unusual," said Dr. Agrawal, handing me a bottle of fat iron pills. "These will cause constipation, but not to worry."

My baby would be born during pilgrimage season, which put an end to my Richard Burton fantasies. As a die-hard adventuress, I was quite surprised to realize I didn't mind. "At last you are pregnant!" Mariamu had exclaimed. At last, after so much play time, real life was beginning. I was delighted, I was scared to death, and I was infinitely thankful to be joining the mainstream of the human race. But soon I would have to share news of my seismic shift with the Magaji's wives. With Hasana, who'd left her son with his father six years ago and had been waiting vainly ever since for the Magaji to provide a replacement. With Adama, whose hopes of bearing a child must surely be fading. And with Fatima, who would remain forever childless. I felt anxious, apologetic... guilty. What they so longed for had happened to me without my even trying. I dreaded our encounter. The night after I saw Dr. Agrawal I couldn't sleep, knowing I'd be going to the palace in the morning. I would also have to inform the Alhajia, my other childless friend; though I had more time to prepare for that encounter as she wouldn't be returning from her course until the following week.

But news traveled fast through the lanes of Kaura and when, by way of leading into a much more difficult topic, I told the Magaji's wives that I wouldn't be making the hajj with them after all, Fatima said matter-of-factly, "We know little about the hospital at Mecca. No one we know has ever given birth there. Better for you to go to the government hospital in Zaria. The Magaji used to work there, he has respect for the place."

"So you have heard my news! Who told you?"

Fatima shrugged. "Two, three different people. You are seen with your notebook all over this town...I am happy for you," she added and her broad smile convinced me this was true.

"No matter that you are from America, Nigeria will be your son's home," said Adama.

"*Kaura* will be his home," said Hasana.

"And seven days after his birth we will have his naming ceremony here in this house," said Fatima. "We will roast a sheep and invite many people to eat with us."

"Shall we invite the *bori* dancers as well?" I said innocently.

All three of them looked at me in silence. Finally Fatima nodded. "If you would like to see them we shall invite them also." She added, "And if not this time, then the next time, you and your son will come with us to Mecca."

"What if my son's a daughter with yellow hair and blue eyes?"

"There are plenty of Muslims of that complexion," said Fatima. "Blue eyes, green eyes, red hair, yellow hair—at Mecca you can see all kinds."

May had long ago turned into June and July was only a week away. Great mounds of cumuli rose in the sky, sheet lightning flashed and thunder rolled in the evening; but still no rain fell and as the moon rose the clouds always pulled away to the east. The Magaji, morose in his office, told my husband that the Sahara Desert was thirty miles closer to Kaura than it had been when he was a boy. Each summer the rains arrived a day or two later and finished a day or two earlier than they had the previous year. This was the fault of the *maguzawa* farmers. In the first place, their flocks were too large and in the second, they allowed their goats to eat the bark off trees. Stripped, the trees soon died and nothing grew in their place except weeds and scrubby bushes. Then the soil turned to sand and blew away in the harmattan winds. Not so long ago there had been forests all round Kaura but these days you had to travel up to Funtua to see a decent stand of trees. He wouldn't be surprised if, before he died, the Sahara reached Kaura.

One morning, when it was hotter than ever, I was on the edge of town when I heard drums beating in a nearby *maguzawa* settlement. Soon they were joined by the familiar monotonous arhythmic sawing of single-stringed fiddles, and over the crest of a low hill a hundred yards to my left strode the Magajiya, waving a peacock fan. She crossed a field that had been vainly prepared for planting weeks earlier. She was followed by a couple of drummers, four fiddle players, a man with a calabash rattle, and two praise singers. Weaving in and out of this short column came the mad arsonist from Sokoto, eyes half-closed, head drawn down between his shoulders. From time to time, he pulled up short and, feet together, hands stiffly at his sides, made a series of little jumps. Then, shaking his head as if to clear it, he resumed his loping stride. Trudging well in the rear came the Magaji, turban slightly awry, robe trailing over the furrows in which, because not one drop of rain had fallen yet, not a single seed had been planted. Behind him came a dozen hangers-on and officeholders whom I knew by sight from the palace.

When she reached me, the Magajiya bowed. "You didn't come back to us," she said, looking at me intently. No, because your dancers scared me half to death, I thought, but said nothing, and before I could think of a better response she'd passed on. But the Magaji paused and, pulling out a grubby blue-bordered handkerchief, mopped his face. "No rain, so what to do?" he said. With a sigh he added, "Hoping this will do the trick," and trudged on. He and his allies against the powers of darkness, the vengeful spirits who punish human beings indiscriminately, made three complete circumambulations of Kaura and withdrew to await the outcome of their joint venture.

It did the trick. The next afternoon, just as before, cumuli mounded up to great heights, lightning flashed, and thunder rolled. But this time the heavens opened and within moments the Kaura river was awash and, as children danced and splashed and shouted with glee in racing ditches, a great dense cloud of winged insects whose eggs had been waiting since autumn to hatch, rose up and crashed kamikaze-like into each other and into everything else that moved. Next morning, they lay heaped in death throughout the lanes of Kaura and, as farmers ran to plant their fields, the mad arsonist, cured for the season, donned a new white outfit, said his good-byes to his *karuwai* companions, and hopped on a lorry heading home to Sokoto.

II

LAS TRES MARÍAS

The Cult of the Virgin in Mexico

Due north of Cuernavaca rises a jagged mountain chain that divides the Valley of Morelos from the Valley of Mexico. Between stretches of dense forest, in which smoke from the banked fires of illegal charcoal makers curls above dark trees, extinct volcanoes jut high and bald into an azure sky. The inhabitants of Ojos de María, one of only a handful of villages in those inhospitable mountains, are mostly Nahuatl Indians who scratch out a livelihood raising goats for *barbacoa* stew and yucca plants for the *mescal* with which, on weekends, they hope to lure city people up their narrow rutted road. But when I first knew the place, the rustic restaurants lining the main street were attracting few customers even on the long holiday weekends with which Mexico is enviably endowed, and most households relied on remittances from *el otro lado*, the "other side."

I started my work in Ojos de María in the cold season, when the rosy-cheeked village children rarely showed up at the school, with its ill-fitting doors and broken windowpanes, until the sun had worked its way round the bald volcano to the east and dispelled the dank midwinter mist. Meanwhile, their teachers would huddle round a brazier in the principal's office. As I waited with them for freezing temperatures to edge upward and the children to come straggling in, I'd listen as they harped on their favorite topics: the inadequacy of their salaries, which, with inflation mirroring the country's perennial economic crisis, hardly put tortillas on their tables, and the thankless task of teaching children whose sole objective was to quit school as soon as possible and head for Santa Isolde, the Orange County town to which several hundred Ojos de María natives had already emigrated. When I asked about the history of the village, the teachers offered scraps of information about the sixteenth-century church and the seven chapels, crumbling into ruin in the nearby forest, that marked the Stations of the Cross. But no one seemed to know how the place had come by its name. *Ojo* means "spring" as well as "eye" in Spanish and there were several springs in the immediate vicinity. Who was the María who had given her name to the village? Had the springs belonged to her? Had her eyes been especially lovely? "Perhaps our ancestors knew, but as for us, we have forgotten," said one of the teachers. "Anyway, María is the most common name in Mexico. So many women are named for the *virgencita*, and also many men. I myself am María Jesús."

So it wasn't surprising that all three of my Mexican landladies were named María.

I encountered my first, María Luz de Orozco, one morning when she was watering her garden in the barrio of Santiago, which lay to the west of Cuernavaca's colonial city center. Most of the city's houses, whether they belonged to ordinary working people, commuter refugees from the pollution of Mexico City, or wealthy snowbirds from North America and Europe, were shielded from the world's scrutiny by high walls topped by shards of broken glass. By contrast, fronted by widely spaced iron railings, María Luz's cream stucco house was open to all eyes. Often, when passing through her neighborhood, I would admire the riot of flowers that grew in narrow beds and glazed containers on her patio. But this was the first time I had seen the lady of the house. As she moved slowly down a row of geraniums, hose in hand, she regulated the flow with her thumb so that water sprayed evenly across the scarlet blossoms. When she reached the end of the row, she glanced up and saw me. "So you like flowers," she observed. A diminutive woman in her sixties, bright white hair framed her dark face; she wore a blue-checked housecoat and yellow slippers and, on the third finger of her right hand, a narrow wedding band. I said that up north I had a flower garden but for all the effort I put into it, it wasn't half as colorful as hers. "Soil, sun, and water are important," she said gravely, "and of those three, the most important is soil." After we'd chatted over her gate for some minutes, she invited me in to see her cuttings. Having inspected a hundred-odd impressively healthy plants in the courtyard behind her house (every one of them grown from just a little cutting, as she impressed upon me), I was about to take my leave when she offered me a newly rooted jasmine and a hydrangea which, with proper care, would flower dark blue come spring. Regretfully, I refused them. I had no place to put them, I told her. I'd been forbidden by my American landlord to plant anything in the obsessively ordered Japanese-style garden in which my rented cottage stood. María Luz remarked that for someone who loved flowers to live without them was a great misfortune. She added that if ever I needed a different place to stay, she had a little apartment standing empty: two rooms, a bathroom, and a strip of south-facing veranda on which potted plants habitually flourished.

That evening, I decided I'd had enough of my landlord's rules and regulations. Next morning, I gave him notice, and at the end of the month I moved out of his cottage and into the back of María Luz's house. " 'Señora Orozco' is too formal," said my new landlady. "It's better that you call me Luz. Everyone does, except my mother, but she is ninety-eight years old and living in León with my sister Gloria."

Luz had four sons, five daughters, and twenty-three grandchildren. All her children were married and two of her sons lived with their families on the upper floors of her house. Her husband, Raúl, for many years a labor union organizer, represented a nearby market town in the state legislature. Luz's day began with six o'clock mass at the church of Santiago up the street, after which she came home to water her *plantitas*. Raúl, too, was up and out early to breakfast with his cronies; being busy with politics, he often didn't return until late. "He's out talking," Luz explained. "He'll talk to anyone, and if there aren't any human beings to talk to, he'll talk to cows or birds. He makes people feel they're important. It's that that gets him the votes."

Hardly taller than his wife, Raúl had a trim waist and a full head of iron-gray hair; his clothes were carefully chosen and well pressed, his shoes were always polished, and, whenever I caught a glimpse of him, whether at dawn or at midnight, he exuded an exuberant delight in life.

Every Friday afternoon at three-thirty, the Orozco family gathered at the house for *comida*, prepared by Luz and a rotating crew of daughters and daughters-in-law. Though every Friday *comida* was a special occasion, those Fridays on which Raúl was able to extricate himself from politics to be there too were truly celebratory. Hearing the front gate swing open, a dozen grandchildren would jump up from the long table and race across the patio to greet their grandfather. Hanging on his arms and clutching at his pant legs, they'd pull and push him into the house. While sons and daughters crowded around him and grandchildren fought over who would sit next to him, a beaming Raúl would take his place at the head of the table. With him ensconced and at his ease in the bosom of his family, Friday lunch became a feast.

But though Raúl sat at the head of the table, the house did not in fact belong to him. Nineteen years ago, Luz had made the down payment with money she'd earned as a seamstress, she told me soon after I moved in. Her son, Pedro, who at that time had just started work in a bank, had helped her obtain a loan. With rent from "my" apartment and her own earnings—she sewed uniforms for a large parochial school—she'd managed to make every payment on the loan out of her own pocket. This coming June the loan would be paid off and the house would truly be *hers*. As protection against life's vagaries, every married woman should have her own property, she told me. When I admitted that my husband and I owned our house jointly, she pursed her lips in regret.

☙

With the cold season edging into spring, Luz said she planned to visit the Virgin.

"The Virgin of Guadalupe in Mexico City?" I asked.

"No, not at all." She didn't much care for that place—always there were too many impatient people shoving you, cleaning women chasing after you with floor mops, rude guards telling you to keep moving on. She was going to visit the Virgin of Los Lagos.

Los Lagos was three days' walk from Muzquíz, the little town in Los Altos de Jalisco where she'd been born. In her childhood, her whole family and more than half the population of their village—several hundred souls—would take the pilgrim path to the fiesta of John the Baptist. They sang as they walked across the dry hills of late winter; they cooked over open fires and slept, wrapped in serapes and rebozos, on the cold ground. When, late on the third day, wearing coronets of yellow gorse they'd gathered on the way, they reached Los Lagos, the fair that accompanied this—and every—fiesta would be in full swing.

Round-eyed, they watched acrobats somersaulting and cartwheeling on high wires, and jugglers keeping five, six, *seven* balls in the air. They saw dancing bears and waltzing elephants, and a tiger snarling in a cage. They had their palms read by fortune-tellers and listened, enraptured, to the ballads of black-and-silver-costumed mariachis. A handsome stranger asked fifteen-year-old Luz to dance; and, though her parents had forbidden her to speak to any boy who was not a blood relation, she danced with him. (Her parents, who happened to be off visiting the Well of Miracles, didn't see her and her sister Gloria, who did, didn't tell.) They ate *nopalitos,* smoked trout, and chili-covered peanuts at market stalls, watched plumed rockets soar into the night sky, and slept beside hundreds of other pilgrims in an ancient hospice with granite walls a meter thick. At mass the next morning, a monsignor—one year it had been a bishop wearing a miter and a gold-embroidered purple cope—would bless the statues of the saints that *mayordomos* (her father among them) had carried on their shoulders from altars in villages all over the Bajío region. And then they'd head for home

to review everything they'd seen and heard and eaten at Los Lagos and to count the days until their next pilgrimage.

But for Luz, the high point had never been the fair or the mass
or even the dancing. "Those you find in other places," she told
me. Her main reason for going to Los Lagos was to see the little
Virgin. "She's no bigger than a doll," she told me, "and nobody
knows where she came from." Some said she was Spanish, that
she was the patron saint of a conquistador who'd tied her to his
saddle when he'd ridden into battle against the Moors in Spain
and, once the Moors had been dispatched to Africa, had brought
her with him to the New World. Others said no, she was Mexican, that long ago an Indian convert to Christianity had carved
her out of *occuelto* wood and worshipped her in place of the old
gods.

"They say she works miracles," Luz told me, "that she cures
TB and cancer and so many other diseases, that she stops men
from drinking and allows barren women to conceive." She
shrugged. "This might be true, but speaking for myself, I don't
ask her for miracles. Such a tiny thing, all by herself, century
after century, on the high altar of that great cathedral ... She,
who lost her son in the cruelest way imaginable ... For a mother,
can there be any greater sorrow?" She met my gaze. "One might
say that I go to keep her company," she added with a quick shy
smile.

After she got married and had so many children she didn't
have time or money to visit. "I had to make do with a picture
postcard tacked up on the wall," she told me. But eventually, after her youngest child, Aurora, finished middle school, she was
able to go again. Only by then she was living far away in Cuernavaca, and so instead of walking to Los Lagos she had to travel
there by bus. Her daughters always said they'd like to go with
her; but they were too busy; her husband and sons were too busy
as well.

"Would *you* like to go?" she asked me.

We went by bus to Mexico City, where we caught the night
express, and after riding nine hours and making numerous stops
in roadside towns we drove into Los Lagos at daybreak. Borne

through the streets by a human tide, we reached the great square, with the baroque cathedral, glowing pinkish in the morning light, at its center. Gone were the acrobats, jugglers, elephants, and dancing bears of Luz's childhood. In their place towered a Ferris wheel and in its long shadow, doing a brisk trade at eight in the morning, were carousels, shooting galleries, and stalls that sold miracle water and religious pictures, candy floss, caramelized popcorn, and mangos cut like flowers and sprinkled with chili-pepper. A column of country people wound through the town square, or *zócalo*. The men wore guaraches, serapes, and battered sombreros, the women, aprons over wide skirts and crocheted rebozos wrapped tightly round their shoulders against the morning chill. They carried banners embroidered with emblems and the names of villages—San Juan de Zacatepec, San Juan de Omoluco, San Juan de la Negra Colina—and wooden statues of the saints, their paint peeling, their gold leaf grown dull. While they waited for the cathedral doors to open, they watched a troop of young girls in white cotton overshirts and beribboned pantaloons, their dark hair secured by red bandannas. Modern Aztec maidens, they stamped moccasined feet, shook rattles, jumped, and twirled.

Eyes narrowed, Luz searched for the banner of Muzquíz, her birthplace. "Can you see it?" she asked urgently as we walked toward the rear of the column. So many in her village had died or left for the city. Did anyone remain to bring the *santos* to Los Lagos? But to her joy, she spotted the Muzquíz banner and, right beside it, gnarled Emilio, youngest son of her maternal grandmother's brother, holding San Juan Bautista de Muzquíz in his arms. He'd come by truck with a handful of neighbors, he told us. The truck had let them off on the outskirts of Los Lagos and they'd walked the last three kilometers into town. These days, no one was willing to walk the whole distance.

"The young ones say they have to make a living, how can they spare a week of their time? And the old ones?" Emilio shrugged. "It's my hip that pains me," he said, watching the great west doors swing open.

As bells peeled, half a dozen men ran to the north side of the *zócalo* to fire off rockets, which, with a *whoosh* and a billow of acrid smoke, raced into the sky.

Luz whipped out a mantilla and covered her head. "Come," she said, taking my hand. "Let us go in with the Muzquízeños."

By the time we entered the cathedral, the nave was a forest of banners and every seat was taken in the pews. Holding his *santo* against his chest, Emilio made his way past men, women, here and there a few young children, creeping forward on their knees to join the other *mayordomos* on the chancel steps. But for Luz, myself, and the rest of the Muzquízeños it was standing room only in a side aisle.

One of the advantages of being as tall as I am in Mexico, a nation of small people, is that I can see over the heads of crowds. Now, despite being near the back of the cathedral, I had a good view of the little Virgin. Fair skinned and barely a foot high, in her white silk robe, gold-embroidered cloak, and jewel-studded crown, she stood on the altar in a square glass box. In her outstretched hands, she held a minute orb and a scepter.

"Can you see her?" Luz whispered.

"Perfectly," I whispered back. But Luz, who only came up to my shoulder, couldn't see her at all.

A priest led acolytes and choristers into the chancel. Though he certainly wasn't a bishop and he looked too young to be even a monsignor, he was darkly handsome and words rolled off his tongue like summer thunder. "*De los siglos a los siglos,* from century to century," he told us, "Jesus Christ and the Saints and his Mother, the Blessed Virgin, protected our forefathers, and likewise, today, they protect us. They gave our forefathers the courage to withstand evil, to know what is true and what is right, and to act accordingly. Let us pray that we, too, receive such courage."

Luz didn't take the Eucharist from an acolyte in the side aisle. Ignoring disapproving glances and whispered rebukes, she pushed through the crowd to the altar rail, where, within ten feet of the Virgin, she took the host from the handsome priest himself. Then, circling round to the end of the line, head bowed in prayer and resolve, she made her way back to the altar rail to take the Eucharist a second time. When we met up in the *zócalo* after the mass, she was glowing. "I saw her close-up twice!"

We ate breakfast with Cousin Emilio, saw him and his *santo* onto their truck, and then returned to the cathedral, to a chamber behind the altar in which the Virgin's wardrobe of cloaks and silken dresses—a different outfit for every week of the year—was stored in glass-fronted mahogany cabinets. To the walls of the chamber were nailed hundreds of *ofrendas*—photos, bridal shoes and garters, prayer books, crutches, baby clothes, thick braids threaded with ribbon—left in gratitude for boons *la santissima virgencita* had granted. We visited places in the town where she had wrought miracles, sampled the ham for which Los Lagos was famous, had our picture taken together, bought momentos for people back home, and rode the Ferris wheel, from the top of which Luz declared she could see clear to Muzquíz.

When she showed me the sights she had been bubbling over with excitement. But later, as our bus pulled away from Los Lagos in the early evening, she wept.

"What's the matter, Luz?"

"I'm sad to be leaving her, is all."

"You'll be back next year, won't you?"

"A year is a long time to wait to see her . . ." Slowly Luz dried her eyes and then she said, so quietly that I had to strain to hear her, "But meanwhile I will talk with her . . . as I always do." Had they heard her admission, my neo-Marxist colleagues might have scorned it; but I was deeply moved. In the gathering darkness, I remembered what the great psychologist William James had written at the beginning of the twentieth century. Religion, he was convinced, is not a "mere anachronism" that modern science will ultimately banish (or a mere palliative for the oppressed, as some of my colleagues would have it). Rather, because it helps assuage and defeat human misery, it has played a central role in human history and will continue to do so. I didn't know why Luz, who in her daily life appeared to me to be virtually imperturbable, needed the constant companionship of the *virgencita;* but I was thankful—and awed—that, for whatever reason, she had it.

Though much of my research was in Cuernavaca, I also had work in Ojos de María, six thousand feet above the city, and in Epizote, a small town in the *tierra caliente,* the hot land, three thousand feet below. For several months I commuted, jolting out at dawn in metal-seated country buses and jolting back after dark. But after missing the last bus to the city on several occasions, I began to notice that my welcome from the kind schoolteachers who'd taken me in for the night was wearing out. I'd better start looking for my own place, or places, rather, since I needed two.

Prosperous Epizote proved to be no problem. Founded at the end of the Mexican Revolution by the peons of the hacienda San Felipe, whose owner had hastily departed after the Zapatistas burned his house to the ground, Epizote was laid out in the grid pattern brought by Roman satraps to the Peninsula and thence by Spanish settlers to the New World. Lying below a red-rocked mountain, the town looked across a lake to a plain dotted with the grass-covered pyramids of a long-forgotten temple complex and, far beyond them, to the snowcaps of Popocatápetl and Ixxtacíautl. Though Epizote had sent many sons and daughters to the farms and orchards of California and Oregon and the factories of Michigan and Illinois, it had retained their affections. They visited whenever possible—for funerals and weddings and New Year celebrations and for the fiesta of San Miguel, their patron saint, for which they arrived in pickup trucks and mammoth aging Chevrolets and Dodges. Most aimed to return to Epizote for good someday; and in the meantime they built fine houses with red-tiled roofs and curved balustrades, stocked shops for mothers and aunts to manage, and contributed to the construction of two schools, a medical clinic, a grand basilica that, when finished, would challenge the cathedral in Cuernavaca in size, and last but not least, a jail, used almost exclusively for sobering up drunks. But following the arrival of Alcoholics

Anonymous, with its thrice-daily meetings in the mayor's barn, the jail population had precipitously dwindled so that by the time I came to Epizote, except for during the September fiesta when the town was inundated with "outside" drunks, the jail was padlocked; and the horned and long-tailed Lucifer painted on the ochre wall facing the plaza looked sadly bereft.

Despite progress on other fronts, numerous efforts to open restaurants in the town had failed and so for lunch I'd buy cheese, tomatoes, and fruit from stalls in the plaza and fresh tortillas from the tortillería, and eat them on a bench under a tree outside the empty jail. One day, as she was wrapping my tortillas, the owner of the place, María Rosa de Ayala, told me she had a room for rent. A vivacious woman with a round figure and large sparkling eyes, she wore her long hennaed hair pinned up on her head to keep it out of the dough. Twenty years ago, she and her rancher husband, Nácio, had built a house with money Nácio had earned picking artichokes in Watsonville, California. Now their five children were all grown up and working "on the other side"; and with the money they sent home, their parents had recently built an extension. The room María Rosa showed me had screens on the windows, a narrow bed, two chairs, and an electrical outlet for recharging the batteries of my camcorder; a single shadeless twenty-five-watt lightbulb hung from the ceiling. I would share a spanking-new white-tiled bathroom with Lola and Elena, teenage sisters from a village in the mountains who worked in the tortillería and slept in the room next door. The master bedroom, most of which was taken up by a great pink satin-quilted bed, faced us across a patio in which purple bougainvillea ran riot. Two ranch hands, uncle and nephew, who came from the same Guerrero village as Lola and Elena, slept in a shed adjoining the barn where Nácio stabled his horse.

When I accepted Rosa's offer of full board as well as lodging, I had no notion of the gastronomic delights lying in store. Even on ordinary days, Rosa prepared at least eight dishes—many of which I'd never tasted before—for both ten o'clock *desayuno* and two-thirty *comida,* to which the hired help and Nácio applied themselves with intense concentration. The only sounds would be the smacking of lips and the plop of second helpings falling onto oversized tin plates. The evening meal, sandwiched between prime-time soap operas, was only slightly less plentiful.

At fourteen, lively Rosa had eloped with Nácio, a lanky, brooding youth of twenty-one. Three decades later, Rosa was at least as lively as she'd been as a girl, if not more so; but Nácio, who had metamorphosed from a lanky youth into a craggily handsome middle-aged man, was as given to silence as ever. Opposites attract, I thought, and in this case, the match looked like a winning combination. After supper Rosa and Nácio would sit snuggled together in front of the TV, above which was a reproduction of the painting of the Virgin of Guadalupe that hangs in the cathedral in Mexico City. At nine o'clock, giving Rosa an anticipatory squeeze, Nácio would turn off the TV and, taking his wife by the hand, would lead her into their pink satin bower, noisily locking the door behind them.

Finding a room in Ojos de María, a poorer place than Epizote, proved more difficult. Once the sons and daughters of Ojos de María made it up to Orange County they tended to stay there or, in any event, to send back a smaller slice of their earnings; houses were cramped and dilapidated and no one seemed to have a spare room. But then Vera, my half-Japanese, half-Russian ex-ballerina friend, introduced me to Ana María Cervantes Ortega y Torre at a Sunday afternoon chamber music concert in the Palacio Cortés. Vera told me later that Ana María lived on a grand estate only two kilometers down the road from Ojos de María, and that her three daughters were living in Europe. "So she might welcome your company," she said.

With her diamond earrings and two strands of extraordinarily large and lustrous pearls, Ana María had struck me as a queenly lady. "*My* company? Why ever would she welcome it?"

"At least call her," said Vera, whose children had grown up with Ana María's. "There's no harm in it. But I should warn you," she added, "the poor are very much with her. She's an *aficionada* of Don Sergio, or should I say a devotee." Sergio Mendez Arceo was the bishop of Cuernavaca whose interpretation of the Gospels and ideas about the relationship between faith, social justice, and human rights in the aftermath of Vatican II had brought him, like other prominent Latin American theologians who shared his views, into bitter confrontation with Rome. The news that queenly Ana María was fighting poverty and class oppression surprised and intrigued me. So call her I did, and she invited me up for tea the following afternoon.

With its shadowy high-ceilinged rooms, colonnaded patio, and marble fountains, the *quinta,* as local people referred to it, looked about four hundred years old but in fact had been built in colonial style in 1949 for a Hollywood star and her movie-mogul husband. Ana María and her husband, Geraldo, had bought it when, just three years after she'd moved in, the Hollywood star had divorced her movie mogul to marry a German prince. Eager to be rid of the *quinta,* with its memories of tedious fights and jealousies, she'd let the Cervantes Ortega y Torreses have it for the proverbial song. It came with a lap pool and, for the time, cutting-edge purification equipment (Geraldo, a former pentathlon athlete, had liked to swim two kilometers before breakfast), stabling for ten horses, and fifty-five hectares (Geraldo planned to raise palaminos). But nowadays Geraldo did a little breaststroke in only the hottest weather and had given up horses altogether; and the house itself was far too big for two people, Ana María admitted over iced tea in the loggia. First she offered me a ground-floor suite, but on second thought decided that the chapel was the answer. Despite its bells and turrets, leaded windows, and castellated walls, this was in fact a guesthouse. It had a perfectly functional kitchen, but if I preferred to dine with her and Geraldo, they would be delighted.

Luz de Orozco was charging me the equivalent of two hundred dollars a month for full board and lodging, with five dollars extra for laundry, and Rosa de Ayala five dollars per day. But Ana María refused any payment.

"It's your expertise I'm after, not your money," she told me, smiling.

"Expertise in what?"

"Community development."

Ever since she'd come as a young wife and mother to live at the *quinta,* she'd had "projects," she explained to me. If one had been born in this tragically backward country and one was *committed* to it and couldn't imagine living anywhere else, shouldn't one do whatever one could to improve social conditions? Her focus had always been families with young children, which was all she really knew anything about. (Sadly, her parents had pulled her out of her convent school just days before her *quinceañera,* her fifteenth birthday party.) When her own girls were small, she'd opened a nursery school in Ojos de María. (In preparation, she'd taken a six-month course in Mexico City—how she'd adored being a student!) In addition she'd provided immunizations for the village children and rabies injections for the village dogs. She'd distributed blankets and winter clothes to the women and—though she'd been perfectly aware of Rome's position on birth control—condoms to the men. "I asked myself, has any pope ever seen, as I have far too often, a poor woman, married to an irascible drunkard, struggle to cook and clean and wash for eleven children with the twelfth child on the way? The rhythm method is preposterous! How is an exhausted, illiterate woman expected to keep track of her 'safe' days? And even if she *can* keep track of them, how's she going to keep her husband off her on her *unsafe* days?" Throughout Mexico's long postwar boom, the government had promoted large families. "They wanted an ever-expanding army of placid workers," Ana told me, "to toil in Coca-Cola plants and Nissan factories … The government was just as callous as the Catholic Church. Condoms were hard to find, and if you found them, were absurdly expensive. And birth control pills were illegal."

After three children and one ectopic pregnancy, Ana María had had "everything removed" in a clinic in Mexico City. "That took care of me, but what about *mi gente* [my people] up in the village?" For a decade, she'd had Cousin Melissa in La Jolla, California, ship condoms down to Cuernavaca and distributed them herself. "The women were easily persuaded, but they weren't the ones to use them, were they?" Persuading the men, she'd soon discovered, was a lonely, daunting, even dangerous task. Too often she'd been chased across pastures and down village streets by machete-wielding husbands. "In our criminally un-equal society, an abundance of children was just about the only way they had to prove their manhood." With a shrug, she added, "Is it any wonder that some of them wanted to kill me?" When Pope Paul IV came out with *Humanae Vitae,* his encycli-cal prohibiting contraception, she'd been on the verge of despair. "But then that brave and wondrous soul, Don Sergio, stood up and rejected the encyclical as unconscionable. And soon the priests in this diocese, who'd been telling their parishioners to accept as many children as God gave them, were telling them to have no more than they could properly provide for. If that meant only two, so be it." Thank heaven, it hadn't been that much longer before the government came to its senses and introduced family planning, whereupon Ana María closed her one-woman birth-control program in Ojos de María and turned her atten-tions to an abandoned silver mine, home to twenty-seven squat-ter families.

"Here *we* are, just two of us, living in luxury, and there *they* are—at last count, one hundred and twenty-nine souls," she said. "You should have seen the conditions when I first went there!" She shivered. "The closest water source, a single tap, was thirty minutes away down the hill—which meant that, after filling their cans and bottles, those unfortunate women had a forty-five-minute walk back *up* the hill to the mine."

First, she'd dug a tube well and put in an all-season road; then, having had the area surveyed and come to an "arrange-ment" with the local authorities, she'd contracted with her cook's brother-in-law to build twenty-seven houses on adjacent community land. After the next harvest, when the men, most of whom were employed as agricultural laborers, would be out of work, they'd break ground.

Crossing her fingers, she added, "By this time next year, my people will be living in decent homes. But oh, the backbiting!" She grimaced. "The competition, the inveterate need to do each other down! What I need to do is get them to identify *common* goals and then work *together* to achieve them...If not, all my efforts will be for naught..."

Geraldo's attitude toward her projects was one of skeptical bemusement, though thankfully, he didn't interfere. "What I miss," she said wistfully, "is having an *ear*—someone with whom to discuss our problems, someone with whom to celebrate our small successes. I tell you, Vatican II truly turned the Church on its head..." So many of her old friends with whom she used to discuss her projects had left the priesthood. Father Jaime, for instance. For fourteen years he'd been the parish priest of Ojos de María until suddenly he'd set aside his vows and married Bertha, an ex-nun from the convent down the road. "A lovely young woman...Can one blame either of them? Celibacy can be too a punitive a sacrifice. Now they give crash courses in Spanish to Anglo schoolteachers from Orange County so they can communicate with children who swarm up to California from places like Ojos de María." She paused and then, emboldened, blurted out, "Instead of rent, what I'd like from you is help with getting my people to cooperate with one another. As a social scientist who studies families, I've no doubt you'll have great insights, wonderful suggestions." Her expression was at once eager, forceful, and seductive.

Without having seen the mine or met any of its inhabitants, no thoughts on how one might encourage cooperation came to mind. But I was drawn to Ana María's warmth and spunkiness, her pluck and determination. I'd never met a Mexican woman like her, or for that matter any woman anywhere else. When I said I'd try to help, she clapped her hands in delight and, from a bureau in the *sala*, produced two impressive keys, one to the chapel, another to the main gate—in case the gardener, who lived in the gatehouse, didn't answer the bell. "You must come and go as you please, and once you're settled, may I introduce you to my people?" As she handed me the keys, she added shyly, "Of course you've read Gustavo."

"Gustavo?"

"Gutierrez. His *Theology of Liberation.*" Though I'd only skimmed the book I claimed I'd read it. "How about the Boff brothers?" I admitted I hadn't read anything by either of them.

Only as I was walking away from the *quinta* with Leonardo Boff's *Jesús Cristo, Liberator* in my backpack did I remember that Ana María had said nothing about how her husband might feel about having a lodger. The framed photographs that I'd seen in the *sala* of Geraldo, a rakishly elegant fellow involved in various athletic pursuits, made me doubt that he'd be exactly thrilled to have a perfect stranger living on his property.

When I telephoned our mutual friend, Vera, she laughed. "Why should Ana care how Geraldo feels about it? It's her property not his and besides, he's occupied elsewhere."

She told me that Geraldo, who came from an ancient and aristocratic but impoverished Spanish family, had found his way to Mexico in 1946. "Fed up with living hand to mouth in the Old World, he sought financial security in the Americas," Vera explained, and in seventeen-year-old Ana María Figuerroa Farías, a cattle and copper heiress who was the only child of rich Creole parents, he'd found it. No matter that Geraldo was twenty years older, his antecedents were impeccable, at least in the eyes of his future in-laws who, the socialist ethos of Mexico notwithstanding, were awed by titles and escutcheons.

"In the 1940s, upper-class parents were still arranging their children's marriages," Vera told me, "and poor Ana was far too filial to object to her parents' choice. As for Geraldo, he reckoned he'd be free to do more or less as he pleased on the generous quarterly allowance his future in-laws agreed to settle on him. These days, as he heads for eighty," Vera continued, "Geraldo can't venture as far afield as he used to. But as usual, he's in luck. His current lady, Gigi Armstrong—Texan, several years younger than Ana María, and with no compulsion whatever to do good works—lives comfortably close by on alimony payments. Her house—Swiss chalet style with geraniums in window boxes—is within easy walking distance. You can see it from the road. Perhaps Ana pointed it out?"

"She didn't. She didn't mention Gigi either."

"No? Well, it's her proximity rather than her existence that bothers Ana. Though she'd been a fixture for quite some time Ana still hasn't come to terms with her being so *close*. She didn't mind so much when Geraldo's mistresses were in Mexico City. Even his more local ladies lived far down the mountain and were possible to ignore. But Gigi's place is only two hundred meters from the *quinta* and Geraldo's continually toddling off to see her—without making the slightest pretense of going to his club, like he used to...By the way," Vera added, "you shouldn't worry about him on your own account. As a matter of courtesy, the first chance he gets, he'll pinch your bottom. That done, he'll let you be. He's hard-pressed enough keeping up with Gigi. He couldn't take on anyone else."

"Why has Ana María put up with him?"

"Ah, a true *norteamericana* question. Kick the fellow out! Right? Sometimes Ana gets ill worrying about 'her people,' especially the women. On their behalf, she can be a feminist. She can urge and exhort them to stick up for themselves. But when it comes to sticking up for *herself*—she's not so good at that... Her daughters are a pretty assertive trio, but they're a new generation. They're decently educated and, besides, they live in Europe. One's married to an Englishman, one to a German, and one lives with her Swedish boyfriend in Paris. They don't have to deal with machismo, at least not in a flagrant form.

"Certainly Ana disagrees with the Church about contraception, but she still goes to mass every morning. And most years she takes a trip to Rome for a Papal audience. That's the only time she ever uses her title. Dear Ana, she thinks that as Condesa Cervantes Ortega y Torre she has a better chance of getting His Holiness's attention than she would as Señora Cervantes Ortega y Torre.... She truly believes that eventually—if she's persistent and prayerful enough—John Paul will change his views on birth control...Anyway, divorce is out of the question."

"Couldn't they decently separate? She shouldn't have to *live* with Geraldo."

"But don't you see, she does have to live with him! Her resolve to remain unimpaired by the humiliation he's made her suffer has *empowered* her...That's both her triumph and her revenge."

The first evening I spent in the Cervantes Ortega y Torres guest-house, a maid in a pink uniform and immaculate white apron appeared with an invitation to dinner at the *quinta*. Having ex-changed T-shirt and jeans for my one dressy garment, I crossed the garden to the loggia, where I found Ana María, chic in black cashmere pants and sweater, regulation pearls and diamond ear-rings, blond hair smooth and gleaming, and Geraldo, an im-pressively handsome elderly gentleman, whiskey on the rocks in hand, gazing at the stars on the lawn. "Oh, there you are!" ex-claimed Ana María. "We've been arguing about Canopus. I think it's that large yellowish star," she pointed, "and Geraldo says, no, it's *that* one, further to the south. Perhaps you can tell us." I confessed that my knowledge of the night sky went no fur-ther than Orion's Belt and the Big Dipper. "Never mind, after dinner we'll look it up in the encyclopedia. Dearest," Ana María turned to her husband. "This brilliant young woman's going to help me in the mine."

Geraldo bent from his great height—he was well over six feet tall—to kiss my hand. "*Encantado!*" As he straightened up, he murmured in English, "Do you know a great deal about mines?"

"Actually, I've never been down one," I replied in Spanish.

"You know it's not the *mine* she's going to help me with, dear-est. It's the people living *in* it."

"Ah, so she knows a great deal about *people*. Well, that might be useful."

At dinner in a dining room hung with dark religious paintings —Saint Jerome in the Desert, the Annunciation, Saint John the Baptist, Saint Joseph, the Virgin Mary and the Infant Christ, and an eight-by-ten-foot Crucifixion—we sat on straight-backed leather chairs, Geraldo at the head of a table that seated twenty, Ana María on his left and myself on his right. Over dinner— gazpacho, sea bass, Brie, and Gorgonzola with crisp French rolls, ending with meringues and strawberries served by the maid, who, for dinner, had donned white gloves—Geraldo and I identified the few things we had in common: we were both left-handed, were dangerously allergic to bee stings, had once ridden a camel in the desert outside Cairo, and had studied at the same British university, he in the 1920s and I forty years later. "I don't remember meeting any *educated* women," he murmured. But then, he admitted, at the time he hadn't been much interested in educated people of either sex. At the end of his first year he and his college had reached a mutually agreed-upon parting of the ways. "Frankly," he confided, "sitting hour after hour at a desk with a book—" to illustrate, he screwed up his eyes and hunched his shoulders over his sea bass—"seemed to me a pitiful waste of one's youth. Young people should be out experiencing life to the fullest, not cloistered like monastics! Tell me, at eighteen, wasn't that your view too?"

Glancing at Ana María, I noted downcast eyes and a flush of irritation. "Not at all," I lied blithely. "Reading was my great pleasure. I'd gone to university in order to read, and that's mostly what I did."

"How I envy you," said Ana María. "By the time I was eighteen, I'd already had Leonora and Eugenia was on the way...I suffered so terribly from morning sickness, I spent most of that pregnancy in bed..."

With no more to say to a terminally bookish woman like me, Geraldo turned his full attention to his food. Even so, when dinner was over, as Ana María led us from dining room to *sala* for coffee, he was moved to pinch my behind.

At ten-thirty the following morning, I spotted Geraldo, jaunty in a Panama hat, passing my window. At eleven o'clock my doorbell rang. Ana María, dressed in a cream poplin blouse, linen slacks, brown sneakers, and sunglasses, had come to take me to Mina de Cortés; the pearls were gone but not the diamond earrings. We got into her small gray Fiat and were off down the mountain. I glanced at Gigi's chalet, in which, at that very moment, Geraldo was taking his pleasure; but Ana Maria's eyes stayed firmly on the road ahead. A mile farther on we turned onto a track that took us across the mountainside and through several dry streambeds. "At one time, the mine really did belong to Hernán Cortés," Ana María remarked. "He grabbed it from a defeated Aztec noble after the Conquest and he and his descendents kept on mining it for centuries. About ten years ago men who came down from the mountains to work as day laborers in the farms around here started camping in the entrance to the shafts. Once the harvest was in, they'd go back home with their pitiful wages. But hard as life was here it was even harder in the mountains, so after a while they stopped going home and began bringing in their families."

We bounced past a straggling line of women and young girls waiting to fill jerry cans at the water tap near the entrance to the mine, sped between two great granite boulders, and skidded to a halt in a moonscape. Not a weed or a blade of grass grew anywhere. "My daughter Eugenia lives in London. I'm going to introduce you as her *comadre,* her little boy's godmother," said Ana Maria.

"Only I've never met your daughter."

"Does that matter?" Ana María said gaily. "You know how it is here—if one is to be taken seriously, connections are important. If I say you're Eugenia's *comadre,* that means I trust you totally and they should too. Now, shall we get out?"

As the dust the Fiat had churned up settled, twenty children, their play interrupted, raced up to us. "Doña Ana!" they shouted, "Doña Ana! What did you bring today?"

From the backseat of the car Ana María produced a leather satchel. "Toothbrushes," she replied briskly and, reaching into her bag, began handing them out.

"But we asked for *lollipops!*" wailed a ragged child who looked eight but was probably eleven.

"If you're good, perhaps later," Ana María replied. Meanwhile, out of dark apertures in the encircling cliffs men, women, and children were emerging. Ana María beamed and waved. "*Buenos Días!*" she called out, "*Buenos Días!*" Everyone waved back and some began making their way toward us across the stony ground. The first to reach us was a stout woman with a freckled face named Doña Leti. Before stepping forward to give her a hug, Ana María whispered to me, "Leti distributes condoms for the Ministry of Health—my old job." Next came Umberto, a short dark man with a shock of salt-and-pepper hair, who'd been "heroic" during the road construction. Ana María greeted him effusively as well. Then, followed by a jostling crowd of children, we set off on the grand tour.

In one cave dwelling after another, Ana María inquired about gastrointestinal infections, muscular sprains, broken ribs, migraine headaches. Taking notes all the while on a spiral notepad, she asked if tablets were being taken as prescribed and if supplies needed replenishment; to a newly delivered mother she gave advice about sore nipples; she asked the mother of a six-month-old boy if she'd started him on solid food. When the woman said she hadn't, Ana María whipped a box of baby cereal out of her capacious shoulder bag. "Do you know how to mix this, Josefina?" Josefina shook her head. "Can you read the instructions written on the side?"

"In our little place there was no school, Doña Ana."

"Then watch carefully what I do." Ana María asked for a bowl and boiled water. Josefina produced both but when pressed, admitted that the water had only been *brought* to a boil, not kept boiling for twenty minutes as Doña Ana had so often instructed. When water, adequately boiled, had been fetched from a more punctilious sister-in-law, Ana María prepared the cereal according to the directions and had Josefina do likewise. Only then was some given to the infant Jacobo, who spat it out and turned away, mouth shut firmly, tears spurting down his cheeks.

"He refuses," said poor Josefina.

"Of course. But you mustn't let him bully you. Leave him alone for three minutes and then try again." Ana María wiped her hands on her handkerchief before moving on to the next cave, in which a family of seven waited expectantly. Her questions and advice, so freely asked and given, aroused no observable resentment. When she walked in, worn faces broke into smiles that lingered long after she'd left.

At the conclusion of our tour, Ana María made some final jot-
tings in her notebook, unlocked the trunk of her car, and
brought out a supermarket bag containing 113 lollipops, one for
each resident of Mina de Cortés who was old enough to lick it.
She gave the bag to Doña Leti for distribution and said she'd be
back the following Monday. Blowing kisses to the children, she
got in her car.

"So what do you make of my people?" she said as we
bounced away.

"They venerate you, they worship you, you've got them eating out of your hand! They'll do whatever you tell them."

"When I'm there, that's true. But most of the time, I'm *not*
there. I've got twenty-seven families from nine different villages
that harbor hatreds going back centuries. As soon as my back's
turned, they start fighting. *That's* my problem—the problem
you're going to help me solve, my darling! When and how shall
we take our first steps?"

"Could we wait till next week? I've got an important commitment in Epizote this coming Tuesday. And as for what steps
we should take—I'll need to think about that."

In Epizote, Nácio and Rosa were about to celebrate their silver
wedding anniversary and everyone with whom they had trace-
able ties of kinship or godparenthood had been invited to the fiesta. Four hundred guests were expected, some from as far afield
as Yucatán and Sonora, and at least two dozen from "the other
side."

"But Rosa," I'd said when she handed me my invitation, "you
told me you were fourteen when you got married. You're forty-
four now. Fourteen from forty-four is thirty. It's your *thirtieth*
anniversay, not your twenty-fifth."

"It's our twenty-fifth, I tell you," Rosa insisted. "Okay,
maybe I can't read, but I can count!" Her father hadn't seen the
point of education for her or her sister. He said they'd only get
married so after a year or at most two, he pulled them out of
school and took them up to the sierras to live in a hut for eight
months of the year to herd goats and sheep. Sheep were harm-

less creatures. It was the billygoats Rosa despised and hated. They were always butting her, knocking her over, trying to you-know-what. It was mostly to get away from them that she'd married Nácio. Better a man than goat, she'd thought. "It was Nácio's green eyes that decided me. They run in his family. Some white man must've come here from Spain. They weren't just *indios* like *my* family." Illiterate though she was, she was a whiz at figures. Indeed, her arithmetical skills were held in such high regard by her neighbors that in recent years she'd been entrusted with the books of no less than four rotating credit groups.

"I told you I was fourteen when Nácio *stole* me. I never said we got *married*. He was most of the year up in 'Cali,' working and saving to build this house and buy a few head of cattle. He'd come back for fiesta week, give me another baby, and go back up. It was five years before he stayed at home long enough for us to have a wedding. When we went to ask Father Rafael to marry us, I had three kids and a fourth on the way." She giggled. "But only just, thank God. From the photos, you couldn't tell."

When I reached Epizote that Monday morning, vehicles with the plates of many Mexican states were tooling up and down the main street. By afternoon, pickup trucks were rattling into the yard behind the mayor's house, loaded with sacks of rice, sides of pork and beef, squawking chickens, legs tied together, fish splashing wildly in buckets of water, and crates of Coca-Cola, Fanta, and Dos Équis. Beneath a canvas awning, the cooks, headed by Rosa and her oldest daughter, Herlinda, down from Chicago, were wringing the necks of chickens, cutting up carcasses, gutting fish. Since Rosa and Nácio's house was bursting with children and grandchildren who'd arrived over the weekend, I was taken in by Pati and Federíco, who lived across the street. Twenty-five years ago, Federíco, who was Nácio's *compadre*, had been Nácio's best man; and Pati, who was Rosa's first cousin, had been Rosa's maid of honor, roles they were slated to play again on the great day.

By six o'clock on Tuesday morning, Rosa had left Lola, the older of her two helpers, in command in the tortillería and was

measuring out flour and butter, cracking eggs, and beating bat-
ter for four immense wedding cakes. She and her team of daughters and cousins worked right through until two o'clock, when,
with cakes frosted, topped with china figurines, and stored in
the commercial-size refrigerators of neighborhood shops, and
with *mole, pozole, barbacoa,* and *frijoles* steaming on portable
stoves turned way down, Rosa went home to dress.

As the clock on the tower of the basilica struck three-fifteen,
she reemerged in silver lamé and spike-heeled silver sandals.
Round her neck hung a heavy silver cross and on her wrists
clacked half a dozen silver bangles; on her head she wore a coronet of silver leaves and in her arms she cradled a sheaf of lilies.
Beside her walked Nácio in new blue shirt and Levi's from
Chicago, string tie, his best cowboy boots, and a new sombrero.
With their fifteen immediate descendents coming along behind
them—and with Federíco, in pink shirt, white pants, and sky-
blue double-breasted blazer, and Pati, in ankle-length mauve
rayon, hand in hand bringing up the rear—they paraded up the
shaded street, past doleful Lucifer on the wall of the town jail
and across the plaza to the basilica. On the flagstones fronting
the Romanesque porch, an eight-piece band played *cantera*
music and Father Rafael waited anxiously, in *liberacionista*
homespun vestments over which, in lieu of a surplice, he wore
an embroidered Indian shawl.

Increasingly, as their numbers dwindled, priests in rural Mexico were finding themselves encumbered with the care of several
parishes. From Epizote Father Rafael drove out to his other four
parishes in his white VW Beetle to say mass, conduct rites of passage, teach Bible classes, and provide pastoral counseling to
those who didn't ask for it as well as to those who did. Regretfully, he'd been obliged to cancel Nácio and Rosa's anniversary
mass because he'd been called to conduct a four o'clock funeral
at Altomeco, a thirty-minute drive away.

It was with relief that he saw the wedding party enter the
plaza. He stepped forward to welcome Nácio and Rosa, and
then, turning, he led them up the long aisle. With a final flour-

ish of trumpets, the music ceased and four hundred guests fell expectantly silent. Catching the mood, a dozen small children stopped racing about and pushed into pews beside their parents.

At the altar, Rosa, with her sheaf of lilies, and Nácio, sombrero firmly on his head, turned to face their guests and well-wishers. Sons, daughters, and grandchildren filed into pews; Pati and Federíco separated and took their places flanking the bride and groom. Father Rafael gestured to the guests to rise and, when all were standing, sternly reminded them that twenty-five years ago, in this very basilica, in the presence of many of them, he had pronounced Ignacio Ayala González and María Rosa Hidalgo Jiménez man and wife. At that time the basilica had had neither roof nor glass in its windows. Today, it had a fine slate roof and glass, some of it colored, in all its windows. But its brick walls, both inside and out, were still without plaster; and, through lack of a font, baptisms were still being conducted in a chipped white hand basin. Therefore he strongly urged the assembled company to dig deep into their pockets so that the remaining work might be completed with all possible speed. "It would be a sorry day indeed for Epizote," he boomed, "were we to meet five years hence to celebrate the *thirtieth* wedding anniversary of our dear friends, this cherished couple, and the work remained unfinished!"

His words still echoed through the church as he turned to Ignacio Juan Ayala González and María Rosa Hidalgo Jiménez de Ayala and, voice softening, instructed them to reaffirm their vows. This done, he bestowed on them the blessing of the Holy Trinity, whereupon Nácio threw his arms round his wife. To catcalls and whistles, the two embraced passionately, the band struck up a wedding march, and everybody cheered. Then Nácio scooped Rosa up, carried her down the aisle past their wildly applauding guests, out across the plaza and into the mayor's yard, where benches and long tables covered in white cloth had been set up for the *comida*.

By 3:36, Father Rafael, in his VW Beetle, was racing over pot-holed roads to Altomeco to conduct the funeral of a forty-two-year-old heart attack victim who'd dropped dead the previous evening when feeding his pigs. Given the thirty-five-degree-centigrade heat of March, the corpse required speedy burial.

During the *comida,* which was served by the wedding pair's three daughters and a posse of their female cousins, Rosa raced on too-high heels from table to table greeting guests, receiving congratulations, thanking everyone for coming, and making sure they had enough to eat. Nácio's job was to make sure they had enough to drink. When a third round of mescal and tequila had been dispensed, Nácio and Rosa cut the largest of the four wedding cakes and each fed the other a mouthful as cameras flashed. *Cantera* music segued into "The Blue Danube," Nácio threw down his sombrero, and Rosa removed her silver-leafed coronet, shaking out her long chestnut hair so that it curled over lamé-covered shoulders to just above her waist. Hands laced, they stepped out onto the dance floor, a stretch of concrete on which the mayor usually parked tractors and pickup trucks, and to loud and prolonged applause circled the concrete once, twice, three times. Plucking a scarlet hibiscus flower from a nearby bush, Rosa stuck it behind her ear, a signal for waltz music to segue into merengue. Within moments, a hundred couples were dancing—husbands with wives, fathers with daughters, grandparents, teenage sweethearts, small brothers and their yet smaller sisters. People of every age from two to ninety were having a grand time.

My job was to videotape the proceedings. As shadows lengthened and the air cooled I roamed about with my camcorder, hoping to catch the spirit of the occasion so that, decades into the future, Nácio and Rosa and their descendents would watch the video and be reminded of just how much fun they'd had. When finally my cassette was finished and, to replace it, I retreated to the table where I'd left my camera bag, I felt more than a twinge of envy. Being a participant-observer was all well and good, but I'd had enough of observation—if only someone would ask *me* to dance!

"That camera's heavy," said a man who was standing near the entrance to the yard. His clothes—white T-shirt, khaki pants, and light zipper jacket—suggested he was from up north. "You must be tired. You've been carrying it around for hours."

"It's not as heavy as it looks," I said.

"Anyway, you should be in the video too," the man said. "Let me take your picture. I know that camera," he added. "A friend of mine's got one like it and sometimes he lets me borrow it. Stand over there, please." He pointed to a patch of sunlight.

"But I don't want to stand," I told him. "I want to *dance.*"

"Dance then!"

"By myself? I'd feel stupid."

"Why? Nobody's looking. They're all too drunk."

"Now, maybe. But later, when they watch the video, Nácio and Rosa will say I was crazy."

"Never mind about later," the man said. So I gave him my camera and he filmed me dancing alone in a patch of dying sunlight. But just as I was forgetting to feel silly, the music stopped. The musicians were putting down electric guitars and saxophones, emptying spittle out of trumpets, climbing down from the flag-draped stage erected in the spot where the mayor usually parked his three tractors—one red, one green, one blue—and going off for a smoke and a shot of tequila

"Too bad they left," I said as I reclaimed my camera. "I was enjoying myself."

"When the musicians come back, we'll dance, okay?" The man grinned. His hair was cut very short and flecked with gray, and his eyes were greenish-blue.

"Okay." Two hours' worth of tape edited down to thirty minutes would be enough. Watching more than half an hour of any event, even one's own party, could be pretty boring. Anyway, it was after six already and the light was fading. I put my camera into my bag and stowed it under a table.

While we were waiting for the musicians to return, we went over to the bar. I had a Dos Équis and he had a Coca-Cola. He said he didn't drink alcohol and then, switching into English, volunteered, "At one time it got me into a lot of trouble, so I stopped." He hadn't touched a drop for sixteen years. He paused and then said solemnly, "I'm sorry, I didn't introduce myself. I'm Jorge Ayala López. I got in last night from Milwaukee after forty-two hours on the road. I'll be heading north again first thing tomorrow morning. I couldn't take more than five days off of work. You stay with Rosa and Nácio, right?" he added. His English, though heavily accented, was perfectly colloquial.

"Right, and you're Nácio's cousin."

"No, I'm his brother."

"Really?" This surprised me. I'd met Nácio's two sisters but I could have sworn he'd told me he was an only son.

"He hasn't mentioned me?"

"Maybe he has."

"More likely, he hasn't." Jorge paused. "I'm from *la otra casa,* the other house," he said evenly. The musicians were trickling back but when they started up again he seemed not to notice. He was looking into his Coke. Nácio, his sisters, and their mother, Amelia, lived where the tortillería was now, he told me. He and his mother, Perla, lived in a place near the bridge—in the middle of an English sentence he used the word *jacál,* meaning shack—and the elder Nácio went back and forth between them. Amelia, the woman of his youth, was from Epizote. Perla, the much younger woman of his middle-age, was from a town in another state. A rancher who traded in cattle, he'd met her at a market in Guerrero. For a while he'd visited her periodically but when he could no longer stand her being so far away he'd brought her and four-year-old Jorge to Epizote.

"He should never have done it," Jorge said slowly. "He should've left us where we were. Amelia was related to everyone in Epizote and my mother knew nobody... She had no support. From the depths of his heart my dad loved my mother—I do believe that—but Amelia had him by the balls, or rather, her brothers did. They'd had a vendetta with some guys in Altomeco and ended up killing them. My dad believed that if he left Amelia and took my mom and me with him someplace else, they'd come after us and kill us too...

"And so we stayed. Thursday nights, my dad was with us, Fridays through Wednesdays he was with Amelia. One Tuesday he dropped down dead in Amelia's house and when they'd laid him out her brothers wouldn't let my mom and me in to see him. We stood at the back during the funeral mass and when they buried him out in the cemetery we watched from behind a tree."

For a while after the death of his father, Jorge stayed on in Epizote, working on ranches round about. He didn't want to leave his mother by herself. "When she died—it was pneumonia that took her and she was only thirty-eight—I buried her on the hillside a ways down from my dad...Amelia had reserved the plot next to my dad for herself, so that was the best I could do. Then I lit out for the other side."

After some moments he continued, "When I found that invitation in my mailbox—well..." He shook his head in wonder. "It was my niece Herlinda that tracked me down. She's the supervisor of a college cafeteria in Chicago." He smiled faintly. "She's one smart young lady...I said to myself, Nácio didn't invite me to his *wedding*, but hey, he's inviting me to his *silver* wedding. Maybe I'd better go!"

"Are you glad you came?"

"It's okay."

"Have you had a chance to talk to Nácio?"

"No, but I'm talking to you."

"Only I'm not Nácio!"

"Nácio's busy."

"Jorge, he has time for *you*."

The music trailed into silence and as the musicians began packing up, this time for good, Federíco got up on the stage to wish everyone a good night.

"We missed our dance," said Jorge. "I'm sorry. I guess I got talking."

I didn't get back to Epizote for more than two weeks after the fiesta because I was busy with Mina de Cortés.

"Men may be bound by archaic notions of honor and ancestral hatreds," I intoned to Ana María, "but generally speaking, women are less bound and more pragmatic. So let's start with them."

I explained about focus group discussions—not that I'd ever been in one, but in that era, focus groups were the bricks and mortar of community development. Non-governmental organizations (NGOs) were pushing them from Haiti to Bangladesh. What you did was invite people who had "common issues" to sit down together and then you "facilitated" a discussion. Having identified a "core problem," you encouraged group members to air as many aspects of it as possible and then you helped them formulate a solution. Simple enough, at least on paper.

Ana María said, "Let's practice on the maids," of whom she had four.

The core problem, quickly identified, was husbands. Husbands who spent your wages on drink and/or other women. Though Lorena, the cook, was a widow, she recalled vividly all she'd endured with Pepe, may God rest his soul! After two wide-ranging late-afternoon discussions at the kitchen table, we still hadn't come up with a *solution* to the core problem. Nevertheless Ana María felt she was as ready as she was ever likely to be to try out her new expertise in the mine. We agreed that since my stay there was only temporary I shouldn't be a full participant. Rather, my role would be to sit to one side and take notes.

The problem identified by our first group, composed of Doña Leti and her two *comadres,* was human excreta and whether—and if so, where—to dig latrines. At the culmination of an hour's intense discussion, the three women agreed that each would invite a woman from one of the several identifiable factions in the mine to join a second group discussion the following week.

On our drive back to the *quinta,* Ana María was guardedly optimistic. All in all, we'd made a fair start. "We aren't expecting miracles, are we?"

When I got off the bus in Epizote the following evening and made my way up the street to the tortillería, I was looking forward to *chilaquiles* for supper and an in-depth analysis of the party with Rosa and Nácio. But when I walked into the house

Rosa was sitting on the couch in the living room, the TV was off, and there was no sign of Nácio.

"It was a great party," I told her. "The food was great, the band was great, you looked beautiful, Nácio looked like a cowboy in the movies, and everyone had a wonderful time!" I tapped my bag. "I've got the video to show you." Rosa nodded listlessly and said nothing. "Where's *el jefe?*" I asked.

"It's Thursday."

"So it is."

"He's not here," said Rosa.

"I can see that," I said.

"He's never here on Thursdays. Thursdays, he's with *la otra.*"

Feeling as if I'd been punched in the stomach, I collapsed on the couch beside Rosa. "Nácio? Honestly, I didn't know...I never would've thought..."

"Well, you haven't been here on a Thursday, have you?" said Rosa bitterly. After a long moment, she added, "I thought his seeing Jorge would do the trick. You talked to Jorge, didn't you? He told Nácio you did...He's okay, isn't he?"

"What do you mean, okay?"

She shrugged impatiently, "He's *doing* okay, right? It was Herlinda who found him for me...She drove by his house on a Saturday. She says he's got two floors and a two-car garage, and he told Nácio he's got a business cleaning offices—seven employees from Honduras. He married a girl from up there and they've got three kids..."

"What does Jorge have to do with you and Nácio and—?"

"Her name's Brenda."

"With Brenda."

"Ever since he was a kid he's felt guilty about Jorge... When he got drunk, he'd weep. 'Where's Jorge? Is he ruined, is he dead?' And now, even though he knows he doesn't have to feel guilty about Jorge because Jorge's doing okay, right?—he *still* wants a divorce!"

"A *divorce?*"

"Brenda's got Carlitos and Nácio says, now our kids are

grown and gone north, Carlitos needs his father! But what about *me?*" Rosa's eyes blazed. "Don't I need my husband? What about our kids and our grandkids?"

She'd heard rumors years ago, when Nácio was up in California . . . What else could one expect, with him being so far away? But then he came back home and they began making a life together. They rebuilt the house Nácio had inherited from his father and got the tortillería going; Nácio leased more land and bought more cattle; they bought a store in Altomeco, near the Acapulco highway and put one of Rosa's sisters into it. Times were pretty good. "There were a lot of poor people like us, working hard, saving their *centavos.*" They could afford to send Herlinda to *secundaria* in Cuernavaca, and to secretarial school. The next one, Pablo, made it to the university, and the other three did too. "Imagine, with a mother who can barely write her own name!"

Rosa drew a deep breath. "I thought, other women have their problems but not me . . . *Idiota!* Nácio was being careful, that was all . . . This Brenda, she works for the power company, two hours away in Matamoros, and by the time I found out, the boy was already three years old. One day when I was over at the store in Altomeco my sister said to me, 'Rosa, you've been burying your head in the sand!'"

"Did my heart break? Sure, it broke." Rosa gestured to the floor around her feet. "But I picked up the pieces and stuck them back together. And Nácio and I, we made an arrangement . . . Brenda and Carlitos got him on Thursdays . . ." She bit her lower lip. "Then last year, after our youngest had her graduation and couldn't find a job down here and went to join the rest of them on the other side, Nácio started talking about his old man *en serio*—when he was sober—not just when he was drunk. About how, by being too chicken to leave Amelia, the old guy had ruined Jorge's life. He said he wasn't going to let *his* son suffer the same way. Soon he was talking about us splitting up—and not like so many do, by his leaving me and moving in with the other one. No, he wanted to divorce, he wanted *me* to leave *him* and all this"—she gestured—"everything I've worked my fingers to the bone for as well, and go live in Chicago, Illinois, with Herlinda, so he can bring the boy and his mother in *here*!"

"Then why the anniversary, Rosa?"

"That was Father Rafael's idea. Of course he knew about Brenda...I'd gone in tears to him the minute I found out. And he'd said to me, 'María Rosa, think of your namesake and the sorrows she bore without ever losing her courage or compassion...'

"It was during the fiesta of San Miguel last September that Nacío said he wanted to divorce. I went to Father Rafa and told him, 'It hasn't worked out. I'm not the *virgencita*, I'm *Rosa* and I'm angry and bitter and *scared*. And I don't know what to do.' So he said, 'It's up to you, María Rosa. Either you take this lying down or you stand up and fight. If you want to keep Nácio, you've got to show him what he'll be losing if you split up.... Get everyone here and *celebrate* the life you have together!' That's why the anniversary."

Suddenly, turning to face me full-on, Rosa slapped my knee and grinned. "It was a *beautiful* party, wasn't it? Everyone had a good time. Even Nácio!"

April slid into May and, with June fast approaching, the first rain showers fell *chipi chipi* and the men of Mina de Cortés were gone from dawn to dusk walking the furrows, planting maize. Meanwhile, though so far not even one man had joined the group, Doña Leti had almost all the women corralled and talking to one another on Wednesday afternoons. And she, as well as Ana María, was guardedly hopeful that when house construction began in October at the end of the rains, the men would be talking to each other too.

But by October, I'd be long gone. My work done, I was going north in June to write up my material.

On the afternoon of the last Sunday before I left Cuernavaca, Luz and I went for ice cream in the Borda Gardens. From there we were planning to go to six o'clock mass in the cathedral. Luz was going for the mariachi music and I was too. But more than

for the music, I was going for the homily. I'd never had the privilege of hearing Don Sergio himself preach in his cathedral.
He was old now and in failing health, and he only preached on
feast days and holidays. But mostly likely, his substitute would
make the same promise I'd heard many times in churches in
Mexico: the poor will inherit the kingdom and the kingdom
is here on earth. Though there was little indication of its imminent fulfillment, I never tired of hearing that defiantly romantic
promise.

On our way downtown, a short dark-haired woman in a tight
blue dress boarded our minibus. She wore a lot of makeup, and
I noticed a large black mole an inch or so to the right of her scarlet mouth. As she edged past us to the rear, the bus jolted, she
stumbled, fell against me, and dropped her purse. Bending down
to retrieve it, she murmured, "*Escuso*" and I got a strong whiff
of perfume and sweat.

We left the bus at the entrance to the gardens and as soon as
we were through the gate, instead of heading for the restaurant,
Luz made for an ornate iron bench. She sank down and covered
her face with her hands.

"I'll be all right in a minute," she whispered.

"Shall I fetch you some water?"

"No need, no need."

"Can you tell me what's up, Luz?"

"Stupid of me, stupid."

"*What's* stupid?"

"I shouldn't be shocked, I should've got over it," Luz said,
and sat up.

"Got over *what*?"

"Running into her, that woman in the bus, the one who fell
on you... For fifteen, sixteen years I didn't see her, and then one
day I saw her in front of the cathedral, so I knew she was back
and that any time I could run into her again."

"Won't you tell me who she is, Luz?"

"The wife of my oldest son."

"*Pedro's* wife?" But Pedro lived upstairs with Alicia.

"Pedro's not my oldest. *Ernesto* was my oldest and that

woman is—was—his wife." Luz covered her face again and her shoulders shook. "They killed him. It'll be eighteen years next week."

Ernesto had been her support through all her troubles—so many children, so little money, a husband as attractive to women as a lamp is to moths.

"He looked just like his father had when he was young—like an angel," Luz mumbled. Her hands fell to her lap. "But unlike his father, he *was* an angel. From when he was a little boy, he was patient and responsible—he tried to give the others the attention they should have had from Raúl... And then *she* bewitched him." With a bitter smile, Luz continued, "My grandson Luís—Pedro and Alicia's boy—he goes to the cinema with his girlfriend and brings her home for supper. But back then, courting was done in secret. Parents didn't know what was going on."

Ernesto went to work for the railroads, he traveled back and forth to Acapulco. "And then one day he showed up with this woman. They went to city hall and registered and that was it, no mass, nothing. I never met her parents. I knew nothing about her family or what kind of people they were.

"They rented a place in San Agostino but, as I said, Ernesto was working for the railroads, he traveled up and down on those trains. When she was expecting a baby I said to him, you should bring her to stay with us, but he told me, 'She prefers being on her own.' When she had the little girl she called her Rosário after a singer who was all the rage at the time..."

Luz reached for my hand. "One night Ernesto comes back from Acapulco and she's with another man. She picks up a knife, or maybe it's the fellow who picks the knife up... The neighbors, decent people, hear them fighting but they don't like to interfere. Next morning the husband's leaving for work and sees the blood—it's seeped under the door out into the yard. He runs across the ravine to find me and Raúl, but he only finds me... I'm watering my geraniums... The two of us, we run back to Ernesto's place and break down the door." Luz dug her fingernails into my palm so hard that I winced. "And there I see my Ernesto, face down on the kitchen floor, a knife between his shoulder blades."

Flies were buzzing round him in the morning light. They were big and black, they had no regard, no respect for human dignity. The woman and the child were gone. The man, whoever he was, had gone as well, only he'd left his jacket. It was dark brown leather and it looked like new.

"The police came and made a report and after that we never heard from them. They only pay attention to *los ricos,* they don't bother themselves with *los pobres* making their way in the world as best they can, simple people like us...Raúl, he showed up the day of the funeral. I didn't ask him where he'd been and he didn't say..."

Luz and I sat holding hands as, all around us, women chatted and small children played.

"The rest of them don't talk about Ernesto anymore—eighteen years is a long time, and some were quite young when he died. It could be they've forgotten. But as for me, I haven't forgotten. In the morning when I wake up I still miss him so badly, it makes me gasp. I jump out of bed and run up to Santiago. During the mass, I pull in my rage, my sorrow, my despair—and I push it back into its box."

Letting go of my hand, she showed me how she did it. "The box is here," she held her abdomen. "And then I can get on with my day."

After my book was published I went back to Morelos to present a copy to each of my landladies. I found Rosa in her tortillería, Luz dead-heading her *plantitas,* and Ana María just back from *barrio* Mina de Cortés. They all said that they liked the photos, though the dedication, *"a mis Tres Marías,"* provoked some curiosity—"Who are the other two?" each one wanted to know. But the contents were lost on them.

"I can't read," Rosa reminded me, "so what am I supposed to do with a book?"

Luz said, "It should have been in Spanish. Spanish I could read."

Ana María said, "My English, what little I once had, is so rusty! Perhaps Geraldo will read it and give me the gist."

"How are things going?" I asked each in turn and eagerly they gave news of grandchildren, rites of passage, projects, plans.

"How's *el jefe*?"

All three said that *el jefe* was feeling his age—Luz with a quiet smile, Rosa with a broad grin, and Ana María with a shrug and a raised eyebrow.

"He's slowing down," said Luz. "All men do eventually. You just have to bide your time."

III

OBOROGI

Witchcraft in a Kenyan Village

As a child, I'd hear about Gishugu from my great-uncle Malcolm, who owned a farm there. One glass of sherry before lunch on Sunday could be enough to set him yearning for the jacarandas lining his driveway, the roses that bloomed luxuriantly all year long in beds on either side of his front door, the sweet smell of grass after a night's rain, and the view from his veranda, unrivaled in the British Empire, so he claimed. But to me, Gishugu was just a dot on the map of East Africa in our disintegrating pre–World War I *Times* atlas, whose data were at best approximate. I didn't actually go there until long after I'd grown up.

My husband and I decided to work in Kenya because, unlike Nigeria at the time, it was politically stable and we had a reasonably good chance of finishing something we'd started, and also because my husband had already spent time in the country and knew one or two potentially helpful people in high places, which meant we wouldn't be starting entirely from scratch. After considering various possibilities in the western highlands, we chose Gishugu in Buso District for the simple reason that a few miles out from the district headquarters the Gishugu Pyrethrum Cooperative Board had an unused "camp" that they were willing to rent to us. It consisted of two brick iron-roofed bungalows, a shed, several shacks, and three pit latrines with concrete slabs. The bungalows would house us, our children, and our assistants; the shed could be used as an office; our cook, our watchman, and their wives, children, and extended kin would live in the shacks; and everyone would share the latrines. In a lean-to next to the shed was a broken generator which, if fixed, should supply electricity for reading lamps, a typewriter, a short-wave radio for the BBC news, a cassette recorder for Bach, Mozart, Pete Seeger, and Marlo Thomas, and, most essential of all, a water pump. The camp had no telephone; however, the chairman of the Cooperative Board had us believe that, provided we lobbied vigorously, service might be supplied by and by.

Behind the camp was a school and a health post; in front, across the unpaved road that led east to central Kenya, was a rectangle of bare red earth, dusty in the dry season, a quag-mire in the rains, surrounded by a butchery, a vegetable stall, a tailor, half a dozen concrete-block shops selling identical goods (matches, candles, plastic bags of laundry detergent, bleach, bis-cuits, pencils, copybooks, and Bic ballpoint pens), the Tea For Two Hotel, which was actually a brothel, and a police station manned by three officers in fiercely starched shirts and shorts, knee socks, and heavy black boots. Though a few old women in the hills behind Gishugu still wore the beaded animal-skin skirts and mantles of their ancestors, everyone else wore western clothes—the women, dresses and cardigans with bulging pock-ets; the men, shirts with frayed collars, cuffed pants, and British-style jackets. Since the recent advent of free primary education, all the children aged five and over wore school uniforms. No tur-bans or startling-white robes, no silk-covered heads or jeweled sandals; men rode push bikes, not caparisoned horses. (Here, just as in the northern Nigerian town of Kaura, women walked.) A less exotic-seeming group than the denizens of the Gishugu market would be hard to imagine.

From the front steps of the police station you could see the Gishugu escarpment rising nobly to the north and, in the right season, through binoculars, the long blue line of Uncle Mal-colm's jacaranda avenue.

In 1891, freshly sprung from Oxford and saved by an inher-itance from an immediate need to join the family firm in the

City, Uncle Malcolm had set out to see as much as he could of the still-expanding British Empire. By 1899, when he married Helen Cantwell, daughter of Charles Cantwell, Esq., of Trapton Manor, Gloucestershire, he'd already crossed, mostly on foot and horseback (he disparaged trains), large chunks of Australia, Canada, India, and the Malay Peninsula. But he'd never been to Africa, at that time the Empire's latest (and final) chunk; and so it was for Africa that he and his bride, a great walker and an accomplished horsewoman, set out just days after their wedding in Trapton parish church. At Mombasa they disembarked from their Durban-bound steamer, bought two ponies to ride when they got tired of walking, and hired bullock carts, mules, and porters for their provisions. Malcolm's objective was the far reaches of Uganda: he wanted to explore the Ruwenzori Mountains. But three months out of Mombasa, they crested the Gishugu escarpment, 6,789 feet above sea level. Before them lay Lake Victoria, gilded by the evening sun, and to their backs a sweep of hardwood forest and rich grazing land which, because the herds of the Masai, whose ancestral home it was, had recently been decimated by rinderpest, was empty of all human habitation and teeming with game.

"This is it!" Helen reported that Malcolm had cried joyously. "We won't bother with Uganda. This is the place for us. This is where we'll stay."

"I thought we'd come to Africa just to *see* it," Helen protested.

"Change of plan. We're going to settle."

But Gishugu wasn't the place for Helen. It was much too far from Gloucestershire. For a week she refused to speak to her husband, who, gun at the ready should an elephant or rhinoceros charge or a lion or leopard leap out of the bush, was euphorically walking the length and breadth of the land he'd decided should be his. She slept in the kitchen tent, glared at Lake Victoria, wrote furiously in her diary, and took her meals alone on a wobbly table on which, in happier times, the honeymooners had played gin rummy. But on the eighth day she capitulated, whereupon they rode down to Nairobi, bought a thousand-odd acres from the colonial government—which acted on the mistaken assumption that the land was theirs to sell—and headed back up to Gishugu with bullock carts filled with building supplies and coffee seedlings. Helen lasted three years and four months as a settler's wife before, pregnant with her second child, she made for home with Will, her firstborn. In due course Malcolm hired a Scottish farm manager and, with a heavy heart, followed his family; but he'd fallen in love with Gishugu and had no intention of giving it up.

By dint of a determination that surprised his relations who'd long ago dismissed him as terminally footloose, and infusions of their capital as well as his own, he held on to it through drought, pestilence, the Great Depression, two world wars, and a guerrilla insurgency. Though Helen never again set foot on the African continent, Malcolm made sure he spent at least six months on his farm every other year. Once, "caught" in Kenya by the fall of France in June 1940, he was obliged to stay put until the Normandy landings. "Four *extraordinarily* happy years," was how, ever afterwards, he referred to that time.

In my childhood, Gishugu coffee beans, which arrived twice a year in one-kilo burlap bags stamped with a zebra logo, provided the only coffee my parents drank. Malcolm died, aged eighty-nine, in 1958; but my parents stayed loyal to his zebra brand until his sons sold the property to the newly independent Kenyan government in 1964. A decade later I found the jacarandas, branches intertwined, dripping bluish-purple blossoms into the driveway. But potatoes grew where the lawn used to be and Malcolm's much-vaunted roses had been nibbled down to stubs by goats and straying cattle. The thatched roof of the main house wore a dense mantle of weeds; stucco walls, once whitewashed annually at the end of the long rains, were soot-streaked and crumbling; the wife of the veterinary extension officer, its current occupant, cooked on an open fire in the sitting room. The guesthouse was being used to store potatoes; the garage had been divided into stalls for black and white Holstein cows. And under a government resettlement scheme the farm had been divided into ten-acre plots and sold off to Africans who'd pulled up the coffee bushes and planted maize, sorghum, and pyrethrum. Even so, I found the view across low green hills to Lake Victoria—which had recently been renamed Lake Nyanza—even more beautiful than Malcolm had claimed.

Buso Town, the administrative center of Buso District, had only come into existence in 1905, that is, several years after Malcolm bought his farm. Even when we got there many decades later "town" was still a euphemism. A narrow tarmac strip was lined with Indian-owned shops, four bars, two power mills, a mechanic's shop, a petrol station, a post office, Dr. Patel's medical clinic, and a branch of Barclay's Bank. At one end of the strip stood the water tower and the district hospital whose wide verandas swarmed perpetually with patients and their relatives. At the other end was the *boma,* an enclave of government offices and bungalows in which lived the District Commissioner, a handful of junior officials, the bank manager, and the headmaster of the Buso Boys' School. St. George's, the Romanesque-style church, stood locked and silent except for when the Anglican priest visited, which, since he ministered to a parish the size of Yorkshire, he did rarely. Beyond the overgrown graveyard was the Rest House, where touring magistrates and public health officials put up; and beyond that was the Sports Club, which boasted two clay tennis courts, a squash court, and a narrow, murky swimming pool. In colonial times a handful of European settler farms, including Malcolm's, had lined the eastern boundary of the district. On Saturday nights, weather and roads permitting, their owners would drive down to the Club for mulligatawny soup, tilapia and chipped potatoes, and trifle and cream; after supper, together with the Irish priests from the Kiltegan Mission, they'd drink to inebriation and sleep off the effects in the Rest House before heading home on Sunday morning. (The district's other missionaries, Swedish Lutherans, German Mennonites, and American Seventh-day Adventists, teetotalers all and by definition morally superior, gave the Club a wide berth.)

By the time we got to Buso, the settlers, along with the British officials, had left and memories of them were fading. Aside from a few sepia photographs of them holding tennis and squash racquets in the Sports Club bar and the odd wooden plaque recording their donations, they'd left few observable traces in this corner of the world to which they'd been so passionately attached. Of the priestly members of the Saturday night group, only Father Mike and Father Brendan remained, the rest having either retired or, during the great emptying out of the priesthood in the sixties, put aside their vows and got married. But with Kenya currently the darling of international aid agencies, veterinarians, soil specialists, and hydraulic engineers from Germany, Israel, the Netherlands, and, occasionally, Japan swarmed through the district in green Toyota Land Cruisers. Young volunteers from half a dozen countries charged about like knights of old on mud-splashed motorcycles; and after the day's work was done, these foreigners did what their British predecessors had never thought to do: they drank Heinekens and Simba beer in the club with the local big men who hadn't been permitted to set foot there in colonial times.

In the winter of 1955–56, the last that Malcolm spent on the escarpment, the population of Buso District had been about 300,000. Given its altitude, it had always been largely free of malaria and dengue fever; but in the 1960s the widespread introduction of antibiotics and infant immunizations had brought a sudden sharp decline in mortality, and as a result in just twenty years the population had increased almost threefold. Contraceptives, though available in the district hospital, had few takers. Bosu parents were slow to adjust to the new demographics. With life goals little changed from an earlier migratory time when land had been theirs for the taking, they still saw children as potential laborers for their fields and herders for their sheep and cattle; they wanted as many as possible and families of eight and ten were the rule, not the exception. In the seventies, Kenya had the highest fertility rate of any country in the world and Buso women had one-tenth of one percentage point more children on average than women in any other Kenyan district. As fathers divided their land between many sons, farms had become smaller and smaller to the point that anyone who owned three—wonderfully fertile—acres was considered a wealthy man. The land which, when Malcolm first saw it, had lain open and uncultivated was now a patchwork of tiny fields, the hardwood forest had vanished completely, and competition over resources of all kinds was growing frighteningly fiercer. Still, in the evening when the smoke of cooking fires and the laughter of children rose from neat homesteads, it was hard to imagine a more peaceful place.

After spending an unconscionably long time in the moldering corridors of disordered administrative offices in Nairobi, we received government authorization and, with a large plastic envelope jammed with documents correctly signed and stamped, drove out to Gishugu to begin our research. Our three assistants, recent graduates of top girls' secondary schools with ten months to fill before going to university, lived with us in the camp. They all spoke excellent English. But I was determined to give learning the Buso language a serious try and so I began looking for someone who *didn't* know English. (A teacher who did would have provided me with an irresistible temptation to cheat.) Like Swahili, Buso is a Bantu language, which means they have important structural similarities; and since I'd taken a Church Missionary Society intensive Swahili course, which had equipped me to deliver seven-minute sermons (for my final project, a sermon on the parable of the Good Samaritan, I'd received a B plus), Swahili, not English, would be the medium of instruction. The only published materials available in the Buso language were a children's story about an elephant and a translation of the Gospels which, after a decade's work, a Swedish Lutheran missionary lady had just completed. From a brief study of a dog-eared *Buso Grammar,* a gift from Father Brendan, I already knew that Buso had twenty-two noun classes and ninety-six verb tenses. Aside from a list of two hundred–odd words at the back of the *Grammar,* no dictionary existed.

After I'd tried my luck with a couple of local men who I'd soon discovered had neither interest in nor patience for the job, the health post nurse suggested I call on Beatrice, who lived on

Ombui's Hill, out beyond the pond in which some Peace Corps volunteers had tried and failed to start a fish farm. I was told she spoke proper Swahili, not the up-country pidgin variety that, if they knew Swahili at all, Buso women generally spoke. This was because she'd attended a Catholic boarding school in Kakamega and the nuns had been strict. Also, because her *shamba* was small (three fields only) and required relatively little attention and her only child was already in school, she should have time to help me.

I found her in her flower-filled yard on a bench shaded by a frangipani tree. As she unraveled an oversized man's sweater and wound the yarn into a ball, with which she planned to knit a cardigan for herself, she was jiggling to Congo dance music that blared from a small black radio on the bench beside her. But when she spotted me looking over her gate she snapped off the music, jumped to her feet, and, cradling to her chest the sweater and the ball of wool she was winding, hurried to meet me. A stocky young woman in her twenties, she wore a wide smile and a bright pink minidress that stopped six inches above her knees. (Though out of vogue in Europe and America, minis were still current in East Africa; they took a lot less fabric than the shirt-waisters favored by the older women, and therefore, as Beatrice later explained to me, instead of one dress you could afford to have two.) She'd tied a woolen head scarf over her tightly plaited hair and on her feet she wore blue plastic shoes. "Last Tuesday I saw you in the market. They told me you are visiting all the homesteads looking for children, so why didn't you come to my place?" she demanded. "I have a son aged six. His name is George."

"But I was looking for pregnant women, not children."

Beatrice glanced down at her flat stomach. "In that case..."

When I explained I was also looking for someone to teach me the Buso language, she shrugged. "I can try. Why not? When shall we begin?"

"When would you have time?"

"I have time *now*. Here," she thrust sweater and yarn into my arms. "You do this and I will prepare vegetables for supper.

While we work I will teach you how to greet people. Greeting people properly is very important. If you don't make the proper greeting you will be taken for a small child or a fool."

We agreed that three mornings a week Beatrice would accompany me as I went from house to house to observe how mothers interacted with their babies; babies tend to fall asleep, so while I was waiting for them to wake up again Beatrice would teach me her language.

One sparkling morning a month or so later we were walking along a lane when a young boy burst through the dense euphorbia hedge on our left and, flinging his arms wide, shouted something I didn't catch. "A most terrible thing has happened!" exclaimed Beatrice. "*Run!*" she commanded, seizing my hand, and as the boy raced off to alert others, she jerked me back the way we'd come. Only when we reached the mud-walled school, in which rows of boys in bright white shirts and dark-blue shorts and girls in white-collared dark-blue dresses were chanting their "six times" table, did she let go of my hand.

"Please tell me what's up!"

"We cannot go that way," Beatrice mumbled.

"What did that boy say?"

"Because of Lucas..."

"Who's Lucas?"

Beatrice turned away. "Let us go to Mary's house," she muttered. Pointing with her chin toward a stand of gum trees, she added, "There we will be safe."

"Safe from *whom*?" But without another word Beatrice was off again at a run.

Beatrice and Mary had married within a few months of each other. In actual fact, neither had got married, at least not to begin with. They'd simply run off with their suitors, Mary in June and Beatrice in October. Only later, after they'd proved themselves by giving birth to sons, did their husbands bring their fathers the full bride-price, eight head of cattle, by which, according to custom, they were finally and officially married. Both devout Catholics, they never missed mass. Since plans for building a church were still a long way from realization, Father Brendan (who, aside from being beloved, was famed throughout the district for his punning skills and mastery of metaphor) celebrated it at eight o'clock on Sunday mornings in the school playground; and it had been through parish work that they'd become best friends. Their husbands were gone a good deal—Beatrice's was a driver for the government of Kenya and Mary's was a salesman for British American Tobacco—which meant their wives had more freedom to come and go than would have been the case had they been farmers and at home all the time. To begin with they taught catechism to the children but then, prodded by Father Brendan, they started a women's savings group. Beatrice, with only one child to take care of, went house to house collecting the money—a shilling a week from each member—and Mary, who, with a daughter and two sons, was a good deal busier, kept the accounts. Their homesteads were a twenty minutes' walk apart and under normal circumstances they wouldn't have seen much of each other; but their parish work gave them legitimate excuses to meet almost daily. Though Beatrice's new tutoring job cut into her free time, if we happened to find ourselves in Mary's neighborhood, which was often, we'd stop in.

We found Mary washing mud off her legs, having just returned from digging in her maize field. As soon as she'd ushered us into her yard and tied the gate shut, Beatrice told her in Buso all about what we'd been running away from; but still she didn't tell me. Only after Mary had lit a cooking fire, boiled water in a dented saucepan, and given us each a mug of tea with milk and three spoons of sugar did Beatrice turn to me. "Mary and I *married* to Gishugu. We didn't grow up here. We can only tell you what we heard..." She cracked her knuckles. "The Catholic fathers loved Lucas—too much, some people say... They never could see any fault in him..." She went on, "He was the cleverest pupil they'd ever had in their school. They gave him a scholarship and even his uniform. He was the first boy from Buso District to go to Makerere College in Uganda and after that he got a big job in Nairobi that came with a house and servants' quarters, so he took boys from Gishugu to cook and wash his clothes. When he married the daughter of the subchief, he paid twelve cows and ten thousand shillings and took her to the house he was building on the road to Nyabakori. We passed it yesterday, the yellow house with two stories and flowering bushes in front. We didn't stop there because in that homestead no woman is pregnant..."

"He had a Peugeot and a driver," Mary added. "And though he himself was as black as the night, when he came home he'd be sitting in the back of that car, like a white man." Mary's Swahili wasn't as good as Beatrice's but I mostly understood what she said. "By that time independence was coming and many people pressed him to stand for parliament. They said such a clever man would make a very good MP."

And then it happened.

Extracting from the two friends exactly what *it* was took time. Embarrassment and enduring shock made them forget to speak Swahili. But eventually they got the story out. One Christmas morning some people who were passing Lucas's house heard screams.

"My husband's oldest brother, Jacob, ran into the yard and saw Lucas fighting his sister," said Mary. "Her name was Agnes and she was home for the holidays from her school in Sotik. She was in Standard 7, her breasts were still small."

"They were on the grass behind the Peugeot," said Beatrice. "Lucas was wearing a fine blue suit, new for Christmas, and Agnes was wearing her school uniform. In one hand he held a broken Simba bottle. That is how he'd caught the girl—first he cut her and then...He was strong and quick and he snarled like a hyena."

"He slashed Jacob's cheek with that bottle—you can see the scar till this day. But others came and they managed to get the bottle away from him. They broke three of his ribs and knocked out his front teeth and then they left him for dead beside his vehicle."

"But he wasn't dead," said Beatrice. "They didn't kill him because he was their kinsman and to kill him would have been a very grave sin, graver even than Lucas's own sin. Then his father,

Obari Mugambo, hired a vehicle and took him to the asylum at Gil-Gil in Rift Valley Province, which is far from here."

"No Buso man was willing to marry Agnes," said Mary, "so she eloped with a Kikuyu who came to drink beer in Tea for Two, and since then nobody has seen her. The child she'd given birth to by her brother, she left behind."

By the time Lucas returned from the insane asylum Beatrice and Mary had already been married for two years, and Agnes's daughter, who was living with her grandmother—the only grandmother she had, as Beatrice pointed out—was in Standard 3 in the school behind our camp. Every one agreed that she looked just like her father used to look when he still had all his teeth.

"While Lucas was at Gil-Gil," Beatrice continued doggedly, "his father consulted so many diviners and they all told him the same thing. His ancestors were angry because he'd neglected them, and his son could not recover his senses until they'd been satisfied. He sacrificed so many goats..." When Lucas came back he seemed to be normal, only he'd lost not just his teeth but the big job in Nairobi and the Peugeot. And his wife, as well as his sister, had run off with a Kikuyu. The yellow house that he'd never quite finished building was all he had left. "Father Brendan took pity on him and sent him to teach in a secondary school in Luo country." Beatrice had been looking down at her hands but now her eyes met mine. "It was the wife of the headmaster of that school whom he attacked . . . So the ancestors *hadn't* been satisfied after all."

Mary took up the story. "They say Kambas are more skillful at treating madness than Busos, and so Obari Mugambo took Lucas to Eastern Province and left him there with a Kamba healer. But two weeks ago he came back to Gishugu. He got down from a bus in the market and there he stood. Everybody looked at him, everybody wondered, What sort of man is he now? They said to one another, 'We will wait to see what happens. Perhaps nothing will happen...'"

Beatrice drew a deep breath. "The boy we saw on the path said Lucas cut the face of his mother's co-wife with a broken

Simba bottle. And then he did to her what he'd done to the others."

We got back to the camp to find our assistants gathered in the shed we used as an office and Elizabeth, our chief assistant, holding the floor. A broad-shouldered young woman, oldest of eleven siblings, former head prefect of the Kitale School for Girls, in September she would be going to Kenyatta Hospital to study medicine.

"When the boy from Lucas's place came running to the police post, what did those policemen do? They refused to do anything!" she cried, her eyes flashing in fury. "I saw them—each one sitting at his ease, his arms folded so"—she demonstrated— "and I heard the sergeant tell that boy, 'Only a madman would do what Lucas has done and he has done it not once but three times. Go back and tell the family this is *their* business! They must deal with it themselves!' They pushed their caps back, scratched their heads. The radio was on and the sergeant turned up the music. They didn't even rise from their chairs."

A map of the community taped to the wall was dotted with small red flags, each of which represented a household in our study. With a ruler, Elizabeth pointed to Lucas's homestead. Then, drawing a wide circle round it, she announced, "We will no longer go into this area. If we were men we'd have nothing to fear. However, we are ladies." In fact we only employed two men, Matthew, whose job was to run from homestead to homestead checking the daily nutritional intake of every one of the children in our study, and Jonah, who swept out the office and made tea, and in between, if it wasn't raining, ogled the girls who worked in Tea for Two or dozed in the shade of the Norfolk pines that flanked the health post.

Since Lucas's neighborhood was out of bounds now, the seventeen women from there who were in our study would have to be replaced.

By the time we started our research in Buso District, Christian missionaries had been entrenched there for decades and almost everyone under age fifty, and a good many people over fifty as well, had been baptized. Gishugu itself was divided between

Catholics, most of whom lived to the north of the market, and Seventh-day Adventists, most of whom lived to the south. Though the Catholic Fathers were just as focused on saving souls as the Adventists, they harbored a deep respect for tradition. They were loath to condemn polygamy or the consumption of alcohol for ritual purposes and they mostly let divination and the ancestor cult alone. As a result, their male converts continued to have as many wives as possible and to spend what little cash they had on home-brewed beer, local hundred-proof alcohol, and animal sacrifice, rather than on secondary school fees for their children; and, because frequent hangovers reduced their preparedness for the challenges of modern life, their inclination was to let those challenges pass. By contrast, American Adventist missionary pastors believed that almost everything traditional was noxious and therefore a clean break with the past was essential. Not only did they insist that their converts renounce polygamy, alcohol, and animal sacrifice but, from the pulpit on Saturday mornings, they instructed them in elementary economic principles and scientific farming methods, and called on them to prosper, which many of them did. Adventist homesteads were tidier than Catholic homesteads; they dug deeper latrines and kept them cleaner; their fields and cows gave higher yields; and, with the exception of the proprietor of Tea for Two, who hailed from Central Province and had never been seen in a church, every commercial establishment in Gishugu market was owned by an Adventist. But regardless of important differences in other respects, all Christian missionaries had either to accept that circumcision was the essential requirement of Buso adult identity, or get out. When we were working in Busoland, if there was a boy or a girl above age twelve who hadn't been circumcised I'd have been very much surprised.

We replaced the mostly Catholic mothers who lived too near Lucas with mostly Seventh-day Adventist mothers on the other side of the market. They dressed their infants in gender-appropriate pastels, sang hymns while milking their cows and hoeing their maize, pyrethrum, and potatoes, and, if ever they had a spare moment, honed their embroidery and crocheting skills acquired from Dorcas, the Adventist women's organization. Meetings, to which they flocked in their best on alternate Wednesday afternoons, were held in the fine church hall across the garden from the even finer church. I admired their energy and optimism but found their smugness wearing. The church outfits of the Catholic mothers were not as elaborate as the Adventist mothers', but the Catholics were less high minded and moralistic than the Adventists and I found them a lot more fun.

In Busoland birth, death, and arrival at every stage of life in between demanded celebration, with more respect paid to the dead than to the living. As long as the ancestor spirits received the ritual attention they considered their due they stayed reasonably contented; but should rites be improperly performed or, heaven forbid, skipped altogether, they took offense; and, once their anger was aroused, they had countless ways of punishing their descendents. Hailstones could flatten crops, lightning could strike granaries and send precious harvests up in flames; wells could run dry, wives could only bear daughters, miscarry, or, worse yet, become barren; sons could commit fratricide, matricide, *patricide*; livestock and children, the only real wealth, could sicken and die. Most rituals took place at first light, or at least that was when they started. If one was to be celebrated somewhere close to Beatrice's homestead I'd spend the night on a cot in her storeroom so as to arrive on time in the morning.

As the most respected elder in his clan, her oldest brother-in-law, Ombui, who had served in the King's African Rifles in colonial times and, except in the hottest weather, still wore the army overcoat in which he'd been demobilized, usually supervised the proceedings. His overcoat aside, his exposure to the outside world had convinced him that he wanted as little as possible to do with it; and when his relatives and friends had begun going off to work on the tea estates and on European farms in the Rift Valley he'd remained steadfastly at home. Though his wife, Martha, had become a devout Adventist, after a brief flirtation with her church, Ombui had refused baptism and, while Martha successfully applied the economic principles she'd learned from her pastor, he focused his energies on preserving ancestral traditions. When I first met him, he couldn't have been much more than fifty, but he wore an air of authority that I found rather intimidating; and because the Buso he spoke was so grammatically complex, so garlanded with metaphor, even after I'd become a quite competent speaker of the language, I still needed a translator for all but our simplest interactions. Ombui really did use all ninety-six tenses listed in Father Brendan's *Grammar*.

Ritual efficacy depended on everything being done correctly. Since handbooks, common in other traditions in other parts of the world, were unknown in Busoland, Ombui conducted events from memory; and, because his memory wasn't always judged by his peers to be reliable, he often provoked argument. So rituals jerked forward in fits and starts and, if enough elders decided Ombui had made a mistake, even went backwards. This meant I often had to hang around taking desultory notes in a cow pasture or under the eaves of a tumbledown house from dawn until late afternoon. Only when the proceedings had been concluded to the relative satisfaction of all concerned could I retreat to Beatrice's house for a replenishing cup of tea.

"They have the fiercest arguments when they circumcise the children," Beatrice told me. "If it's boys who are being circumcised, the old men argue. If it's girls, the old women argue." They argued out in the fields while the children waited, naked, scared, and shivering, for the circumciser's knife; they argued while the children slowly healed in darkened huts; and they kept on arguing right up to the moment when, ten days later, they opened the door, called the children out into the sunlight, and signaled for the feasting to begin. "*Everything* has to be done right, that's why they have so many arguments. But you'll have to wait until December to hear them shout and stamp their feet and even *spit* in indignation." By December, the main harvest would be in and there would be money for the meat and grain and for the beer with which proud parents entertained the hordes of friends and relatives who came to help them celebrate their offspring becoming fully constituted members of the Buso tribe.

Beatrice's husband, Kepha, was often away during the week;

but on Saturdays and Sundays he was at home. Slim and over six feet tall, Kepha was outrageously handsome, or so I'd thought the first time I saw him when, before I'd even met Beatrice, I'd spotted him at the petrol station in Buso town, filling up the Land Rover he drove for the government. His cheekbones were high, his nose was straight, his eyes were lustrous, and he had the whitest, most even teeth I'd ever seen.

When I realized Kepha was Beatrice's husband, I'd thought, Poor Beatrice, being married to a prince can't be easy. But mercifully he seemed unaware of the attention his superb good looks attracted. He and Beatrice had caught each other's eye in the market center near Beatrice's home, and after a few brief conversations—in which Kepha had towered over Beatrice and Beatrice had looked modestly down and away to the left—Kepha had decided Beatrice was the girl for him. Only the chances of Beatrice's father accepting his proposal were negligible. Not only was Kepha a Seventh-day Adventist, not a Catholic, but as the youngest of five brothers, he had very little land; and, having dropped out of Standard 6 for lack of school fees, he had only one marketable qualification—his driver's license. Beatrice's father was hoping to do a lot better for his oldest daughter, the product of the Ursuline Convent School, Kakamega, and the apple of his eye. In fact, he had already entered into marriage negotiations with the father of Francis Xavier Nyamwange. An only son, young Francis was in his second year of teacher training and was looking to inherit five acres of rich bottomland.

So Kepha and his friends had simply stolen Beatrice. One midday, as she was walking from the power mill to her home with a bucket of maize meal on her head, his friends had grabbed her and dumped her onto the backseat of Kepha's Land Rover, whereupon, with a great grinding of gears, Kepha had sped away to Gishugu with his loot. Beatrice claimed that the theft had been entirely Kepha's idea. "I got into that vehicle because he had three big men with him and I was one small girl," she told me. But I didn't for one moment believe her. From the delight on her face when he drove into their yard at the end of the day, it was obvious she'd met him halfway.

In addition to driving, which he did with skill and passion, Kepha loved gardening. After losing his father when he was eleven, he'd been raised by an uncle on a Kericho tea estate whose British manager hired Kepha to work in his garden. Though his job was lowly—he mostly watered the rose beds in the dry season and weeded them in the rains—by careful observation he learned from the head gardener how to care not only for roses but for all the flowers, shrubs, and trees on the place. And when he grew up and received the scant acreage that was his patrimony, he divided his land into three: one-third he planted with maize, sorghum, and potatoes; one-third with pyrethrum; and one-third he made into a garden. His brothers told him he was crazy to waste his precious land on *maridadi* (decoration). But he ignored them. He planted the seeds and cuttings he scavenged in the course of driving for the government all over western Kenya; and, given the climate and his green thumb, they flourished. A dark-red floribunda rose rambled over the house he and Beatrice had built together after he'd paid her father eight cows and two goats and their elopement had metamorphosed into marriage. Purple, scarlet, orange, and white bougainvillea grew in great mounds over a rough pergola, and lemon trees and papaya dotted the grassy yard beyond his beds of zinnias, marigolds, onions, and spinach. When I arrived to spend the night on Saturdays and Sundays the battered gray vehicle he drove for a living would be parked beside the bottle-brush bush, Kepha would be puttering in his garden, and Beatrice and George would be on the bench under the frangipani tree, shelling beans. An idyllic scene.

But, as I soon discovered, the idyll was a mirage.

George would be seven on his next birthday and still he had no follower.

"Alone of all the women in this neighborhood, I do not conceive," Beatrice burst out bitterly as she and I were drinking final cups of tea by the light of a hissing propane lamp before bed one Wednesday evening. She told me she'd weaned George at eighteen months, the very same day as her sister-in-law Martha had weaned *her* son, Enoch. Two months later, Martha was hav-

ing morning sickness; eight months after that, when Martha delivered, Beatrice cut the umbilical cord and buried the placenta,
stoked the fire to heat water, helped the new mother wash herself and her purplish infant daughter. But still Beatrice wasn't
pregnant and when she went to the government hospital with
George tied to her back, hoping to see a doctor, she only got to
see a male nurse who chided her, "Why are you complaining?
Don't you have your son? There are women coming here who
have no child at all!" and brusquely sent her away.

So she'd counted out her pyrethrum money and gone to see
Dr. Patel, the Indian doctor, in his pink-washed private clinic
across the road from Barclay's Bank in town. But Dr. Patel happened to be on leave at Mombasa with his wife, his two sons,
and his wife's parents, and Beatrice had no intention of unbur-
dening herself to his Luo nurse.

"She was fat and when she walked she made a disgusting
noise." Beatrice put her palms together and made a sound like
bellows fanning a fire. She shivered. "Those Luo women, they
keep everything," she added in English. The Ursuline Sisters
had taught her quite good English as well as excellent Swahili;
but by the time Beatrice revealed this truth, ten weeks after
taking on the task of teaching me the Buso language, speaking
English together seemed out of keeping, and we used it only for
emphasis.

"Everything?"

"Because Luos do not circumcise their daughters, even
grown-up women have those things hanging down just as small
girls do. Only they are big women and their things are big as
well, so that when they walk about on a hot day they make that
shameful sound."

"I haven't been circumcised either," I admitted.

Beatrice looked at me, astounded. "Why ever not?"

"It's not an English custom."

"Don't white people ever circumcise their children?"

"Some circumcise their sons. A few do it for religious reasons;
but mostly they do it for health, to avoid infections. My son, for
instance, was circumcised in the hospital when he was three days

old. But my daughter won't be circumcised. Daughters never are."

"Then how do European girls get sense?" Beatrice asked after a lengthy contemplative silence.

"Did *you* get sense, all of a sudden, when you were eight years old?"

She shrugged. "Before that I was just a child. In the house, I did whatever my mother told me. At school, I did whatever my teachers told me. And the rest of the time I played. But then came my circumcision ceremony and afterwards, when I walked out from my mother's kitchen into the sunlight, all the women sang and danced and ululated, and my father gave a great feast!"

"But how were *you* different?"

"Those things between my legs weren't there anymore. When the old grandmother cut them off with her harvest knife, did I cry out? No, I didn't! I was frightened to death but I didn't show it. Already, at eight years old I had courage."

"And you had sense as well?"

"I was *beginning* to get it." She looked at me quizzically. "How did *you* get it?"

"Like Luo women, I suppose—just through living."

"When you walk you make no sound, even on a hot day," she observed. "But then, you're not fat. You're thin."

Beatrice never went back to try to see Dr. Patel because the Canadian visa he'd applied for came though, he closed his clinic, and moved his family to Edmonton, Alberta.

When George turned five, Ombui took matters into his own hands, Beatrice told me. "How much longer will you wait?" he asked Kepha. "Something we have or have not done has made our ancestors angry. It is your responsibility as well as mine to do whatever is necessary to put right whatever is wrong." To begin with, Kepha was adamant. As an Adventist, he was forbidden to consult diviners, let alone sacrifice animals. But Ombui kept pushing, pushing. "So long as the ancestors are angry they will threaten not only *your* well-being but the well-being of us all," he said. Four brothers, four sisters-in-law, their children. Ombui counted them up on his fingers. "What right do you have to endanger thirty-seven people, their cattle, goats, and chickens?"

Eventually Kepha caved in.

"He and Ombui consulted Kerubo at Goembu."

"You didn't go with them?" I said.

"Of course I went, but Kerubo didn't speak to me. She only spoke to my husband and my brother-in-law."

"But *you* were the one who was suffering."

"That's what you say, but Buso people would say that my problem is a *family* problem that only men can solve. Anyway, Kerubo didn't ask to speak to me, only to Ombui and Kepha. She is proud and fierce, as I think you know. Is she not Getuka's friend?" Getuka, the "investigator," is what the local people called my husband. Because divination interested him particularly, he visited Kerubo regularly and once or twice I'd gone along.

As a young woman, Kerubo had come very close to death, so she'd told us, and when with a diviner's help she'd recovered, her husband's ancestor spirits had ordered her to train as a diviner herself, a process that involved many sacrifices and presents to her teacher and took her twelve years to complete. By the time I met her, she was an imposing stern-faced woman in her sixties who'd had a successful "practice" for decades. In the morning she'd dig in her *shamba* like any other housewife; but by early afternoon, she had donned beaded necklaces and bracelets, her professional regalia, and was ready to receive the anxious men and women who came daily seeking her help. Eyes closed, face averted, she would listen as supplicants whispered in her ear what it was that burdened them; and then, with a rattling of gourds, she'd go to work. First, across a black goatskin, she scattered a pouch full of cowrie shells, pebbles, tamarind seeds, buttons, and beads of different colors, shapes, and sizes, by which the ancestor spirits communicated their demands—through her—to their descendents. Then, she swayed back and forth until, with a piercing shriek, her eyes jerked back in their sockets, the spirits entered, and she went into a trance. As she puzzled out the meaning of the pattern that her buttons and cowrie shells had made, she muttered, groaned, cried out, and sang wild snatches of old songs. When eventually she made sense of what she'd seen, with a dramatic shaking of the head she banished the spirits, emerged from her trance, and in a ringing voice deliver her diagnosis. Had she been faking her trance? Had she undergone some sort of fleeting psychosis? In the years since I'd been stunned and frightened by the *bori* dancers in Kaura, I'd become convinced—by William James, among others—that certain people can gain access to states of consciousness beyond the ordinary. Though I myself mightn't have the talents or discipline to do so, I believed that some others, including Kerubo, assuredly did. They weren't fakes, they weren't crazy. Rather, they had particular psychological propensities that I didn't share.

Beatrice reported that Kerubo seemed to have found her case particularly puzzling. She'd thrown her buttons and shells six or seven times ("Each time she asked Ombui for more money") before uttering her pronouncement: when the mother of Ombui and Kepha had given birth to twin girls, their father had hadn't carried out the necessary rituals.

"Kepha asked Ombui if he remembered those twin sisters," said Beatrice. "And Ombui replied that he did not. 'They must have died before I was born,' he said. Then Kepha said, 'How can we know if Kerubo is telling the truth? It could be that she's lying.' But Ombui respects those diviners, even those who are so old and blind they can barely see the patterns their cowrie shells make. He never doubts their words, and he follows *exactly* their instructions regarding time and place, the animal to be sacrificed, even the songs that should be sung."

Kerubo told Ombui to sacrifice two goats, one brown with white forelegs, weighing twenty-five pounds, and one white with black markings.

"Ombui found two goats with the features Kerubo had described in a distant market, paid for them, tied ropes round their necks, and led them home. Then he called his brothers. Three of them, Kepha, Jonathan, and Justus, are living on this hillside; but the last one, Barongo, works in a tobacco factory in Kuria country. When George had just turned two years old, he rented out his land, sold his cows, and took his wife, Gochere, and his five sons away. So Ombui had to send his oldest son, David, to call him back for the sacrifice. But Barongo swore at the boy and chased him off, and Ombui had to go down to Kuria himself to fetch him. Barongo swore at Ombui also, but Ombui sat in front of the house where Barongo was staying and refused to leave until Barongo agreed to leave with him.

"They arrived here late in the night, in fact already the sky was beginning to grow light, and immediately Ombui started sharpening his knife for the sacrifice. Afterwards he divided the meat and each brother received a portion. Barongo, as the second brother, took the forelegs; Justus, as the third brother, took the right flank; Jonathan, as the fourth brother, took the left flank; Kepha, as the youngest, took the hind legs, and Ombui, as the oldest, took the head and the heart. And then everyone on this hillside ate, except Barongo, who wrapped his share in a gunny sack to take back to Kuria...Before the sun had risen above our gum saplings, he'd left."

Beatrice shook her head mournfully. "But for all that, here you see me just as I was, with only one child..." In a hoarse whisper she added, "And now Jonathan has told Kepha he should take another wife—*another wife who will bear him more sons.*"

I was shocked. "He'd never do that to you, Beatrice! Kepha's *devoted* to you. Anyone can see that."

"Two wives on this small piece of land!" Beatrice's eyes were blazing. "If he brings her, I shall fight her! Not for even a single night will she stay here!"

"Kepha loves you. Why should he care what Jonathan says?"

"Because all these Buso men can think about is *sons*! You can see them all around here." She gestured. "There are men with five sons, even men with *ten* sons living on two acres. Everyone's hungry, there's no money for oil, or tea, or sugar, let alone for school fees. But because they have sons, they believe they are *chiefs*!"

Kepha came to see me in the office. He'd like to speak with me outside, he said, so I followed him onto the veranda. He told me that at the Adventist hospital at Goma Bay on the shores of Lake Victoria Nyanza there was an American lady, Dr. Margery, who could cure barren women.

"Would you go with us? If we go by ourselves, that lady will not consent to see Beatrice. She is too busy. Every day women come from all over Nyanza, from Western Province, even from the Rift. But if you, a European lady just as she is, come with us, I think she will agree."

I knew Dr. Margery by sight as well as reputation but had never spoken to her. Though I'd occasionally found myself standing next to her while we both waited to be served in Kassim's grocery store in Kisumu, her morally superior expression hadn't encouraged conversation. (To keep on doing good works for thirty years in one of the remoter spots on the planet, might a conviction of one's moral superiority be essential?) After I failed to receive a reply to any of the three letters I'd written requesting an appointment, we decided to take our chances and one Thursday morning set off to Goma Bay. I drove our yellow Datsun with long-legged Kepha, who'd wangled the day off, beside me and Beatrice, in her Sunday best navy-blue mini, in the backseat.

When we reached the hospital, a cluster of brick buildings with red tile roofs set back from the lake, the grounds were swarming with people: mothers with crying babies; sons with aged parents in their arms; boys with bandaged head wounds; women on makeshift stretchers in the throes of childbirth, feverish children, blind children, cripples. Kepha led Beatrice and me to Gynecology, where a strong smell of disinfectant hung in the air. I didn't fancy claiming the white woman's privilege; but that's what I'd come for after all, and so I pushed my way through the crowd of waiting women. At the desk in an office heaped with medical charts the woman I'd seen in Kassim's shop was interviewing a patient in the Luo language. Wispy gray hair escaped from her scraggly bun; the back of the hand with which she was writing notes was splotched and mottled, and in the

February heat of Goma, three thousand feet below Gishugu, her glasses had slipped to the end of her nose. When it looked like she'd finished taking her patient's history I knocked sharply on the glass panel of her office door, whereupon she glanced up and, pushing back her glasses, stood up. "What can I do for you?" When I explained that it was my friend Beatrice, not I, who needed her attention, her face clouded; but before she had a chance to turn us down I launched into a speech about how long and how much Beatrice had suffered and how far we'd come, and I didn't stop until her expression softened and she'd agreed to squeeze Beatrice in at the end of the day.

As we waited in the shade of a giant flame of the forest tree, Beatrice kept saying, "She won't see me, she won't see me. The doctor in Buso hospital didn't, the Indian doctor didn't. Why should this lady?" But this time she was in luck. Shortly after five o'clock, Dr. Margery ushered Beatrice and me into her examining room. "As I don't speak Buso," she said to me, "I'll tell you what I find and you'll explain it to her and the husband."

"My friend speaks English and Swahili. You can tell her yourself." But Dr. Margery didn't seem to have heard me. Meanwhile, behind a screen, Beatrice, who had never in her life had a gynecological examination, was exchanging her Sunday best for a hospital gown. Once she was up on the examining table she reached for my hand and gripped it tightly; and when the doctor pulled up her gown, spread her legs, and, with latex-covered fingers, began the examination, she flinched, shut her eyes tight, and bit her lower lip.

"Some of these tribal customs are truly inhuman," Dr. Margery remarked loudly, one white woman to another. "This poor lady has nothing left! No labia. No clitoris. Everything's gone. Want to take a look?"

But I'd already seen enough, thank you. Just a couple of months earlier, Beatrice and I had been chatting with Ruth, Ombui's hugely pregnant daughter-in-law, when, right there in her own yard, Ruth had gone into labor. "Shouldn't we call the midwife?" I said. "No!" Beatrice retorted. "The labor is already *hard*. The baby will be here long before that old woman." When we'd helped Ruth into her kitchen, Beatrice ordered, "Just light the fire and heat some water!" A decade later, when western women began campaigning against "female genital mutilation" in sub-Saharan Africa, my consciousness of the issue would be raised; but after Beatrice had caught the infant girl as she emerged squalling from the birth canal and I was put to sponging off Ruth's "nice naked hole," what I saw there—or rather what I *didn't* see—interested but didn't exactly shock me. This isn't to say that I hadn't been shocked when, years earlier, I'd first learned about female circumcision. Ngozi Onjugu, the ebullient Ibo girl whose room was next to mine in the dormitory of the college where I'd taught in Nigeria, was getting married over the Christmas holidays to her beloved Nathan; and just as she was leaving for home, she'd informed me off-handedly that three days before the wedding she would be circumcised. Of course I knew that *boys* were circumcised—in those days, virtually all middle-class English boys were circumcised in infancy— but, having never before heard of any such thing being done to *girls,* I was dumbfounded. Observing my reaction to what she considered mundane information, Ngozi cheerfully offered to show me what was going to be done to her next Wednesday morning (today being Friday), an offer I hastily refused.

Since then, having had a lot of relativist training, I'd learned to take things pretty much as they came. Also, after delivering Ruth's baby, Beatrice and I had had several conversations about sex from which it became quite obvious that, though she had no clitoris, Beatrice knew perfectly well what an orgasm was, and indeed, had them often. In other words, my dear friend wasn't *that* badly off. Even so, I knew I wasn't up to taking a look at her "nice naked hole." I felt it would be an inexcusable invasion of her privacy; so I turned the invitation down.

"You should *see* the state little girls can get into after some decrepit old creature has carved them up with a rusty knife," Dr. Margery continued. "Any decent government would make circumcision illegal, but not this one. This one doesn't have the guts." Fortunately, her disgust didn't interfere with her professional performance. After the manual examination, she took four X-rays and asked me to follow her into a small room, where she put the films up on a screen.

"My friend should also see them," I told her.

"Does she even know what an X-ray is?"

"I'm sure she wants to see them."

Frowning, Dr. Margery adjusted her glasses. "Well, if you say so," she conceded. When Beatrice had joined us, the doctor, using a wooden pointer, showed us that both of Beatrice's fallopian tubes were blocked. "This means conception is impossible. Sad, in such a young woman...The cause?" She shrugged. "Infection. Probably gonorrhea." Turning to Beatrice, she said in Swahili, "Have you been moving around?"

For some seconds Beatrice didn't grasp her meaning. When she did, she swallowed hard and said to me angrily in Buso. "Tell the woman no! What does she take me for?"

"She's been faithful to her husband," I told Dr. Margery.

"In that case, this is his fault, not hers."

"Does it matter whose fault it is?"

Dr. Margery shot me a quizzical glance. "You know, in this society women get blamed too often, so it's kind of nice to know when the woman's in the clear...I'm sorry, but you're going to have to tell the husband I can't help her. There's really nothing to be done."

While we waited outside Gynecology for Beatrice to get dressed I gave Kepha the bad news. I said, "Beatrice was infected." I didn't have the heart to say "by *you*." But he knew this was the case, and of course Beatrice, who understood English and had heard what the doctor had said to me, knew too. The silence in the car on our long drive back to Gishugu was leaden, and when I let Beatrice and Kepha out at the end of their lane, they waved a wordless good-bye and trudged off up the hill toward their house.

There were two rainy seasons in Busoland, April to July and September to November. In May, when the rains were especially heavy and the sun mightn't show its face for days at a stretch, the noses of small children ran perpetually and rasping coughs

could be heard in every homestead. A few old men donned
stained raincoats purchased from the peddlers who sold used
clothing from America and went out to beer parties; women tied
batiked Indonesian cloth and ragged blankets round their shoulders and, slipping and sliding on muddy paths, went, barefoot,
about urgent domestic business. I too had urgent business—
mothers to visit with and interview, babies to weigh and measure and observe. Umbrellas, which people used as sunshades in
the dry season, were worse than useless in equatorial downpours, so if I got caught between homesteads I'd run for shelter
to the nearest hut and gossip with the other shelter seekers while
I waited for the rain to let up. Provided they stuck to standard
topics—birth, death, planting and harvesting, cash crop prices
—I could understand pretty well what people were talking
about. But the longer they hunched in the dark of shuttered
kitchen, the more likely they were to turn to basic preoccupa-
tions; and then I sometimes lost track. Or rather, what they
talked about I found so disturbing, I'd start feeling dizzy and distracted. Had I really heard right?

I was beginning to grasp that going to church, as almost
everyone in Gishugu did regularly, had little to do with salvation
and all to do with protection from one's neighbor's malevolence.
As Bosu people lived alongside their closest kin, their neighbors
were likely to be brothers, sisters-in-law, and parents. It was
with them that they competed for land, water rights, rushes for
thatching, firewood, wild plants to make sauces to eat with
maize-meal porridge; it was against their success and failure in
every aspect of life that they measured their own; and, all too often, they were scared to death of them.

If your cow gave good milk or your fields a bountiful harvest;
if your daughters grew tall and straight; if your son did well
in the school-leaving exam; if ever in any way you showed that
you were proud of an achievement, you could provoke jealousy
and that jealousy could kill you, your wife, your children, your
livestock, and your crops. Stick your head up and you'd get it
cut off.

"Look at Mokeira's daughter," people whispered as rain beat down on thatch. "She came top in Standard 4 last December and by Easter the child had lost the power of speech—bewitched by the wife of her oldest uncle..."

"Do you know what happened to Marcus? He used the five thousand shillings he'd brought home from working in Nairobi to buy a Jersey cow, and within the month that cow was dead, poisoned by his twin brother."

"Did you hear about Lucas? His success made his father's brothers' sons so jealous that they set out to destroy him, and destroy him they did. Once he was a big man riding around in a big white car. But *now* look at him! After he raped his mother's co-wife, his father chased him out of Gishugu to wander the countryside, begging for food and stealing maize out of strangers' *shambas*. Chief Mwamba has vowed that if ever he comes within ten miles of Gishugu market he'll have him castrated..."

People lived in terror of *oborogi*, witchcraft, and they feared the sorcerer's magic they bought to protect themselves almost as much. Too often it boomeranged and instead of warding off your enemy, it came back to kill you.

By the time the storm had passed and I walked out of the hut onto the rain-washed hillside, my stomach would be churning with anxiety. Was Peter, the simple-looking fellow who idled in the shade with Jonah, our office tea maker, really the most powerful sorcerer in the district? Was Rachel, the cheerful mother of nine who sold roasted peanuts in twists of newspaper in front of Tea for Two, really the head of a witches' coven? And if Peter *wasn't* a sorcerer and Rachel *wasn't* a witch, why were people so terrified of them, as well as of their own brothers and sisters-in-law, even their own parents? Why was there so little trust and so much terror in this lovely, peaceful-seeming place? Fierce as it was, I didn't think that competition over limited resources was a good enough explanation.

With a few exceptions (the unconscious, defense mechanisms, transference, repetition compulsion), I hadn't found

Freud's ideas too helpful as I struggled to understand what I was seeing and hearing in Busoland. I'd read that, as England lurched out of the Middle Ages into modern times and the beginnings of class stratification, witchcraft accusations had been epidemic; that back then, just as in mid-twentieth-century Busoland, victims had almost always been the well-to-do, perpetrators almost always impoverished. That wealth provoked jealousy among those at the social margins, and jealousy provoked malevolence, and from malevolence sprang the devil's work had been universally believed. In the seventeenth century, a woman who lived in the village where I grew up in the English Midlands had been accused of witchcraft, tried, and convicted. In my childhood, villagers still talked about her and her two accomplices, who had suffered death by drowning in a nearby pond. It was hundreds of years too late to know much about the psychological conditions that had encouraged projection and paranoia in early modern England; but in Gishugu I spent my days watching small children and their caretakers and so I had a front-row view of early childhood experience, which went a long way to molding adult personality, or so I thought. I wondered, since Freud had hardly treated any children, what did he really know about early childhood experience? He'd only had his own memories and those of his adult patients to go on; and memory is notoriously unreliable. And so I more or less abandoned Freud in pre–World War I Vienna, and turned to Donald Winnicott, a psychiatrist, and John Bowlby, a pediatrician, who had been psychoanalytically trained in post–World War II London. Like me, they worked with real live children.

Quite often I would spend a whole day, from sunup to sundown, watching a mother and her baby going about their quotidian business. Though the child would do everything he could to attract his mother's attention, never once, cute as he surely was, did she look him in the eye; rarely, despite his persistent gurgling entreaties, did she address one word to him. By the time he was weaned and released to the charge of an older sister or cousin, at eighteen months, he'd stopped even trying to get his mother's attention. As the mother of young children myself, this resignation and withdrawal was painful for me to watch. I knew it was *shame* that constrained these Buso mothers, just as it had the Hausa mothers whom I'd observed in Kaura years before; and Buso mothers were quite articulate: "We must behave this way in order to teach a child respect for his elders. Through respect comes his grasp of the difference between right and wrong. And besides," they'd add, "why talk to a child who himself cannot answer you?" In due course children raised this way would learn to speak the Buso language fluently, even if their mothers rarely spoke to them; in due course, cognitive abilities unimpaired, they would go to school and some of them—like our extraordinarily able assistants—would do brilliantly. But according to my new gurus, being raised this way could have disastrous psychological consequences: distrust, a permanently splintered personality, an inveterate need to project one's own aggressive impulses on others.

I realized that the fact that I was *watching* inhibited these mothers. For all I knew, when they were alone they ignored stern cultural prohibitions; and certainly the warmth of nights spent tucked in bed with their small children might compensate for emotionally distanced days. Still, "maternal unresponsiveness leads to paranoiac tendencies" was the best explanation I could come up with for the preoccupation with witchcraft that confronted me almost everywhere I went. But my husband soon pointed out that even though Hausa mothers might hardly ever have looked their children in the eye either, witchcraft didn't preoccupy the adult Hausa people we'd encountered to anything like the degree it did the Buso. Competition between co-wives had to be the root cause, he insisted. In the quite recent past, when land was plentiful, a Buso man could widely separate his wives; but these days, given acute land shortages, a woman often had to live within a few feet of her co-wife, or even in the same house. Proximity gave rise to *engareka,* deadly jealousy, and jealousy to *oborogi* witchcraft. And so we argued back and forth until eventually, renouncing all reductionist explanations, we agreed that this Buso preoccupation had to have multiple causes, and perhaps we'd never identify them all.

☙

After Beatrice returned from Goma Bay an uneasy calm settled on Ombui's Hill. As usual when the long rains began, the brothers and their wives planted their crops, weeded their fields, and weeded them again; but before their maize was ready for harvesting, Jonathan's wife, Margaret, miscarried in the fifth month of pregnancy, and Miriam, the six-year-old daughter of Ombui and his wife, Martha, caught meningitis and, three days later later, died in hospital in Buso town. Within an hour of her death, the stunned parents brought their child's body home in a taxi; within two hours, her aunts dressed her in the flowered frock she'd worn to go with her mother to the Adventist church each Saturday and laid her in a hastily constructed coffin in her parents' living room.

When neighbors heard the news as it was called across lanes and over hedges, they came in from the fields and bathed hurriedly. Dressed in their best, they climbed the hill and streamed past Martha, who lay inert in Beatrice's arms in the yard, into the house. Round the coffin they shuffled, old women in shirtwaisters bent in anguish, their miniskirted daughters-in-law howling in grief; behind them came men of all ages grave-faced and silent. Out in the yard again, weeping women flung themselves to the ground behind Martha and men went to stand, heads bowed, arms akimbo, behind Ombui and his brothers. Meanwhile Ombui's schoolboy sons, David and Joshua, were digging their small sister's grave. When it was finished Ombui signaled to them to fetch the coffin and one by one the grieving women stifled their anguish.

In the sudden silence the Adventist pastor stepped forward to say a few last sorrowful words. Then David and Joshua spaded the earth over the coffin, filled the hole completely, and were stamping down the earth when suddenly their mother emerged from her stupor, jerked herself out of the arms of her sister-in-law, and, stumbling across the yard, threw herself on her daughter's grave. "Witches killed my child, witches will kill all of us, everyone on this hillside!" she screamed, and in her grief she clawed at the freshly turned earth, rubbed handfuls of it into her hair, arms, and cheeks, tore copper earrings from her earlobes, ripped the bodice of her dress.

Next morning Ombui took first one bus to Buso town and then a second as far as it went into North Mugarango; then he walked three hours to the homestead of Michomo, the most famous diviner in Busoland. When he'd whispered in the old man's ear about the child who had died in his homestead and about his brothers' children who had died in the womb, Michomo threw his cowrie shells, squinted at the pattern they made, and asked Ombui to give him five shillings. Again, he threw his cowries and demanded ten shillings more. When Ombui had handed over a crumpled bank note, Michomo squinted and puzzled, puzzled and squinted, until finally he announced that Barongo and his wife, Gochere, were responsible for the misery on Ombui's Hill.

When her fifth son was born, so Michomo revealed to Ombui, Gochere said to her husband, Barongo, "Husband, you have so little land. How will you provide for our sons?" to which Barongo admitted he didn't know. "Your mother bore your father five sons," she reminded him, "and I have borne *you* five sons. With your brothers' land, we would have land enough for our sons." Now, Gochere came from a family of witches, Michomo told Ombui. She remembered the spells, the incantations, and the magic potions her mother and her grandmother had taught her to make when she was a girl; and by and by she taught Barongo all the witchcraft she remembered. On a succession of moonless nights Gochere and her apprentice husband stole out with rags imbued with a magic potion; they hid them in the walls of their brothers' houses, each house in turn; and when the last rag had been hidden they went away to Kuria country to wait for their magic to work.

"One day, when your four brothers and their families are dead, Barongo, as sole heir, will return to claim his inheritance. With twelve acres, he will own more land than anyone else in Gishugu," said Michomo.

When Ombui got home he called his brothers and their wives

together and, in the room where, just two days earlier, their neighbors had circumambulated his daughter's coffin, he gave them Michomo's diagnosis. To have their suspicions confirmed and the source of their anguish identified was a tremendous relief, Beatrice told me later.

Kepha, who was the first to speak after Ombui had finished, said, "When we met those two on the path and we greeted them, so many times they walked on as if they hadn't heard us. We'd say to ourselves, we have done nothing to offend them. They hate us for no reason, it is their nature. We were always so afraid of what their baseless hatred might make them do to us."

Jonathan's wife, Margaret, said, "When my daughters were circumcised, Gochere refused to help with the preparations. She complained that back pain was keeping her from doing any work. But earlier that same day I'd seen her weeding her coffee bushes. There was nothing wrong at all with her back!"

Justus said, "Once Barongo's oldest son, who at that time was in Standard 6, pelted my three timid daughters with rocks, chased them into my house, and padlocked the door so they couldn't get out, not even to go to the latrine. On our return from town many hours later their mother and I found them quaking in terror, and the youngest one had soiled herself. When I demanded an explanation, Barongo claimed that my daughters had been the ones throwing stones and his son had locked them into the house to protect himself! But we knew Barongo was lying."

Ombui said, "More than once, Barongo refused to contribute to the cost of the rites the rest of us performed for our father. Or even attend them. His heart is black, there is no doubt about it. Black as night."

Michomo had not only identified the source of the family's misery; he'd also provided a plan: they should send for a witch smeller to smell out and remove the magic that Barongo and Gochere had concealed in their houses. But witch smellers had never been common; nor had they ever come cheap. So far as Ombui could remember, even when he was a young man there had only been only four or five in the whole district, and now he knew only of two, one of whom, having recently fallen off a steeply pitched roof and broken his left hip, had retired. That left Gachombo, who lived on the Luo border and, as a side line, grew an especially powerful strain of marijuana, some of which he traded but most of which he kept for personal use. This meant he was often out of commission.

Given no alternative, Ombui and Kepha went to see him. For two hundred shillings he agreed to come the following week, but as he refused to commit himself to any particular day, the three employed brothers were obliged to arrange to take a whole week's leave from work.

On the following Wednesday afternoon Gachombo came loping up the lane to Ombui's homestead. His appearance—ragged sweatshirt emblazoned with the words "Queen's Park Rangers," dirty blue shorts, tire-tread sandals, dusty hair standing in clumps on the dome of his head, a scraggly beard, and eyes that looked in different directions—did not inspire much confidence. Nevertheless Ombui took his ladder down from the rafters and sent his son David to round everybody up. With more than two dozen men, women, and children—including David with the ladder and myself taking notes—following along behind him, Gachombo crossed and recrossed Ombui's Hill, stopping many times at each house, granary, latrine, and kitchen to sniff at walls, knock on doors and shutters, and gambol like some strange four-legged creature across thatched and iron-sheeted roofs.

It was from the roof of Jonathan's wife's kitchen that he produced his first trophy, a small child's undershirt which, with a triumphant cry, he tossed into the yard below. From Justus's latrine he took a gourd, just five inches in circumference, whose mouth was stopped with a miniature corn cob, and from the thatched roof of his granary, a man's green sock. With a trill of delight he extracted another sock—this time a gray one with a heel darned in black—from the roof over Ombui's living room. In Kepha's homestead, which he'd left until last, Gachombo ran back and forth from house to kitchen to granary to latrine in a frenzy of excitement so intense that I half expected him to levitate and take flight. In a final sweep around the yard, as the sun was sliding into Lake Victoria Nyanza far below us to the west, he extracted a pair of men's underpants from Beatrice's granary and a medicine bottle containing a dark-brown mixture from the wattle fence round the latrine. And just when we all thought he was finished, he grabbed the ladder from David, clambered onto the roof over Kepha and Beatrice's bedroom, and from between corrugated iron sheets drew out a scarlet brassiere. In the waning light, he waved it in triumph, the assembled company looked down in embarrassment, and Beatrice covered her face in shame. "A present from Kepha when he first brought me here," she whispered to me. "The witch Gochere stole it long ago from my clothesline..."

Gachombo heaped his trophies in the corner of the yard and, with a glowing coal Beatrice brought out from her kitchen, set the little pile alight. As we watched, it flamed briefly, burned low, and within a few moments had turned to ashes.

Ombui and his brothers, and their wives and children, scattered to their homes to sleep the deep sleep of the saved while, having pocketed his fee, Gachombo set off for Gishugu market to spend some of his take in Tea for Two. As we walked the couple of miles to the market together under a rising moon, I would have liked to ask him about his professional training, but my attempts to engage him proved fruitless. Either his exertions had tired him out or, more likely, he didn't understand what I was saying. And even if he understood, why should he, the only surviving witch smeller in Busoland, share his secrets with a strange white woman? At the hotel he bade me a cordial good night and I went on my way to our camp.

Next morning the market was abuzz with the news: Barongo's house had burned to the ground.

I hurried to Ombui's Hill, where many of the same people who, just a week earlier, had attended little Miriam's funeral, were standing around the smoking ruins. But Beatrice and Kepha were not among them and next door their homestead was deserted.

I found Beatrice at work in the furthest corner of her *shamba*.

When I called to her from the edge of the field she didn't look round. Only as I came within a few feet of her did she straighten up and stand back from the row of beans she'd been weeding.

"What does this mean?" I asked her.

"What does *what* mean?"

"The fire, of course."

"After Gachombo burned those things we thought the fire had gone out and we left the place and went to our houses. But the fire *wasn't* out. The wind carried a spark to Barongo's house."

"You and Kepha didn't try to put it out?"

"Our well is very deep. To bring up even one bucket of water takes a long time."

"So you let the house burn!"

Beatrice stared at me defiantly. "Without a house, why should they come back here? No, now they are gone for good.

"Unlike you," she said evenly, "I have only one child, and that lady doctor told me he is all I'll ever have. So I must protect him. I think you understand that very well," she added and bent once more to her task.

IV

THE SAINT OF KATHMANDU

Treading Where the Buddha Trod

"You should come with us to Lumbini, Lord Buddha's birth-place," said the Saint of Kathmandu as she swept by me after evening devotions in the nunnery. Pausing at the bottom of the stairway to her quarters, she turned and, bright black eyes lock-ing with mine, added, "Will we meet tomorrow? The buses leave at six"—an order, not an invitation, I realized, and so, putting my life on hold, next morning I returned to the nunnery. By the light of a twenty-five-watt bulb strung up over a shuttered shop beside the gate I noted a sleeping cow, a pack of mangy brindled dogs hunting through rubbish in the gutter, and three women in ragged cardigans and faded cotton saris sweeping the crumbling sidewalk with stick brooms. No buses, not a single pilgrim. I was wondering how to proceed when two nuns in long pink dresses showing strips of orange underskirt slipped by. They wore brown knitted hats and gloves, pink shawls wrapped tightly round their shoulders, thick brown socks, and canvas shoes and, with blood-red Singapore Airlines zippered bags in hand, were heading purposefully south. Heaving on my backpack, I hurried after them.

"Are you going to Lumbini?" I asked as I caught up.

"Where else would we be going this early in the morning?" the older of the two replied briskly.

As we made our way through rutted lanes, men in black caps, woolly scarves, and made-in-China winter jackets and women tightly shawled like the nuns emerged from dark doors and alleyways. By the time we reached the broad street in front of the king's palace where half a dozen buses were parked we had a whole troop following behind us.

Scanning the crowd that milled around the buses I spotted clumps of brown-robed Theravada monks as well as pink-robed nuns and then the Saint, as I called her privately, though the local people called her Guruma, meaning "mother-teacher." A short, stout fair-skinned woman, she was peering at a list of names through steel-rimmed glasses; but then she looked up, saw me, waved, and in that dark January dawn her broad face glowed.

In bus number three, I was glad to find a place next to the door with room to stretch out my legs. My companion on the narrow metal seat was a woman almost as tall as I and a good deal heftier; she was dressed in a blue-and-white-checked nylon sari, the "uniform" that Guruma's female devotees donned for religious events. With a sigh of satisfaction, she settled herself on two-thirds of our seat, took an orange from her capacious handbag, peeled it, and pressed half on me. "No time to eat at home," she remarked in Nepali, and, oblivious of fellow pilgrims pushing up against and clambering around her, consumed her half, one segment at a time. The seeds she wrapped in a scrap of paper and tucked into her handbag.

By seven o'clock every pilgrim had been accommodated, every zippered bag and string-bound box had been stowed, dawn was breaking, and the winter mist was lifting. The buses cranked up and, with multicolored Buddhist banners streaming from luggage racks, roared away.

Lumbini, just four miles on the Nepal side of the Indian border, is the place where, in the sixth century BCE, the Buddha was born under a *sal* tree, his mother, Mayadevi, having been caught short en route to her natal home, to which, according to custom, she was returning to deliver her child. By twin-engined plane, it was a thirty-minute hop over the Mahabharata Mountains to the town of Bhairawa and a thirty-minute taxi ride from there to Lumbini. By car, one could cover the distance—180-odd kilometers on a relatively well-maintained two-lane road—in four hours. A commercial bus might take seven hours and we took almost twelve.

Ninety minutes after setting off we stopped in a roadside town clogged with brilliantly painted haulage trucks and littered with rubbish to queue up for the filthiest latrines I'd yet seen in Asia. Ninety minutes after that we squeezed into an earthen-floored restaurant in another roadside town for a lunch of gritty rice, mushy vegetables, and watery yellowish dal. A group of cheerful monks sat at one long table; at another table sat a group of equally cheerful nuns. For the monastics, who at ordination had taken a vow not to eat after noon, this was the last meal of the day; but we lay people needed to stop in several more seedy towns to buy soft drinks, bananas, boiled sweets, and roasted peanuts. In addition, because many pilgrims were in their eighties, we stopped at least once every hour so that the men could pee into the drainage ditch beside the highway while the women, stumbling in among leafless trees, could hitch up saris and squat, backs to the buses, in a vain gesture of modesty.

No one seemed to mind about the time our journey was taking. Though we were on pilgrimage, a serious merit-making endeavor, we were on holiday as well. With devotional songs playing at maximum voltage on the tape deck, we chatted, snacked, dozed, gazed at the bone-dry winter scenery as it changed from barren mountain to forested foothill and from foothill to desiccated plain, and traded life stories.

My hefty seatmate, a schoolteacher named Chandra, informed me that she had very bad karma. Who knew what she'd been up to in her former lives? At any rate, in *this* life, she'd certainly paid for it! As a student in the training college, she'd been no judge of character; in fact she'd been no judge of anything. Instead of marrying the young man her parents had carefully chosen for her, she'd eloped with Keshor. All *she'd* cared about was his looks—he'd been as handsome as a Hindi film star—and, as it emerged in short order, all *he'd* cared about was drinking... She'd vowed to Avalokiteshvara, the bodhisattva of Compassion, that none of her children would marry for love... She'd secured husbands of good character for her daughters and, just six months back, a bride from an impeccable family for her older son. With school closed another two weeks for the winter holidays and a daughter-in-law to take care of the house, Chandra had been free to join this *tirtha yatra* (sacred pilgrimage). And once she'd got her younger son properly married she'd have *two* daughters-in-law to take care of the house. "And then I'll *really* be free!"

"Free to do what?" I asked.

"Free for *dhyan*, meditation," she replied happily. "Six years ago, I was crazy," she confided. Keshor had been drinking all day and regularly beating her and the children. Twice she'd stopped on the bridge over the Bagmati River, which, that monsoon season, flowed deep and strong and so inviting, and considered throwing herself in. "The third time I stopped, I *would* have jumped if my cousin-sister Prabha, walking home from her job as a teller in the Nepal National Bank, hadn't come upon me staring at the water." Prabha had grabbed her, stuffed her into a three-wheeler taxi, and brought her straight to Guruma... It was Guruma who had taught her how to focus her mind, control her anger, stifle her despair, become peaceful. Keshor drank as heavily as ever—why shouldn't he? His government job was permanent. Even though he only showed up on the last day of the month to collect his salary, they couldn't fire him. But whereas once she'd been in rage and anguish from morning to night, now she was *calm*—well, most of the time at least. They didn't get into fights like they used to because when Keshor cursed and threatened, she simply walked away. (Chandra, with her powerful shoulders and broad hands, may once have given as good as she'd got, I thought.) All the same, the house wasn't good for meditation, what with Keshor shuffling about, banging into things and shouting, the television blaring, the telephone ringing, kids yelling outside in the courtyard...

"A lady I met in Guruma's nunnery took a three-month retreat in a hut in the Burmese jungle," said Chandra. "I, too, would like to take a three-month retreat one day, though in my own case, I wouldn't want to do it in the jungle. I'm afraid of snakes, monkeys, and vengeful spirits. No, I'd prefer a meditation hall—with screens on the windows to keep out mosquitoes and flying ants."

My life story was bland in comparison with Chandra's. Though I, too, had married for love, my husband didn't drink excessively and had never beaten me; and my children, over whom I had no control whatever, would certainly marry for love as well. As for meditation, I was only a beginner. My mind still raced in a hundred directions. Peace, I told Chandra, was nowhere near at hand.

"Practice, all it takes is practice," she said cheerfully, adding, "and the guru is very important too. Who is yours?"

Though I'd never had a guru exactly, two people had tried to point me in the right direction. For years, my English friend Eleanor had been urging me to be mindful and "let it go," whatever "it" might be. "But I can't stop thinking," I'd tell her despairingly. (If I did, wouldn't my world crash?) "I'm not saying you should, or even can, stop thinking," she'd say reasonably, "only that you shouldn't *hold on to* your thoughts." And here in Nepal, a monk named Vipassi, with whom I studied the Pali Canon, had noted my salt-and-pepper hair and tactfully suggested that I should start preparing myself for a good death. "So what can I do?" I'd asked him. "Watch your breath as it comes in and goes out again," he'd said, and settling into the full lotus position, he'd demonstrated. "I can't sit like that," I'd protested. Looking mournfully at me over his glasses, he'd observed, "Europeans are too much used to chairs." He hadn't let me off the hook, however. Meditation in anything other than the full lotus position would be ineffective. Physical pain and its mastery were an essential aspect of the discipline. But now, seven months later, I still couldn't maintain even the *half* lotus for more than five minutes.

"Guruma will teach you better than those people," said Chandra. "Only ask her."

But as we rattled through the late afternoon, I thought I

wouldn't. The monk Vipassi had been right—I *did* need to prepare for a good death. But as he lay dying, hadn't the Buddha
told his disciples, "Seek your own salvation with diligence"?
Not through grace—his or God's or anyone else's—but through
your own efforts. Having spent a lifetime studying, hadn't I already benefited from the attentions of an inordinately large
number of teachers? Salvation—or, at any rate, peace—was
what I was after; but I was seeking it in my own way.

It wasn't till after sunset that the buses lumbered into the
park surrounding the Buddha's birthplace. Clutching bags and
bedrolls we disembarked and found to our delight that here, on
the edge of the Gangetic Plain and at sea level, the temperature
was a balmy fifteen degrees warmer than in Kathmandu. Stiff-
ness and fatigue vanished as we pressed through iron gates into
the floodlit grounds of Gautami Mahaprajapati Vihara, named
for the Buddha's aunt and stepmother who'd raised him after his
mother's death, when he was one week old. Smooth-skinned
young nuns, freshly shaved heads gleaming under the floodlights, wove among us with great gray kettles and we sipped our
sweet milky tea from small metal cups as beaming Guruma
handed out almond-flavored biscuits.

The Lumbini Development Trust, to which several Pacific
Rim states had generously donated funds, had offered land in
the park to every country with a sizable Buddhist population.
Several governments had already completed the construction of
monasteries in myriad architectural styles, and installed monks
to care for the pilgrims who, given the increasing ease of international travel, were starting to trickle in. But for all that the
Buddha's birthplace lies within its borders, the great majority of
Nepal's population is Hindu. Buddhists are a small minority,
composed of people of Tibetan stock on the Himalayan rim and
Newars in the Kathmandu Valley who, millennia ago, migrated
down from the mountains. When the government of this—until
2006—officially Hindu nation showed no sign of producing
funds to build a Buddhist monastery, Guruma took on the project herself. But instead of a monastery she would build a nunnery, a haven for women in this sacred place. Now, after years

of collecting money house to house and intermittent bursts of construction, her dream had become reality, and a crowd of three hundred monks, nuns, laypeople (some with small children in tow), dancers, jugglers, and musicians had gathered for the consecration.

Ladies piled into dormitory rooms in the nunnery itself and gents trooped off to a nearby monastery whose golden pagoda reached far into the night sky. Along with two nuns and three lady devotees, I was assigned a plank bed with a straw mattress in a top-floor room. After rolling out my sleeping bag and noting gratefully that the faucet in the bathroom produced a trickle of water, I descended the steep concrete stairs to a vegetarian supper. Seated in the open on long rush mats, we were served by the team of young nuns, who, in preparation for feeding three hundred, had been cleaning rice and chopping vegetables since noon. Guruma herself sat between two little girls, sisters aged about five and seven. She urged them to eat, she served them second helpings of curried okra, she joked and giggled with them but, given her vow not to take food after midday, ate nothing herself; and soon she was up and, pail in hand, collecting discarded biscuit wrappers that tumbled across the compound in the evening wind.

Beneath a moon that hung huge and silver in an indigo sky, a musician riffed on his harmonium while his companions brought out flutes and fiddles and set up drums; the lead singers settled cross-legged on cushions and behind them, stomachs replete and gurgling, pilgrims filed into rows of white plastic chairs.

Guruma climbed the broad steps of her brand-new white-domed stupa and as she adjusted the microphone the crowd fell silent. "You are welcome," she told us, "all of you are welcome. May you find peace in this place!"

After we had taken refuge in Buddha, Dharma, and Sangha, the preamble to this, as to every Buddhist ritual, the musicians launched into the opening measures of a familiar song and soon the reinvigorated pilgrims were swaying in rhythm and singing of compassion, sympathy, and love.

I noticed several elderly men who had been standing at the edge of the crowd melt into the darkness beyond the floodlights, heading for the gate. Well, who doesn't need a stroll after a twelve-hour bus ride, I said to myself, and edged toward the gate. Once outside, I saw that the truants, hands clasped behind their backs, heads poked resolutely forward, were snaking their way between the buses that had brought us down from Kathmandu and across the parking area to a graveled road. At a discreet distance, I followed them through a stretch of densely shadowed forest that opened into moonlit grassland and led over a dry riverbed, past a water tower, and a small flat-roofed temple—into fairyland.

A thousand butter lamps flickered in perfectly ordered rows on trestle tables. They illuminated monastery ruins, a stone-flagged temple pond, the *sal* tree under which Mayadevi had given birth to the Tathagata, and one of a series of pillars erected in northern India in the third century BCE by the Buddhist emperor Ashoka, many—like this one—inscribed with decrees reflecting Buddhist teachings. Burgundy-robed monks darted between the tables, lighting lamps and adding ghee as women wearing striped aprons over long brown tunics and shaggy-haired men in thick woolen pink-sashed coats watched from the shadows. Loaded down with coral and turquoise ornaments, prayer wheels in hand, these pilgrims murmured mantras while behind them on the roof of the Tibetan monastery two monks, silhouetted against the moon-drenched sky, blew balefully on six-foot silver horns. Only then did I remember that ours was not the only celebration. Loshar, the Tibetan New Year festival, was just beginning and pilgrims from across the Himalayan region and even, despite the hazardous journey, from Tibet itself were converging on Lumbini.

One of the old men in the group I'd been following told me that in his youth, before the Chinese invaded Tibet, he'd spend several years in Shigatse working for his father's brother, who imported Indian textiles and exported Tibetan salt and wool. "In those days we'd go to the temples of the Tibetan monks and we'd call them to our house to give them alms, and every year we gave them lunch on the anniversary of my grandfather's death." Even now, so many years after he'd come back to Nepal, he still gave alms to the Tibetans. "And so do my friends," he added, indicating his companions. "In their youth they lived in Shigatse as I did, or in Gyantse or Lhasa."

"And your wife, does she also give to the Tibetans?"

"She has no interest, she was never in Shigatse, we didn't take our wives," he said and with his chin he pointed back toward Gautami Vihara. "She is with Guruma. She has ears only for her."

I'd heard that often before. Though the majority of mothers in my current study were Hindus, a substantial minority were Buddhists; and, as I interviewed them about marriage and motherhood and how they raised their children, they would often invoke Guruma as a source of wisdom not only about religion but about everything related to family life. "Everyone talks about Guruma. Who is she and where will I find her?" I'd asked a young mother named Sabbu one morning. "At four o'clock this afternoon she's coming to our courtyard," Sabbu had replied matter-of-factly, mentioning that since the day was a Buddhist festival, Guruma would be giving a teaching there. "You should come to hear her." And, along with the five hundred residents of Sabbu's courtyard as well as several hundred people from "outside," I'd come. Because Guruma had spoken in Newari, I'd understood very little of what she said; but even so, I'd found her aura of firmness and warmth compelling. A few days later I made my way to her nunnery and, after an audience that she conducted, thank heavens, in Nepali, I offered to tutor her young nuns in English for their secondary school certificate exams. When she accepted my offer, to my delight, I found myself on board, a member of the team. *In.*

Now, pulling myself away from the magical scene at the *sal* tree, I returned to the nunnery, where the musicians were still playing and the pilgrims still singing; and by the time Guruma had chanted, told a story, at which everybody chuckled, and, to wind things up, led us in fifteen minutes' meditation, it was midnight.

My spot on the long plank bed in our dormitory room was between the wall and two nuns, Sumeda and her friend Khema, both of whom I'd got to know quite well in Kathmandu. Khema, who had given up her career as a government economist to "go into homelessness," spoke excellent English. She and her brothers, the children of a wealthy businessman, had been educated by European nuns and American Jesuits. "The sisters would fine us five *paise* whenever they caught us speaking our own language," Khema had told me. "That's why I speak English properly. They were strict but also they were kind, and they taught us a lot we could never have learned from anyone else in Nepal in those days. About human rights and *women's* rights, in particular. Before the revolution of 1990, nobody knew that women should even have rights. We did, though, because Sister Elizabeth, our social studies teacher, told us."

The three lady devotees with whom we were sharing the room, a mother and two amply proportioned married daughters, were wives of prominent members of the Newar Buddhist community, Guruma's longtime devotees and, as Khema whispered to me, substantial contributors to Gautami Vihara; in fact their names were on the donors' plaque over the door of this very room. Though Khema and Sumeda knelt to pray at length before sleeping, the ladies lay down, covered faces with shawls, and were out like lights. Unfortunately Mama was a champion snorer. This didn't seem to bother the others but it certainly bothered me. If I slept at all it was only in snatches and too soon it was four o'clock, time to get up, splash water on our faces, and make our way down to the dharma hall for meditation. Though I'd fully intended to go to the dharma hall, in the sudden blessed silence after my roommates' departure I fell asleep again and slept like a log until, more than two hours later, the swell of voices rising from the courtyard woke me.

After breakfast Guruma and her team set to washing cups and plates in icy well water while we pilgrim/tourists paraded from one monastic complex in the making to the next. In the early sunlight we gazed at soaring scarlet columns, castellated walls, and golden serpent finials; we were awed by the number of toilets in the Korean monastery and by the sheer size of the Japanese guesthouse; we peered into a huge hole, the future Vietnamese temple; and in the brand-new Burmese meditation center we gawked at a line of men in handwoven sarongs, white undershirts, colored jackets, and odd little hats circling slowly, slowly, oblivious to their audience, oblivious to everything except their own breath. Chatting merrily, we strolled back to the nunnery to await the arrival from Rangoon of the great meditation master, U Buddhaghos Sayadaw. And wait we did, for a couple of hours; but just as we had concluded that his flight down from Kathmandu to Bairawa had been canceled, a white Mercedes belonging to Guruma's richest devotee burst out of the trees and with a scattering of gravel scrunched to a halt at the nunnery gate. The sayadaw, brown-robed and of impressive girth, descended and, flanked by two stripling monks, advanced to the stupa, a bright, white dome-shaped shrine, where he delivered a lengthy discourse on impermanence, which Guruma, who had studied many years in Burma, translated into Newari one chunky paragraph at a time. When finally he cut a white silk ribbon and—to cries of *sadhu, sadhu*—declared Gautami Mahaprajapati Vihara consecrated, it was just seventeen minutes short of noon. The sayadaw was hurried off to lunch in a well-swept space at one end of the nunnery storeroom—funds for the construction of a dining hall had yet to be raised—where Guruma served him nine different dishes, whose preparation she had personally supervised.

Our own generous lunch out in the courtyard was followed by half an hour of blissful indolence. But then we were rousted out of the chairs where we'd been warming ourselves in the sun, fell into line—I found myself with Chandra, my seatmate on the bus ride down—and trooped off to do obeisance to the Buddha at the *sal* tree. Monks and nuns, shading shaven heads with capacious umbrellas; mothers hand in hand with small children; gnarled grandfathers; Guruma's myriad uniformed devotees; acrobats and dancers; musicians playing fifes, drums, and stringed instruments—all were headed by the three great gods of the Hindu-Buddhist pantheon, white-bearded Brahma the Creator,

Vishnu the Preserver blowing his conch shell, and Siva the De-stroyer and Lord of the Dance, a strange loinclothed, dread-locked fellow brandishing an iron trident as he looped wide circles across the stony road.

But when we reached the Buddha's birthplace I saw that it had been stripped of last night's magic. The Tibetans had van-ished, a trestle table had been knocked over by a foraging cow, and butter lamps lay scattered, cold and blackened, on the scrubby grass. Goats scampered through the monastery ruins; crows cawed and argued round the temple pool and beneath the *sal* tree, which daylight revealed to be festooned with tawdry sun-bleached prayer-flags; a phalanx of somber black-robed Japanese pilgrims knelt in prayer. None of this dismayed my companions. For most, this was their first visit and they were thrilled to see with their own eyes the place they'd been hearing about their whole lives. They didn't seem to notice that Maya-devi's temple was squat and ugly; they ignored the plastic bags floating on the surface of the pool, the coils of barbed wire round Ashoka's pillar, the litter overflowing from the rusting dustbin by the gate. As we circled the garden, Chandra greeted with delight one long-familiar object after another and then, as we turned northwards, she cried, "Do you see *that?*" In the distance a perfectly triangular Himalayan peak jutted above forested foothills, snowy white against a cobalt sky.

After we had made several slow circumambulations our pa-tience was rewarded: the Japanese pilgrims, rising from their de-votions, marched off behind their priest toward their monastery and we replaced them at the foot of the *sal* tree.

The following night was devoted to chanting twenty sutras in their entirety. This great endeavor was led by teams of monks and nuns who spelled each other, one sutra at a time. Part de-votional and part protective ritual, it began at eight o'clock and, amplified to deafening levels by a sound system that only broke down twice, ended just before sunrise. By then, though some people, myself included, had long since sidled off to bed (where rest was possible even if sleep was not), many others, following along in their handbooks and joining in wherever they could, had stayed the full course.

One place we'd left out of our tour of the park on our first morning was the World Peace stupa, one of many that the Japanese were building around the globe. On our last morning, I asked my nun roommates, Khema and Sumeda, if they'd like to see it, but both shivered. They wouldn't want to go near the place, they said. So shortly after sunrise I set off by myself. At that early hour, the laborers who would soon be mixing cement and climbing bamboo scaffolding hadn't shown up yet and except for a flock of egrets dipping and soaring across the winter field and a herd of deer—five does and two bucks, sporting magisterial antlers, who paused in their grazing to stare at me—the place was deserted.

On another serene morning only six months earlier, the Japanese monk in charge of construction had been hacked to death by three men who'd vanished, leaving him lying in a pool of blood. In a tin box in the small house a few hundred meters from the stupa were several thousand rupees, money to pay his laborers that the monk had withdrawn from Grindley's Bank in Bhairawa the previous afternoon. But the killers hadn't touched the money, indeed they hadn't gone to the house at all but had fled into a nearby strip of forest. Their sole purpose had been murder. Who were they? Maoist guerrillas who, from their bases in the western hills, aimed to destroy shallow-rooted democracy, overthrow the monarchy, and establish a Marxist state? Hindu fundamentalists who, regarding Buddhists as apostates, had murdered one as a warning to the rest? Thugs hired by cabinet ministers or even members of the royal family to "eliminate" the monk because he knew too much about their theft of Development Trust funds? Despite the media attention that the murder provoked and the protest march that Guruma and other prominent Buddhists had led through the streets of the capital, the government investigation had quickly fizzled. The cabal that ran the country had no intention of opening Pandora's box. From Guruma's karmic fallout perspective, whether or not the state saw to it that justice was done was unimportant. She'd assured me that the perpetrators of this monstrous crime—whoever they were—would be reborn in hell, and the monk in heaven.

As I watched the deer and the egrets and the mist rising from the river behind them, a yellow-robed figure, the murdered monk's plucky replacement, emerged from the small house on my left. Seeing me, he smiled and, palms together, namaskar'd.

Later, as I was queuing up to board a bus back to Kathmandu, Chandra hailed me. "Already you are leaving?"

"Shall we sit together?" I called back.

She shook her head vigorously, reached into her bag, pulled out some pink material, and held it up for me to see. She made her way over. "I will stay here ten more days for meditation, I will put on this nun's dress," she told me. "You must also stay."

"But I've got work to do."

"What work could be more important than meditation? If you were knocked down by this bus, would you wait till you'd finished your work to go to hospital?"

For one long moment, Chandra studied my face. Then she pointed across the courtyard to where Guruma stood, razor in hand, beside a wooden-handled pump. Several women, arms and shoulders bare, saris hitched up to their armpits, were pumping water over their loose hair. Heads were much easier to shave if the hair was already thoroughly wet. But how many years would it take for that hair, a married woman's glory, to grow long again?

"Does your family know you're doing this?" I asked, but a shrug was Chandra's only response and, turning on her heel, she left me.

Soon I was climbing into the square cab behind the driver's seat, along with two handsome monks and two pretty nuns, both of whom were my English tutees. Since their monastic vows forbade them to touch members of the opposite sex seating arrangements were going to be tricky. First the driver, who looked sixteen though one hoped he was older, hauled two empty gas cylinders into the cab. But they left no room for us passengers, so he hauled them out again. After various alternatives had been tried and abandoned, the problem was solved by having the two monks sit together with a small girl—premenarcheal and still not fully female—between the first monk and one of the nuns, and by wedging my backpack between the second monk and myself. That done, everyone grinned in relief and we drove off.

On our return journey, instead of devotional songs, we had Hindi pop music blasting away on the tape deck. It emerged that, though their vows prohibited participation in or even being present at any sort of "entertainment," the tapes had been supplied by the young monks seated at the back of the bus. "This music is for the driver," the nun sitting beside me informed me off-handedly. "Otherwise he could fall asleep, the bus could crash, and we could all be killed." As we had no elderly people with us, we only needed to make three pee stops instead of nine and we made Kathmandu in under eight hours. When we passed the police post on the rim of the Kathmandu Valley, the driver snapped off the tape deck and the monk on the other side of my backpack began an energetic chanting of the *Mangalasutra*.

In Indra Chowk two weeks later, I ran into Guruma returning to her nunnery after taking lunch in the house of a devotee. She told me she'd arrived back in the city the previous evening.

"How was meditation?"

"You ought to have stayed with us!"

"I couldn't spare the time," I mumbled.

Guruma shrugged, too bad. "On Sunday I leave for India."

"Another *tirtha yatra*?"

"For *tirtha yatra*, this is the best season. In India, it's still quite cool but soon it will be too hot for Nepalese pilgrims—Nepalese people are hill people and they complain a lot in the heat. We've just come from Lumbini, where the Buddha was born, and now we'll visit the places where he lived and taught and reach ultimate enlightenment. And two Americans will travel with us," she added.

"Americans?"

"From Washington, D.C. They sent me so many e-mails and so I agreed. But what about you? Will you come also?"

Cocking her head, she looked at me expectantly. She would cherish my company, her strobe-light look seemed to insist, more that anyone else's in this world.

Once, on the temple trail across south India, an old Brahman guide had brought me and my husband into the presence of a famous holy man. "Do you want *darshan*?" our guide had asked, and before we could reply, he'd decided the answer was yes (who in the world didn't long for eye-to-eye contact with this great sadhu?) and, stepping forward, he'd whispered in the man's ear. The sadhu turned and looked at me. For four seconds—no, only three, though it seemed like an eternity—I held his omniscient, searing gaze, which demanded devotion and, in exchange, offered regeneration, recovery—a whole new life. But then the old Brahman was tugging on my sleeve and it was my husband's turn under the strobe light. I didn't forget my encounter with the divine. I told myself it had been staged, that it was laughably theatrical, that I'd been duped somehow. Even so, I wanted to repeat it and a couple of years later, finding myself in a city that the sadhu was scheduled to visit I went to the ashram where the newspapers said he would be staying and positioned myself in the front of the waiting crowd. His vehicle rolled up and he descended, a powerfully built hirsute man wearing only a dhoti and rope slippers on a raw winter day. ("He cannot feel cold because he has heat from yogic practices," whispered the woman standing next to me.) Before he went striding into the ashram he paused to survey the crowd. But he didn't meet anyone's eyes (not even mine!) and after he'd gone inside, I felt a sharp shock of disappointment.

"You really want to go off again?" said Vidya, my university lecturer friend.

"Why shouldn't I?"

"What about your research?"

"My assistants know what to do," I said a bit defensively.

"They'll do fine without me." This was true of course. However, since all five were high-caste Hindus who appeared to find my interest in Buddhism odd if not downright baffling, I expected that when I told them just why I was going to India I'd receive a bemused response.

"Do you know what you're in for?" Vidya persisted.

I grinned. "An adventure!"

"Do you know what a Newar pilgrimage is like?" Vidya persisted.

"I just went on one, didn't I?"

"And how long was it? Only two-three days! This one will be two-three *weeks*. The same bad food for breakfast, lunch, and supper. Plank beds—if you're lucky enough to find a bed at all—and no privacy."

Vidya had done graduate work in the States, where he'd learned that all Americans, including trekkers, Peace Corps volunteers, and eco-freaks—even anthropologists—who found their way to Nepal, needed *personal space.*

"I got used to bad food and crowds in Mexico, and sleeping in pilgrim rest houses on stone-cold floors."

"Mexicans aren't Newars," Vidya pointed out. "Mexicans are Christians and they pray. These Newars are Buddhists and they *meditate.* You're quite a restless person. Can you sit for many hours like they do?"

"I can try."

"And then there's shopping."

"For mementos? That's to be expected. No big deal."

"I mean, *serious* shopping," he said gloomily. "You don't believe me? Well, you'll see." He brightened. "Anyway, you'll need an Indian visa and there isn't time to make the application."

"I got one when I was in New York at Christmas," I said smugly.

"Go then!" Hands raised to chest level, palms facing outwards, he said, "But afterwards don't say I didn't warn you!"

When I climbed onto the bus the following Sunday I saw that Guruma was the only nun on board and the forty-odd laypeople were all locals. Those devout Americans must have backed out. Being the only foreigner on an adventure was a privilege to which I was quite accustomed, and which I relished and was reluctant to forgo. I throve on being the only "observing eye" at the party. So as I negotiated my way to the only vacant seat, down an aisle blocked by sacks of rice, baskets of potatoes, onions, and eggplant, a gas stove, and cooking pots, I was delighted that I wouldn't be spending my time discussing American Buddhism with two dharma seekers from Washington, D.C.

This was going to be a self-service pilgrimage—no team of young nuns to cook and clean up after us like there'd been at Lumbini. Under the command of Ratna, Guruma's general factotum, *we* would be the cooks and bottle washers.

Guruma had taken in Ratna, an orphan boy of about eight whom she'd found sleeping in a doorway in Asan Toll, and raised him in her nunnery. By the time he was twelve he was fixing water pumps and generators; by fifteen he had acquired an encyclopedic knowledge of automobile engines; by eighteen he was a whiz at TVs and public address systems. Several years ago he'd moved from an alcove off the nunnery kitchen to a hole-in-the-wall appliance repair shop that Guruma had helped him set up; but he was always ready to leave his shop in the care of his wife's elder brother and head for the holy sites. He was indispensable, and not only as a mechanic. His self-confidence and sunny disposition persuaded Guruma's devotees to pay attention to him and, much of the time, do what he said. Though most in this particular group were middle-aged women, four of their husbands were also along, as well as two young girls in jeans, shoes with platform soles, and form-fitting sweaters. No musicians, no jugglers, dancers, gods, or little kids. Only prosperous people who, having trustworthy hands in which to leave households, shops, and businesses, could be gone from home for three weeks.

After many months of daily Newari lessons, I could still communicate only with my long-suffering teacher. This was a source of shame to me. Reasonably fluent in Nepali, the national language, I could more or less get by with anyone who'd been to school; but western-style education had only been introduced quite recently and most of the women on this expedition hadn't been to school. Even if they understood Nepali, chances were they wouldn't understand me with my foreign accent. Guruma and Ratna spoke Nepali but they were sitting at the front of the bus; the husbands, being businessmen, surely spoke it and the teenagers surely did as well; only I wasn't sitting anywhere near them. My seatmate was a silver-haired Newar lady wearing armloads of bangles; and as we chugged up to the rim of the Kathmandu Valley and then, brakes squealing, took the hairpin bends down the other side, instead of interviewing Guruma about her early life as I'd hoped to be doing, I attempted to converse with my seatmate and failed miserably. She didn't understand what I said in either language and, aside from her name, the courtyard in which she'd been born, and the courtyard where she'd married, I hardly understood a word that she said either. By the time we reached the Trisuli River, whose waters, turquoise flecked with white, were racing to join the distant Ganga, we'd both given up and I was fingering my Walkman; and before we reached our first toilet stop at Naubise, craving had defeated restraint and I was wired.

Emerging from the foothills at Narayan Ghat, we raced west and then south to the border at Raxaul, where everyone was required to get out of the bus. But whereas the others went through immigration and were back in their seats in no time, because I wasn't a Nepalese citizen I had to show my passport and have my visa inspected by a line of khaki-uniformed Indian officials, a glacially slow process. While I waited on a wobbly chair for twenty minutes, a turbaned Sikh sporting a swagger stick withdrew with my passport to an inner office. "We're checking for drugs smugglers and terrorists," he said gruffly on his return.

"Do I *look* like a terrorist or a drug smuggler? I'm a *pilgrim*!" I protested. But the Sikh, who seemed to be finding my canceled China visa of great interest, made no response.

Suddenly Guruma was beside me, patting my arm. "It's just their work," she whispered, "they're compelled to behave like that," and she waited with me while I simmered down and three

more immigration officers flipped through my passport. At last
the Sikh grabbed it, stamped it portentously, handed it back and
I was free to cross into India.

Starting in Kushinagara, where the Buddha passed away at
age eighty-five, we would zigzag across the North Indian plains
to Bodh Gaya, where he attained enlightenment, finishing up at
Sarnath, where he gave his first sermon.

"Why do we visit the place of death before that of enlightenment?" I asked as we walked to our bus. "Shouldn't we go the
other way round?"

"I'll tell you why," said Guruma. "Bodh Gaya is two long
days' journey from Kathmandu and people would find sitting on
the bus for all that time very tedious. Kushinagara is a lot closer
so we will go there first."

We reached our destination only to find that the government
rest house where Guruma had planned for us to stay was filled
with Thai pilgrims; and so we lurched on to a gray concrete hall
with a gray concrete floor and, in the rear, a smoke-streaked
cookhouse and two evil latrines with doors that didn't latch. In
no time Ratna had divided us into four kitchen crews, each made
up of one gentleman and nine ladies. We were to work in rota-
tion, he told us—on for one day, off for three. The crew I was
assigned to was on that first evening and as we hauled supplies
from the bus to the kitchen I noticed that one of the off-duty
husbands was videotaping our labors with a late-model video
camera. He introduced himself as Rajendra Acharya—a Nepali
Brahman name, I noted, and wondered how a Hindu happened
to be on a Buddhist pilgrimage.

It emerged that Rajendra and his wife, Bobina, were the two
Washingtonians.

Pursuing me from bus to kitchen and back again, Rajendra
gave me a rapid-fire account of his American experience to
date. While he was in engineering school in D.C. he'd identified
a hole in the market begging to be plugged. "Americans like our
Nepalese curios," he told me as he zoomed in on Bobina kneeling to light the gas stove. After graduation, he'd started import-
ing religious statues—switching to English, he told me sotto

voce that gods and goddesses in sexual union were his biggest sellers—along with Tibetan *thanka* paintings, silver jewelry, singing bowls, brass water pots, prayer flags, incense, and meditation paraphernalia. After a slow start his business had taken off and now it was booming. He sold through three stores in the Washington area and also a catalog, and in April he was going online. Bobina kept the books, and now they had green cards ("which cost me too much money"), they were making their first trip home to Nepal since they got married.

"My wife studied with Guruma when she was a girl," he told me. "She's always saying how much she misses those Saturday classes. So when her sister wrote that she was planning to make this *tirtha yatra* my wife insisted we make it too. To be honest, I'd have preferred to spend our vacation hanging out with my friends in Kathmandu. Only you know how it is in America. If the husband doesn't keep the wife happy he has hell to pay. So we left our kids with their grandma and came along."

After we'd eaten Chow-Chow instant noodles and finger-sized bananas, drunk hot water with lemon, and cleaned up, we sat for puja (prayer and chanting) in the room where we would later sleep. Then Ratna distributed reed mats and blankets and as soon as we'd each found a spot to lay them—mine was between Guruma and one of the teenagers—he snapped off the light. But though I'd dozed during puja, sleep had vanished. Never had concrete felt harder and even though not a drop of rain had fallen since October, now, in February, mosquitoes were ubiquitous. They dove past my ears, alighted on my cheeks, forehead, eyelids. I pulled my blanket over my head but a few moments later, close to asphyxiation, threw it off again. Meanwhile, cordoned off at one end of the hall, the men—Ratna, our driver, and the four husbands—were snoring like foghorns. My elderly roommate in Lumbini had been a first-class snorer but she'd been the only one, whereas here there were six of them.

Guruma had fallen fast asleep, regardless, the moment her head touched the folded shawl she was using as a pillow. For a while, as snores rolled through the hall and mosquitoes whined assiduously, I watched her sleep the sleep of the blessed. She was sixty-four years old, but in the dim light filtering through barred windows her face looked as smooth as a young girl's.

Closing my eyes, I began to count my breaths. When I reached one thousand five hundred and fifty I switched to counting the different kinds of flowers that bloomed from March through November in my garden in New England. After flowers I tried world capitals and European rivers, but nothing did the trick. Remembering the desolation of sleepless childhood nights, I longed to take hold of Guruma's shoulder, as once I'd taken hold of my mother's shoulder, to shake her out of sleep and demand that she let me lie beside her—not just *near* her as I was already, but *touching* her. Skin to skin, sleep would come.

But instead I got up and picked my way between the rows and out to the evil latrines. On my way back I stood for a while in the yard and listened to night sounds—cattle chewing the cud in a nearby pen, a petulant bird, a lorry shifting gears in the distance, and the first triumphant cock's crow. Only then did I realize that, behind me, the cacophonous snoring had ceased.

Before dawn we were up and off to the narrow barrel-roofed temple that housed the great recumbent statue of the Buddha at the moment of death and final liberation, an object of awe and wonder to pilgrims since ancient times. Thirty feet from head to toe, he lay on his right side, head resting on one cupped hand. It had been here, in the hour of his death, that he'd addressed his disciples and for the last time impressed the fundamental truth upon them: Everything is impermanent, decay is inherent in all things.

But a hundred Thai pilgrims had made it into the temple before us and were already absorbed in deep meditation, leaving precious little room for us. Packing us in around the feet of the Buddha, in a loud whisper, Guruma instructed us to meditate on death and putrefaction, which, as well as I could, I did. But soon after the sun rose she got to her feet and led us out of the temple and across a blanched field to the stupa. Rising brownish-gray like the rump of a sleeping elephant, it marked the place where the Buddha was cremated, and apart from a couple of spindly legged cows, we had it to ourselves.

After we'd circumambulated and were seated on the dusty ground, Guruma addressed us. Her voice solemn, she told us the story of the Buddha's passing, and how there and then his sorrowing disciples had recited and recorded his teachings so that the truth he'd taught them would remain in perpetuity. Because the story was familiar I could follow it, more or less. As soon as Guruma had finished speaking a distinguished-looking lady called out, "Now tell us *your* story!" whereupon Guruma transformed herself from solemn guardian of the canon into skillful raconteur. I soon lost the thread of the story; but after breakfast, finding her on a bench behind the rest house reading a Hindi newspaper, I asked her what she'd said.

"I was telling them what I was like as a girl," she replied.

"What *were* you like?"

She shrugged. "Whatever my father wanted me to do, I did the opposite . . ."

The first major confrontation had been over education. Her father, Mani Kaji, was a goldsmith; he did beautiful work that was much sought after, even by the family of the maharajah of Nepal, even by the king and his two queens. Mani Kaji wanted his sons to know how to read, but in those days the few schools in Nepal were for the sons of very big people and so he hired a Buddhist priest as a tutor. "I was ten when that old priest started coming to the house to teach my brothers. 'Why only my brothers? Why not Parami,'—that was my sister, she was three years older than I—'why not *me?*' I asked my father. 'Why should you girls learn to read? You'll only get married,' was his answer. In fact Parami had no interest in studying, it was only I who did. I kept whining and complaining until finally, to be rid of me, he bought me my own slate. The day I joined my brothers on the veranda was the happiest day of my life!

"Then my mother—her name was Lakshmi—wanted to learn to read along with us children but my father forbade it. He said it wasn't right for a woman her age to be sitting with young kids. Soon after, she heard that a young monk who'd recently returned from abroad was teaching some children and even one or two married women in the temple, so she asked that monk to let her study with them. My father was happy she would be going daily to the temple. You see, she let him believe she was going to *cook* for the monk, and to his mind that was good because she would earn merit not only for herself but for the whole family.

"In fact the monk wasn't just teaching reading, he was also teaching Buddhism. In those days our priests didn't bother to teach the people anything about the dharma so actually, most of them knew nothing about it. They recited prayers they'd learned by heart without even knowing what the words meant; they performed all sorts of ceremonies for people and thought only about getting paid for their services. But the monks were different from the priests. They were educated men, they understood the scriptures, and they were willing to help ordinary people understand them too. It was from him, Bhikkhu Sugandha, that my mother first heard the *truth*.

"To start with, I'd been happy with the priest who was our teacher, but that didn't last. Once we'd learned to read and write a little, he didn't seem too interested in teaching us anything else. Mostly, he liked to gossip with our watchman. My brothers didn't care—they'd sneak off to play, leaving me fuming.

"My mother suggested to my father that instead of studying at home, I go with her to the temple. My father really liked that idea. Under the monk's influence—cooking and cleaning and washing his robes for him—I'd become a properly compliant Newar girl."

Bhikkhu Sugandha had had many adventures, Guruma recalled. He'd traveled all over India, he'd ridden in trains and even on elephants; he'd sailed in a small wooden boat down the Ganga and in a steamship across the sea to Burma, where he'd studied. During the World War, he'd seen Japanese soldiers and English soldiers fighting each other; he'd seen the gilded pagodas of Rangoon and Mandalay; he'd walked on jungle paths through dense forests and once met a tiger face to face. But it wasn't his adventures alone that enthralled her.

"The Lord Buddha taught the dharma in many different ways depending on who was listening. Our monk had the same talent. He would take a complicated idea and explain it so that even a small girl like me could understand."

In the meantime her sister Parami had turned sixteen and was of an age to be married and, no matter that his younger daughter hadn't had her period yet, Mani Kaji decided to marry off both his girls at once so that instead of two wedding parties, he'd only have to give one and he'd save a lot of money.

"Before long the matchmaker found two boys who belonged to our caste—their families weren't rich and they weren't poor either, but pretty much like us. When everything was settled, my father called us into his workshop and told us we were to be married in just fifteen days! Parami sobbed and wailed, but it was just for show. She was always peeping out at young boys in the street and saying that this one or that one was good looking. Her head was full of romance. I sobbed my heart out also, but *my* tears were *real*. The very thought of marriage disgusted me.

"I told Bhikkhu Sugandha, 'I *never* want to get married. I'll *kill* myself if they stop me from studying and send me off to live for the rest of my life in some stranger's house!' Oh, how I wept! When I'd quieted down a bit he said, 'Well, do you want to be a nun?' I said, 'What is that?' In those days there were very few of them in the city and I'd never seen even one. 'A woman who has left her house, one who is homeless,' he told me. 'She never gets married. She goes off into the world to study and to spread the dharma. You are a very good student. In only one year you have learned to read and write Pali, the language of our scriptures, and even to speak it quite well. You should continue your studies so that when you are older you could teach the dharma, especially to women. In Buddhism, women are very much neglected. You could help correct that deplorable situation. Soon I'll be going down to India to meet my guru. Let's see if I can arrange for you to go with me.'

'My father will never permit it,' I told him.

'No, surely not, but your mother, Lakshmi, might.'"

Married at age seven, Lakshmi had had to accept the young husband her father had found for her and the suffering that came with married life—being treated like a servant by her mother-in-law and by the wives of Mani Kaji's older brothers. But her greatest suffering had come from motherhood. She'd endured twelve pregnancies, two miscarriages, ten childbirths, and the deaths of five children. All those deaths, she believed, were punishment for sins she'd committed in her past lives. Only by earning merit—merit that would cancel out bad karma—did she have hope of being happier in her next life than she'd been thus far in this one. And giving a child to the monastery was one of the most meritorious acts a parent could perform.

"My mother was very eager for me to become a nun," Guruma continued. "Even so, she was worried. 'You'll be going very far from home,' she warned me. 'Well, I can't stay here, can I?' I replied cheerfully. Though I knew what I was running away *from* I had but the faintest idea of what I was running *to*. I only knew the courtyard I'd been born in and the streets and temples round about. I was a talkative and quarrelsome and—" she shrugged, "yes—a spoiled child. 'And you'll have to cut your braids off,' said my mother. She knew I was very proud of my braids, which reached to my knees and were the envy of all my girl cousins. 'Nuns shave their heads like monks,' she added. I was so excited at the thought of going off into the world that I said I wanted to shave my head right away. 'No, no! You must wait till you reach India,' cried my mother. 'If you shave your head here your father will buy you a wig and lock you up in his workshop until the day of your wedding. You must tell no one about this.' 'Not even Prasanna?' Prasanna was my youngest brother and my best friend. 'Especially not Prasanna! He can't keep a secret for one minute.' 'He'll be so sad without me,' I said, but then I remembered that if I got married as I was supposed to, Prasanna would be sad about that as well. Either way, I'd be leaving him."

Lakshmi knew that on the day Bhikkhu Sugandha was leaving for India Mani Kaji would be away from the house for a few hours, making the final marriage arrangements. As soon as he'd gone out she took from its hiding place the small bag in which she'd packed a few things and, just as they did every morning, mother and daughter set off for the temple. But this particular morning, instead of sitting in the dharma hall with his students, the monk was waiting at the gate, and with him was the Tamang boy Lakshmi had hired to guide him and her daughter through the mountains. As mother and daughter knelt at the monk's feet, the boy swung the monk's bag on his back and started through the gate with the monk following behind.

"I knew my mother was weeping and I couldn't bear to look at her face. I was weeping also, but I knew that my father would soon return to the house and discover I was missing. He would compel my mother to say that I'd left to become a nun in India, and then he'd send people out on horseback to catch me. We needed to get as far along the road as quickly as possible. So I jumped up, wiped away my tears, and ran after the others."

At that time the road to India was just an unpaved track. A few lorries managed to grind their way over the mountains, but most merchandise had to be carried in and out of the Kathmandu Valley on a mule or a man's back. When Guruma set off on her adventure, Nepal was still in the hands of autocratic rulers. Anyone coming in or going out of the Valley was required to register with the police. "Only *we* couldn't register," Guruma explained to me, "because if we did the police would ask Bhikkhu Sugandha for a letter from my father giving him permission to take me to India, which of course he did not have. So a mile or two short of the police post the boy led us off the road and up the escarpment through the forest. Once, while we were taking a rest—the climb was very steep—we spotted two horsemen through the trees below us, so we had to hurry on. Whoever those horsemen were, they didn't catch up with us.

"We came out of the Valley all right, slept the night in a Tamang village, and in the morning headed south. That second day the mountains were lower and not quite so steep and soon they were only hills. Meanwhile the temperature was climbing steadily higher. On the morning of the third day we had our first glimpse, through a gap in the hills, of the Terai plain and in the evening we reached it. In the weeks before the monsoon rains arrived, the heat was like a furnace. In all my life I'd never been so hot or so exhausted. How could I continue walking? Why couldn't I lie down in the shade and sleep? Then I remembered why I'd come so far already and why, before I could rest, I had to go a lot further."

The Tamang boy turned back toward the mountains and Bhikkhu Sugandha and Guruma crossed the border. "We couldn't cross together because the border guards would have thought the monk had stolen me and thrown both of us in jail. So I made the crossing with some farmers who were returning from their fields, and the monk crossed over by himself. Once we were on the other side and out of sight of the border guards, we met up again and boarded a bus. I'd never ridden in a bus before—from that point on, almost everything I saw and did was new. Late on the fourth day we reached this place, Kushinagara, where Bhikkhu Chandramani, our monk's guru, was teaching."

The Buddha lived his entire life on the Gangetic Plain and for more than fourteen centuries after his death it remained a Buddhist land. But then Muslims from central Asia began sweeping down into North India during the dry season to pillage the monasteries. Those few monks who escaped the sword ran away to Nepal and Tibet and by the beginning of the thirteenth century, the monastery at Kushinagara was deserted and in ruins and the villagers were carrying off the bricks to build their homes. The Muslims destroyed the Hindu temples also and slaughtered many priests; but their sons survived and with them their religion, and slowly Hinduism recovered. But Buddhism never did, and the Lord Buddha's teaching was forgotten in India.

"But then, about a hundred years ago, Bhikkhu Chandramani came from Burma to Kushinagara. Slowly, slowly, he put the place in order, and then pilgrims started coming and he took care of them. When I met him," said Guruma, "he'd been living here for fifty years and he was a stooped old man. I stood before him, a small girl in a dirty blouse and a torn skirt. 'I don't want to get married,' I told him. 'Nor do I want to live in my house. I've come here to shave my head. Have you got some scissors?' I spoke in Newari—at that time it was the only language I knew. Over the years, a good many Newars had come to study with this old bhikkhu and he'd picked up some of our language. Looking at me over his glasses, he replied, 'You are very young and you have come a very long way and before you shave your head you should have supper.' He led me to the kitchen and told his servant to prepare a meal for me. But as soon as I'd eaten and for some reason the boy had slipped away, I took hold of a knife and ran outside. By then the moon had risen, it was almost as light as day."

On their way into Kushinagara, Bhikkhu Sugandha had pointed out the Buddha's cremation stupa. "I thought it would be good to take leave of householder life in the Lord Buddha's presence and so, with that knife tucked into the waistband of my skirt, I found my way to the stupa and, standing just where I stood this morning, I sliced off one of my braids. I was just about to slice off the other when I heard a scream. On a high branch of a great *peepal* tree a man was standing—I could see his head and shoulders outlined against the moon. A madman! I thought. He's going to jump down from that tree and murder me! I shut my eyes and began counting my breaths as our monk had taught me...

"Well, though the madman kept on screaming he didn't come down from his tree. So after a while I stopped my meditation, opened my eyes, and sliced off my other braid. Then I hacked off as much as I could of the rest of my hair and returned to the monastery. By then, thinking I'd been stolen and was being taken to Calcutta to be sold into a brothel, Bhikkhu Sugandha had gone running to the bus park to look for me, and Bhikkhu Chandramani was alone. He was so thankful to see me that at first he didn't notice that most of my hair was gone. But when he did, he cried out, 'My child, what have you done?' 'I came here to shave my head,' I told him. 'If you've got a razor, may I borrow it to finish the job?'"

Taking up her newspaper, Guruma said with a faint smile, "That was a long story, wasn't it? Our pilgrims had heard it all before but they asked to hear it again."

From Kushinagara, we jolted on to Vaisali, which in ancient times had been a city celebrated for its gardens and lotus ponds. Vaisali had special meaning for Guruma because it was there that the Buddha first ordained women. On the long bus ride I sat with Rajendra's wife, Bobina. She told me with a dazzling smile and in American-accented English that she loved the United States and she wouldn't *dream* of moving back to Nepal. A month's vacation was just about bearable but to live there permanently? She would *die*!

"I find Nepal entrancing," I told her.

"Why shouldn't you? To you, everything's exotic—the mountains, the temples, the carved doors and windows, the cows lying down in the middle of the street. Maybe even the smells. And when you've had your fill of the exotic you can fly away. But Nepalese women are *trapped*. For them, Nepal can be deadly. The men all suffer from the Asian Disease."

"What's that?"

"It deludes them into thinking that all women are inferior to all men."

"When I was a girl in England, the disease was widespread there as well."

"Maybe, though a lot less now, I bet... But in Nepal change comes slowly, slowly. As a daughter, I still can't inherit my father's property, as a married woman I have to prostrate myself to my parents-in-law daily and do just as they say. All Nepalese people care about is *ijjat, ijjat*—honor, prestige, reputation, keeping their good name. If the neighbors should see me talking to a man who isn't my relative, they'll gossip about me forever! The list of "don'ts" for females is a mile long—and the "do's" are all about putting males first."

"But you flew away."

"With Guruma's help, yes, I did... In dharma class when we were small, she used to tell us, 'Girls are just as intelligent as boys and just as capable. People who tell you this isn't so are lying!' In secondary school and university we went on studying with her and if we wanted to speak to her privately we could find her in her room most evenings, between five and six. Whatever she was doing—the accounts, or writing a letter, or even a book—she'd put it aside to listen to our problems. Let's say we wanted to keep on studying but our parents wanted to pull us out of school because a marriage proposal had come from some stupid boy. Or we wanted to get a job but our parents wouldn't permit it because of shame—we'd shame our families if we worked in an office with strange men. Or supposing we *did* get a job but our boss threatened to fire us if we didn't have sex with him... Whatever was on our minds we could discuss with Guruma. And she would say, 'If you know what you want and believe in yourself, *no one* can stop you.' I can't count the number of times I said to myself, Bobina Kansakar, you must be brave like Guruma!"

Bobina refused several marriage proposals, finished her degree, and found a job in an organization for refugees from Bhutan for which, to her disgust, she earned only two-thirds the salary that a man in a similar position earned. "Still, working out in the world was ten times better than being married off." At twenty-seven, when she'd long since stopped receiving proposals and expected to be an old maid—most Newar girls were married by twenty—Rajendra came back from America to attend his cousin's wedding. While he was home his family was planning to get him married but he met Bobina at his cousin's wedding party—she was invited because she worked in the same NGO as the bridegroom—and for him it was love at first sight. "On my side, yes, I liked him. But I needed to make sure America had cured him of that disease."

"Well, had it?"

She grinned. "He still had *traces* but after we'd met twice for coffee I figured I could handle him, and even though he only knew three words of Newari and I'm Buddhist and he's Hindu, I agreed to marry him. Of course we realized there was no way of getting our parents' consent. So we went to see Guruma and she said, 'There's only one solution—you'll have to elope. And since, as the Lord Buddha said, everything, even parental disapproval, is impermanent, eventually things will work out.' She called in some of the other nuns and they all chanted the Mangalasutra and Guruma blessed us. Then we went to the Tripureshwor temple and had the priest there give us his blessing as well, and after we'd registered our marriage in the town hall we went to Rajendra's house.

"His parents hit the roof, as they say in America. They were mortified because they'd just settled on the perfect Brahman girl for him—her grandfather had been a counselor to King Mahendra, just like Rajendra's had. The marriage negotiations had almost been completed, and now their bird had flown! His father claimed that no one in the family had ever married a Newar; maybe in the bad old days someone had had a Newar *concubine,* but a wife—never! As for my dad, when he realized his daughter had married a Bahun—one of the *conquerors!*—he collapsed. My mother thought he was having a heart attack and rushed him to a clinic in Bagh Bazaar but the doctor said it was shock and sorrow, pure and simple, there was nothing wrong with his heart, and sent him home with six Valium tablets... Except for my sister Pavana—she's sitting up there—" Bobina indicated a woman wearing a purple sari seated nearer the front of the bus—"they carried on as if the end of the world had come. It was just my bad luck that Rajendra had to go back to the States almost immediately—it was December and half his annual sales are made in the two weeks before Christmas—so off he went, and since I couldn't go back to my house, Guruma let me stay in the nunnery while I waited for my U.S. visa. I think you know Khema and Sumeda? Well, I slept on the floor in their room and that's how I spent my honeymoon—in a nunnery without my husband! And when my visa came through, it was Guruma who saw me off at the airport. Pavana wanted to come but her husband stopped her..."

"*Did* things work out?"

"Well, for the first two years we wrote to our parents every other week but we never received a word in reply—not even a card at Dassain—until Babu was eight months old. Rajendra is the only son and Babu is the only grandson—that is, the only one who *counts* to my in-laws. In fact, Rajendra's sister has two sons but they belong to her husband's family. One day we got this phone call from one of Rajendra's uncles. He told us he'd just got back from the Kathmandu airport after putting my father-in-law on the plane to London—he'd be arriving in Washington at 2:35 the following afternoon. And sure enough, he did! The furthest he'd been before that was down to Tamil Nadu in India for a checkup in Vellore mission hospital."

"Was his visit a success?"

Bobina grimaced. "In the daytime we were working, Babu was in daycare, my father-in-law had no one to talk to, and he doesn't understand much English, so TV was a bust. And oh yes, he complained about the heat—it was August—and American chicken was too soft and tasted of nothing and the vegetables weren't fresh. He stayed just long enough to get over his jet lag. Then he got on the plane and went home. But at least the ice was broken and as soon as word reached my dad that Rajendra's dad had been here, he sent my brother Chabi over. Chabi showed up with a dozen little shirts my mother had sewn for Babu and three boxes of Indian sweets for us."

"So things turned out all right in the end."

"Well, you know how it is—you solve one problem and then you're up against another... *Dukha, dukha.* Isn't that what life's about? Now we've got Rajendra's sister's son living with us. He's going to the community college near our house—at least he's supposed to be going, but he's flunking. I think he's not very smart but Rajendra thinks he's into drugs..."

Except for a sixty-foot-high pillar surmounted by a lion, erected by the Emperor Ashoka, and a partially excavated mound nothing remained of Vaisali's ancient glory. Sitting with her back to Ashoka's pillar, Guruma gave us that day's history lesson, which Bobina translated for me in whispered fits and starts.

Once, when the Lord Buddha was camped not far from his ancestral home, Kapilavastu, five hundred women with his widowed stepmother, Mahaprajapati, at their head asked to be admitted to his new monastic order. He said to himself, "If I accept these women and then I'm unable to protect my monks from their carnal desires, my mission will fail," and he turned them down. But the women refused to take no for an answer and when he broke camp and set off eastwards with his monks, they followed. Catching up with him at Vaisali, with their clothes all dusty and in rags and their feet cut and bleeding, they came to beg again for ordination and again he turned them down. But then someone posed a challenging question. "Is a woman capable of attaining enlightenment?"

The Lord Buddha was obliged to answer. "Yes, just as capable as a man."

"In that case, aren't men and women spiritual equals?"

"Indeed, that is true." Backed into a corner, the Lord Buddha agreed to ordain the women, though only on condition that, as nuns, they accept a more stringent set of rules than those he'd imposed on his monks.

Regrettably, the Lord Buddha was a product of his times, Guruma told us. Though he admitted that women and men were *spiritual* equals he couldn't accept them as *social* equals. He never really trusted his nuns. Were they not impulsive undisciplined creatures? Wasn't this the immutable female nature?

Since childhood, she herself had believed that, given the chance, women would prove themselves the equals of men in every respect, a belief that Bhikkhu Sugandha, her beloved teacher, had strongly encouraged. But the truth was, twenty-five centuries after the Lord Buddha ordained the first nuns, the great majority of men, whether monks or laymen, continued to protect themselves from their own shortcomings by the fallacious belief that males were superior to females. In some countries—Burma, for example, where she'd spent many years in her youth—this prejudice was not quite so evident; but in Nepal women still ran up against it at every turn. Her insistence, as a young nun, on standing up for herself had got her into plenty of trouble until one day wise Bhikkhu Sugandha sent for her. "Actions speak louder than words," he'd told her and he'd advised her, "The only way to convince a man that you're his equal is to do equally good—and, if possible, better—work."

"So swallowing my pride and my anger, I went about my business. Instead of arguing with the monks, I decided to teach the dharma to anyone wishing to hear it, in particular to girls and young women who risked being thwarted and subordinated by wrong-thinking men." For some moments after Guruma finished speaking there was total silence but then one of the blue-jeaned teenagers began to clap. Tears streaming down her cheeks, Bobina followed, and then Rajendra, and soon everyone was clapping; and four crows perched on the lion on the top of Ashoka's column cawed vociferously and whirled away.

After Vaisali, we crossed the Ganga at Patna and touched down at Emperor Ashoka's palace at Pataliputra before riding on to Rajagriha, which in the Buddha's time had been the capital of his most powerful patron, King Bimbisara of Magadha. The Buddha spent many rainy seasons teaching and preaching in King Bimbisara's bamboo grove and many dry seasons meditating in caves on Vulture Peak, the mountain that jutted high above it. One stunningly beautiful morning, Guruma led us up to one of those caves, where she told us stories about the Buddha's life in such ringing tones and with such dramatic gestures that she had some of us wondering if she hadn't witnessed the events she was recounting with her own eyes. Then we slithered back down the mountain to pack up provisions, cooking pots, bedrolls, and belongings, load the bus, and bounce on to Nalanda, the great Buddhist university. In its heyday, Guruma told us, ten thousand students and two thousand teachers had been housed in eight colleges, studied in the nine-story library, worshipped in magnificent temples, and spent their leisure hours in parks and gardens beside lakes teeming with fish. But then, as the twelfth century came to a close, Muslim armies had sacked the university and left it in ruins, a corner of which the Archaeological Survey of India was now excavating.

After wandering through the foundations of the library and a couple of temples, all of a sudden I felt desperately thirsty; so I left the group and went to buy a bottle of water, which I drank in the shade of a *sal* tree. As I looked out across a sweep of desiccated land which, eight centuries before, had been a lake, I realized it was Ash Wednesday and I'd missed mass in the chapel behind the school the Jesuits ran up in Kathmandu for the children of the Nepalese elite.

A decade earlier in Calcutta, in St. Paul's Cathedral, full and overflowing at Ascension-tide, instead of watching others take communion, I'd resolved to take it myself for the first time in a very long while. As I'd made my way to the altar rail, I imagined that when I reached it, the Anglican priest would step back and denounce me. "This woman doesn't belong here!" Then I would have to admit to him and to the entire congregation that I hadn't recited the Apostolic Creed with the rest of them because, at forty-five, I didn't believe it any more than I had at twenty-three. Nevertheless, *The Life of Christ* (The Movie) was still playing in my head; and so I'd come to the altar to pay homage to an ideal. But the priest hadn't seen me for what I was, an apostate; or if he had, he welcomed me anyway. I glimpsed the glimmer of a smile as he handed me a wafer. Or was that my imagination?

Once back in the fold, or at least on its periphery, I wasn't particular about where I paid homage. Though Anglican churches could be found in former British colonies like India, Zambia, and the United States, in other countries where I spent my time they were either harder to track down or, as in Nepal, nonexistent. But Catholics were pretty much everywhere, so mostly I went to mass; and never once, even in Mexico, where I almost always towered over the rest of the congregation, did anybody, priest or layman, ask me what I was doing there. In my youth, religious traditions had been rigidly separated. No longer. The Jesuits up in Kathmandu were meditating and doing yoga, *evam me suttam,* so I'd heard.

Finished with their tour of the ruins, the rest of the group bought bottled drinks and joined me under the *sal* tree. As we lolled in the shade, one of the teenagers, a girl named Nita who was planning, she'd told me, to be a women's rights lawyer, asked Guruma if she knew of anyone these days who'd actually attained enlightenment. With a wrinkled brow, Guruma replied that one old monk, who'd been meditating for sixty years in the Burmese jungle, was *reputed* to have done so and become enlightened, an *arhat*; but she only had it on hearsay. "In the Lord Buddha's time, monks and nuns by the hundred attained enlightenment." But since then anger, hatred, and conflict between people, within families, communities, and states, had increased exponentially. "*We* are living in the *Kali Yuga,* the dark age. Enlightenment may no longer be possible."

Whereupon Nita's cousin-sister Nanu, who planned to be a dentist, asked, "Without hope of attaining enlightenment, why should I do as my parents tell me, why should I care so much about respect and self-control?" What was the payoff, she urgently wanted to know.

Head to once side, Guruma regarded the girl in silence. "We try to be respectful, compassionate, even-tempered, generous," she said slowly, "so that mostly we make good karma, so that"—she gestured—"we reduce our bad karma, and when the end comes we are peaceful rather than tormented, and in due course attain a good rebirth."

We pilgrims had fallen into a rhythm. Prayer, meditation, history lessons, sightseeing, dharma talks (about ethics, philosophy, and how to get on with our relatives). But the mundane took up a good deal of our time as well. After breakfast we would take our baths around the public tap. Watched by a line of dark-skinned children fascinated as much by our northern fairness as our near-nakedness, we thirty-seven women, *longhis* tied tight under armpits, scooped water out of buckets with rusting powdered milk cans, passed round cakes of soap, and washed as discreetly as we could under the circumstances. Then, slathering lotion on limbs and faces, we would withdraw to let the men in our party take their turn. When there was both water and time enough we did laundry. In the sunshine and close to zero humidity of the Indian spring, clothes dried in a matter of minutes. My companions wore a seemingly endless succession of beautiful nylon saris pulled from compact zippered bags;

whereas, by day three, in my fraying hand-loomed Mexican shirts and khaki pants, I was permanently disheveled, they remained immaculate.

One grungy rest house merged with another and it became difficult to distinguish between sacred sites as well. Despite the Archaeological Survey of India's efforts to excavate, restore, and convey a sense of ancient glories, all monastic ruins began to look pretty much alike. But seeing these holy places was less important than the mood that being in them evoked. Pilgrimage was addictive and I began to imagine myself, like pilgrims I'd encountered in remote monasteries on the Tibetan plateau, traveling from one sacred spot to another for the rest of my days. Like sheep we followed our shepherd, and even though some of us swatted mosquitoes and slept fitfully at night, and in the morning awoke with limbs stiff and aching, for close to twenty-three hours out of twenty-four we were peaceful.

But one hour of our day was invariably hectic. Though we cooked and ate breakfast and supper in the rest house, we took our lunch in truck stops, where the simple fare—curried cauliflower, chickpeas and potato, minced spinach, yogurt, chapati, rice, and dal—was always a good deal tastier than anything we produced ourselves. And after lunch we would head for the bazaar, where the women fanned out like locusts, moving through the stalls to pounce upon made-in-China goods, most of which were also available in Kathmandu.

"Why do they want to buy this stuff when they can get it at home?" I asked Guruma.

"Here prices are better," she replied genially just as a woman beckoned and she hurried off. Since few of our dedicated shoppers knew Hindi, let alone Bhojpuri, the dialect of Uttar Pradesh and Bihar, Guruma's services as translator were constantly called upon. Everyone wanted shoes—sandals, black patent leather heels, lace-ups, house slippers, babies' booties. Bras and panties were also in great demand; and every purchase involved prevarication, fierce bargaining, and—at least half the time—a change of mind *after* the conclusion of the sale. Sometimes this occurred when we were already en route to the next holy place, which meant doing an abrupt U-turn. Throughout these negotiations Guruma was saintly. Is she watching her breath, I wondered as, to accommodate the twelfth matron to be torn by indecision on one particular afternoon, she patiently switched back and forth, back and forth between Newari and Bhojpuri. Eventually, with everyone more or less satisfied, we would climb back on the bus with our loot. Capacious bags brought along especially for the purpose were bulging, and soon every nook and cranny under the seats and in the overhead racks had been stuffed with *stuff* and Ratna and our bus driver had begun lashing the overflow onto the roof. Given a realistic fear of thieves, every evening when we reached our sleeping quarters, all our loot had to be untied, taken down again, and, along with everything else, carried inside.

From Nalanda we drove south through fields bright with spring wheat to Gaya, a cremation place most sacred to Hindus, where we stopped briefly for tea and a stroll on the ghats, steep steps beside the river, past the great temple that housed a footprint of the god Vishnu. Though several people in our party expressed a desire to see the footprint, a sign above the door read "Hindus Only," which, with the single exception of Rajendra Acharya, none of us was. (Rajendra went inside with his video camera and, on reemerging, pronounced the footprint a fake.) Just a few miles further on we rolled into Bodh Gaya, the most sacred of all Buddhist places. A sprawling, dirty, unprepossessing town on a meandering tributary of the Ganges, which at that time of year had all but run dry, it was surrounded by monasteries and rest houses, a few of them spanking new and densely decorated but most, including the Burmese monastery where we would be staying, grungy and decayed.

After the dust and clamor of the streets and the assaults of beggar children, the garden surrounding the Maha Bhodi stupa was an oasis of tranquil loveliness. In a wash of pink, cream, and purple bougainvillea, scarlet flame of the forest, and blue jacaranda, maroon-robed Tibetan monks performed prostrations, and here and there between crumbling monuments emaciated towheaded western youths in running shorts rose to full Nordic height and, as if readying for a dive into a swimming pool, held steady before falling to their knees, stretching forward in prostration, pulling back, rising, and repeating the process 108 times.

Following a preliminary circumambulation of the temple and a glimpse of the *vajrasana,* the Diamond Seat, a marble slab topped by a yellow satin cushion that marked the spot under the Bodhi tree where Sakyamuni, sage of the Sakya tribe, attained enlightenment, we assembled in the shade of an ilex to receive our day's history lesson. And after supper, we returned to the temple, whose great sandstone tower was now floodlit, for an all-night meditation session. Along with pilgrims from all over the Buddhist world—but minus Rajendra and another husband who had bravely announced they were going to bed—we seated ourselves beneath the luxuriantly thriving direct descendent of the original Bodhi tree. I had intended to see the night through; but despite hourly walks in the garden, by half past two in the morning I'd had enough and, leaving the others lined up straight-backed behind Guruma, I crept away between long rows of flickering oil lamps to the same tree where we'd had our afternoon lesson, wrapped myself in my Kashmiri shawl, and fell into a dreamless sleep. I awoke around five-thirty and in the predawn darkness crept back to my companions, seated as straight as ever, and took my place among them. As the dawn rose, the floodlights were extinguished, some Sri Lankan monks began chanting, and my companions opened their eyes, stretched, and, wearing beatific expressions, scrambled to their feet. If any were aware that I'd cheated, nobody said anything about it and neither did I.

A three-day stay at Bodh Gaya gave us time—when we weren't meditating at the temple—to do laundry, take afternoon naps, read, listen to music on our Walkmans (Bach's sons for me, Hindi-pop for the teenagers), make phone calls to Kathmandu, and hike across the dry riverbed to the granite mountain on which, after leaving the luxurious life of his father's palace, Sakyamuni had practiced rigorous austerities for six long years before realizing he was on the wrong track. As the brief Indian spring pressed on toward summer, pilgrimage season was drawing to a close and on the open land behind the Bhutanese monastery, Tibetan entrepreneurs had already begun to dismantle their tented restaurants, in which, since autumn, they'd served banana pancakes, bran muffins, cheese enchiladas, muesli, yogurt, and blended fruit drinks to westerners on the dharma road. One noon, while our companions lunched on curried vegetables at stalls in front of the Maha Bodhi Society guesthouse, Rajendra, Bobina, and I slipped away to a partially dismantled Tibetan restaurant to eat the season's very last banana pancakes with yogurt and warm honey.

Next morning, our eleventh out from Kathmandu, we set off westward on the final leg of our journey, to Benares and nearby Sarnath, where the Lord Buddha delivered his first sermon to the five ascetics, his companions during his fruitless ordeal on the granite mountain. Having attained Buddhahood, he might have kept his knowledge of nirvana and how to reach it to himself had his friends not pursued him, as he wandered up the Ganga in his newly enlightened state, and begged him to share it. In the Deer Park at Sarnath he gave them the Four Noble Truths—all life's experiences from birth to death engender suffering; suffering is rooted in craving, attachment, pride, and false beliefs; but these may be eradicated by living a moral life and practicing meditation; doing so conditions one to see the impermanence of all things and ultimately brings release from *samsara*, the cycle of rebirth.

As we trundled across Dufferin Bridge at Benares and looked south along the river, a stir rippled through the bus. It wasn't the great sweep of the ghats with their palaces and temples or the soaring minarets of the Aurangzeb mosque that provoked excitement, but rather, the prospect of *shopping*. At Sarnath itself we had no time to gaze at Ashoka's pillar or the Dhamekh stupa, an outrageously phallic two-tiered construction poking fifty meters into the sky. As soon as we'd dumped our belongings in the rest house we got right back on the bus and headed for the

Chowk, the great bazaar at Benares. Ten ladies in our group had imminently marriageable daughters each of whom would need several brocade saris for her wedding; and the rest were hell-bent on buying for themselves. Hoping to set limits on their wives' appetites, the four husbands came with us. It was shortly after two when we plunged into the Chowk, whose narrow lanes were lined with sari shops and thronged with frenetic humanity; and by the time we staggered out—craving temporarily assuaged and laden with paper parcels—crying "Tea! Sodas! Chat! Samosas!" the sun was setting.

Guruma, who had spent the past four hours bargaining and translating, led us into a tea shop and, leaving Ratna to handle our orders, made off to the toilet out back. When, after twenty minutes, she hadn't reappeared, Bobina and I went in search of her.

We found her lying, eyes closed, in a strip of deep shadow in one corner of the yard, her brown cotton shoulder bag placed neatly beside her. "I felt pain here and here," she whispered as we crouched beside her. She pressed hands to throat and breast.

"Why didn't you tell us, Guruma? Why are you so hard on yourself? Why won't you ever take rest?" wailed Bobina. "You stay here, and I'll fetch a doctor," she said, and jumped to her feet.

Guruma's eyes flickered opened. "I don't need a doctor," she said sharply, "and I've taken enough rest." Rising to a sitting position, she moved her head from side to side, lifted her arms straight out in front of her, flexed her fingers, wriggled her toes.

"Don't move!" cried Bobina, one staying hand on Guruma's pink-clad shoulder. "We'll carry you to the bus!"

"How could you two weak women carry me? I'm too heavy."

"We'll call some others."

"No, you will not!"

"Do you still have pain?" I asked.

"Now not so bad."

"Is this the first time you've had it?"

She shrugged. "Oh no, it comes quite often."

"What does your doctor say?"

"That I have a weak heart, high blood pressure, and my cholesterol is 322." With a snort of indignation, she added, "He also tells me I should leave the nunnery only when necessary, and I tell *him*, 'That means at least three times a day!' " Patting the shoulder bag lying beside her, she said, "But my tablets are always with me. I take two white ones morning, midday and evening, and two blue ones before I sleep. Help me get up because I'd like to drink tea now. And not a word about this to the others!"

"What shall we tell them?"

"I'll tell them the truth myself—that I've been resting."

Sarnath was the end of one journey and the beginning of another —the inward journey of a ten-day mediation retreat. I'd known from the outset that it was scheduled, and on and off along our zigzag route I'd debated whether or not to sign up. Rajendra and Bobina needed to return to Kathmandu to rejoin their children, and the two girls, who would be starting a new school term, would be traveling back with them. I'd rather hoped that there would be some pressing reason for me also to return to Kathmandu; but when I telephoned Parvati, my chief assistant, she told me she had everything under control.

"Don't hurry back," she said. "Haven't you been wanting to take such a course for some time?"

Cumulatively over the past two weeks I'd spent at least thirty hours in meditation, sometimes with a cushion and sometimes without, but never for more than a couple of hours at a stretch. Was I up to sitting cross-legged from long before dawn until long after dark with only short breaks for light vegetarian meals and trips to the toilet? Could I stand the pain, the physical torment? What if I was bored out of my mind? When I returned at five o'-clock from the long-distance telephone office I still hadn't decided.

Though the retreat wasn't scheduled to start until after supper, my companions were already in meditation mode. The women had exchanged brilliantly colored saris for subdued cotton *salwar kameeze*s (long, loose shirts over wide trousers), and

Ratna and the three remaining husbands had donned track suits. Most were walking slowly, eyes downcast, from one end of the rest house grounds to the other, apparently oblivious of the many Tibetans who, having spent the winter at Sarnath, were noisily packing up before heading back to monasteries and refugee camps in other parts of India.

"Well, are you going or staying?" asked Bobina. "Rajendra made our night bus reservations this morning but now you've left it so late, you might have to stand all the way to the border," she added, just as Guruma, seemingly recovered from yesterday's bad turn, rounded the corner. Bobina and Rajendra namaskar'd, thanked her, and asked if they could bring Babu and Nanu to the nunnery to meet her when she returned to Nepal at the end of the month.

"I'm sorry you can't stay here with us," said Guruma. "I know our English friend is particularly sorry to see you go."

I opened my mouth to say "Guruma, I'm going with them!" —but then I swallowed hard and said nothing. The decision had been made.

Two hundred yogis assembled in the meditation hall to hear the rules read in several languages. (Anyone who didn't feel he or she could abide by them was invited to leave but nobody left.) Then we were asked to take the eight precepts—no killing (even of insects), lying, stealing, sexual activity, alcoholic beverages, entertainment (reading, writing, listening to music), or touching money (our valuables had been placed in plastic bags and locked in a safe), and no solid food after midday. We also took a vow of silence and, having been instructed to avoid eye contact with other human beings (no mention was made of dogs, of which there were many wandering about the grounds), were assigned places—men on the left side of the hall, women on the right.

To my dismay, I was separated from the Nepalese, and instructed to move my belongings to the section of the rest house reserved for female westerners, of whom there appeared to be about thirty; worse yet, while my friends remained with Guruma, I was assigned to an English-speaking Sri Lankan monk named Bhikkhu Buddharakshita, who had studied for seven years in Australia. Freed from a householder's anxieties, he, like many monks, looked extremely young but was probably over forty.

After a short restless night with my new companions—given our vow of silence and the almost total absence of circumstantial evidence, I never discovered the name or country of origin of a single one of them—I was awakened by the tolling bell by which time would be measured for the rest of my stay at Sarnath. The first three days would be devoted to a preliminary exercise with which I was quite familiar that involved *anapana,* focusing on one's breath; and every evening we listened to a dharma talk which, in the case of the westerners, was delivered by a rather engaging monk from Bangladesh.

To my relief, the physical experience was easier than I'd anticipated; in fact it wasn't really difficult at all, given that we never had to sit for more than ninety minutes and each sitting period were followed by a half hour's walking meditation in the grounds. It was the emotional experience for which I was unprepared. Rather than getting *bored,* as I'd thought I might be, I became increasingly *angry.* Though to begin with I was merely annoyed at having been summarily separated—on racial grounds —from my friends and Guruma, annoyance soon deepened into indignation and indignation into rage at this entire rule-bound process. When, during our two-minute meeting on the first day, my teacher, Bhikkhu Buddharakshita, asked me how long I was able to maintain one-pointed concentration, and I replied, 'Thirty seconds,' he looked disappointed. When I gave the same answer on the second day, he was concerned enough to ask if I was confused.

"About what?"

"You grew up as a Christian, didn't you? You wrote that on your form. But being a Christian and doing meditation shouldn't confuse you. You don't have to be Buddhist to meditate. *Anyone* can practice meditation."

"I'm *not* confused," I told him. "I'm *angry*—about having to obey so many rules. We're all adults here but nobody trusts us to have good judgment. I feel like I'm eleven and back in my boarding school—and being subjected to discipline for discipline's sake."

"These rules are not gratuitous. They have a purpose. They are to prepare you for acquiring insight into how things really are. Isn't that why you're here, to acquire insight?"

"I'm not sure why I'm here."

By day three I could barely concentrate for even thirty seconds and during our meeting on day four—that morning we had moved on from *anapana* to *vipassana,* the acquisition of insight, and for the past eight or nine hours had been scrutinizing physical sensations in our feet—I told Bhikkhu Buddharakshita that I didn't belong in the course and wished to withdraw.

"I haven't been sufficiently helpful to you?"

"*Bhante,* this is *my* failure, not yours!"

He looked at me coldly. "Withdrawal is not possible," he said.

"It's not that I expected the course to be easy," I continued. "I didn't, but it's turned out to be much harder than I thought and I'm not up to it. It's as simple as that."

"I believe you heard the rules?"

"Yes, I heard them."

"They included one that forbids a yogi to withdraw for any reason other than life-threatening illness. Do *you* have a life-threatening illness?"

"Of course not!"

"In that case, you are obligated to remain here and continue working diligently on the assignments," he concluded and, to indicate that my two minutes with him were up, he looked down at his lap.

That evening, between drinking hot milk—the yogi's non-supper—and listening to the nightly dharma talk, I sought out Guruma. "I feel like I'm going to explode," I told her. "I can't stand it. If I don't quit now, I might really go crazy!"

She didn't seem surprised. Meditation was easy for Nepalese people, she said. Their forefathers had been practicing meditation in one form or another since the Lord Buddha's time. "They just slip into it. But you westerners are different. Meditation is new to you, and before you can accept it you have to read every-thing and think about everything and question everything. Re-ally, you give yourself a very difficult time..." She observed that because I had no life-threatening illness and—so far as I knew—my husband and children didn't either, if I insisted on leaving, I would have to break the rules.

"I'm afraid so."

"Then if you wait here, I'll fetch your money and your pass-port from the safe." She patted my forearm "Next time you'll do better."

In the morning I took the bus up to Raxaul, where the same Sikh who had stamped my passport on my way into India almost three weeks earlier stamped it again on my way out. From there I took a night bus up to Kathmandu and as soon as I got back to my house I telephoned Bobina.

"Was Guruma disappointed with you?" she asked when I told her my story.

"If she was, she didn't show it."

"I bet she said that even anger is impermanent."

"Something like that, yes."

[v]

EL SHADDAI

Charismatic Christianity in Hong Kong

Just as I was beginning the coffee-making process on Sunday mornings, our maid, Isabel da Costa, dressed in a sea-green pantsuit, springy hair pulled back in a neat knot, silver crucifix round her neck, bulging white and blue plaid shopping bag on her arm, would pop her head round the kitchen door. "I'm going to church, Mam," she'd say, eyes bright with expectation for what lay ahead. "You have a nice day, and I will too."

Initially when we received notice that the university had assigned us a "furnished four-bedroomed fifth-floor flat with spacious living room, dining room, six air conditioners, balcony and view of South China Sea," I was delighted; but within moments I was seized by dread. Who was going to take care of such commodious digs? Who would dust the furniture and polish the floors? Who would negotiate the dry cleaners, the fish market, the greengrocers? To me, lacking even a single word of Cantonese and with a book to finish, the prospect was daunting; and, apart from mixing gin and tonics, my husband wasn't likely —or any better equipped—to pitch in. On a visit to Hong Kong in the early 1990s, we'd seen Filipina maids crowding the sidewalks and squares of "Central," as the downtown of Hong Kong is generally called, on Sunday afternoons. But when, on New Year's Day several years later, we flew into the astonishing new airport, how one set about securing the services of such a person was still a mystery.

As it turned out, Ella, whose stepmother was the sister of my boarding school roommate, taught economics at the same university, lived in an adjoining block of flats, and employed two Filipinas, Laura and Isabel. Hearing through the family grapevine of our imminent arrival, she'd obtained a key to our flat, and when we arrived with our twenty-three boxes of books, two laptops, brand-new seven-octave German keyboard, and—since we planned to acquire new wardrobes from an Indian tailor on Nathan Road—one modest suitcase each, we found Ella reading the *Guardian Weekly* on the living room sofa, Isabel hovering in the front hall, the fridge stocked with essentials, and chicken soup simmering on the kitchen stove.

"Obviously you need a helper and I happen to have one to spare," Ella, a pretty, if chunky, divorcee of about forty, said cheerily. "Try her out, and if she suits you, do please keep her. I've written down my phone number." She indicated a scrap of paper on the coffee table. "Just give me a ring if you have a problem with her—or for that matter with anything else. I've got to run now." And, with a rustle of newspaper, she was off.

After serving us the soup, followed by cheese, biscuits, and fruit salad, Isabel brought two cups of instant coffee. "We have no coffee pot," she told me, "and many other things the university does not provide." From her pocket she produced a list of missing household items. "Tomorrow we will go to Ikea in Causeway Bay," she said in carefully enunciated English. "They have a good selection, reasonably priced."

Aside from being an assiduous house cleaner, ironing adept, parsimonious shopper, and expert darner of socks, Isabel was a comprehensive Cantonese-style cook. Just about the only daily decision I needed to make was whether to have fish and chicken or fish and pork for dinner. After a few feeble attempts to resist regression, I settled into having all my domestic needs met.

A few days after our arrival, while jogging beside the Pak Fu Lam Reservoir in the late afternoon, I spotted Ella walking briskly in the middle distance with Jim, her Tibetan mastiff. Drawing level with her, I thanked her again for her generosity. "Isabel's wonderful. You did us a very good turn."

"I should be thanking *you*," Ella replied. "Look at me—two stone overweight! Do I really need Isabel's four-course dinners? Besides, I didn't have room for her. I only took her in as a favor to Laura. They belong to the same church—one of those charismatics, so I believe, though I've never actually been there. Once Laura did ask me to go with her, but whooping and hollering's not my cup of tea.

"Anyway, one morning last spring Laura came barging into my study. I'd already had my eleven o'clock coffee and it was still too early for lunch. I had a pile of essays to mark before my class at two and I wasn't happy to see her. 'So now what's up?' I growled. She told me some tale about a friend of hers who'd been dumped in the street by her Chinese employers. 'That's too bad,' I said. 'Such things do happen,' and turned back to my essays. 'But she's *in the kitchen*,' said Laura. 'She had nowhere else to go, so she came to me.' 'You mean to *me*,' I corrected her. 'She's scared to death of Immigration,' said Laura. 'If she doesn't find another job in *two weeks*, they'll send her back to the Philippines.' To cut short a rather complicated story, I let Isabel stay and she moved into Laura's room and I gave her a new contract, which settled the immigration issue. But my kids are at school in England so there isn't enough work for two helpers and Laura's room's *tiny*... What with all three of us menstruating in the same week, the atmosphere in the flat was getting tenser and tenser. Since Isabel moved over to your place life's been so *relaxed*!"

"Did you find out what happened with her employers?"

"No, I never did. Of course I asked her about the fall-out but she just muttered and looked at the floor. When she first showed up at the flat she did have a bruise or two. She's cute, so I suppose the husband was after her and the wife suspected and gave her a hiding. That's how fallings-out often happen here."

Female domestic workers are the Philippines' major export and its main earners of foreign currency. In 2000 at least 150,000 were working in Hong Kong, where most lived in rooms just large enough for a cot and a chair in the rear of what, until

Shanghai's recent explosion, were some of the world's tallest, most expensive apartment buildings. From dawn until long after dark they cook, clean, shop, walk dogs, and take care of children for a government-guaranteed minimum monthly wage of about US$450, most of which they send home to their families. In an economy ruined by Ferdinand Marcos and, after he was ousted in 1986, almost terminally stressed by a population that burgeoned in the wake of Corazon Aquino's pro-life policies, even—especially—for well-educated women, there is little work to be had at home; and so, after finishing up their two-year contracts and taking a few weeks' holiday in the Philippines, most Filipina "domestic helpers" (as the government of Hong Kong has designated them) sign up for another two-year stretch—and then another and another. In the Gulf States, where the government provides little protection from financial exploitation or physical abuse, life as a maid is perilous. Italian employers are reported to be kind but likely to "forget" to pay wages. Israelis pay quite well but, since the beginning of the second intifada, Israel has become too dangerous. By just boarding a bus to go to the supermarket, you risk being blown up. Though Los Angeles has the best working conditions, if the applicant is single or childless, a visa is virtually unobtainable, the assumption of the Immigration and Naturalization Service being that, once she's in the country, she will "go illegal" and stay for good. Despite Beijing's efforts since the 1997 Handover to undermine it, the rule of law still prevails in Hong Kong SAR (Special Autonomous Region: "one government, two systems"). So Hong Kong, only a short plane ride from Manila, is viewed as the best place to work as a maid.

Six days shall they labor; on the seventh shall they rest.

By eight o'clock on a Sunday morning, Filipinas by the tens of thousands are heading into Central by bus, subway, ferry, and tram. Within sight of the harbor with its dark-blue rolling waters they spend their precious leisure hours on the clipped lawns of city squares, in the underbelly of the glass and gray steel Hong Kong Shanghai Bank, in the sharply delineated shade of skyscrapers, and on the elevated walkway linking the luxury shop-

ping complexes of Central and Connaught Road with the Star
Ferry Pier. In tight clusters they read and write letters, pass
around photos of children being raised by sisters and mothers
on the other side of the South China Sea, play cards, trim hair,
polish nails, embroider tablecloths and tea towels, eat *adobo,
paksiw,* and *halo-halo* out of plastic containers, read Filipino
magazines and listen to Filipino music, and doze through the afternoon, heads on friends' laps. At points during their long and
lazy—but *frugal*—day off, they may call home from phone
shops on Des Veoux Street, send off money orders, and browse
alley stalls for jeans and T-shirts. Many go to church. St. Joseph's
on Garden Street offers mass every hour on the hour and every
hour it's swamped. Holy Communion at St John's Anglican
Cathedral on Battery Path is swamped as well. Though the great
majority of Filipinas are Roman Catholic, to some, given that
the English liturgy is almost identical, having a Protestant dean
rather than a Catholic father dispense the bread and wine isn't
something to worry about. What's important is *receiving* it.

When Isabel came to work for us she'd been in Hong Kong
for thirteen years. "It'll be fourteen in June," she told me. Her
son, Ernesto, was back home with her mother; she didn't mention a husband and all she volunteered about her "previous employers"—before Mam Ella took her in—was that things had
started out good enough but had gone from bad to worse to terrible. It seemed that when she left the household she'd had time
to pack only one small zippered bag with a few clothes, a Bible,
and a photo of her son, a gap-toothed boy in school uniform,
which she'd tacked up on the wall of her room in our flat. She'd
also brought with her a pocket radio that she kept on the kitchen
counter tuned to a station that she listened to many hours a day.
Whenever she passed through the swinging door between the
kitchen and the dining room, she'd be followed by a burst of
hymn singing or the voice of a preacher holding forth in a mixture of Filipino and American-accented English. From the
snatches of English I caught, the preacher sounded like Pat
Robertson or Jimmy Swaggart. Inspirational, folksy, sometimes
hectoring.

"That's DWXI, my church's station," Isabel replied when I asked her about it.

"What church is that?"

"Oh Mam, it's Catholic, it's El Shaddai."

"I've never heard of El Shaddai."

Isabel gazed at me in wonder. "How is can that be, Mam? Ah, now I understand—you're *Protestant*. On Sundays you go to St. John's, like Mam Ella. Even so, for sure you've heard of Brother Mike."

"I have to admit, I haven't. Who is he?"

"Our leader, Mike Velarde. Please, Mam, wait one second…" She darted off, rubber thongs thwacking across the parquet floor, and returned with a newspaper clipping. Above a page-length article in Filipino was a colored photograph of a dark-skinned, broadly smiling man. His jet-black hair was immaculate, his regular teeth dazzling white. For a moment Isabel gazed raptly at the photo. "Brother Mike was on the verge of death from heart disease when he said 'yes' to Jesus," she said softly. "In the evening he was dying and next morning he was well! To say thank you to Jesus for this miracle, he vowed to bring as many people to Him as possible.

"That was twenty years ago," she added, turning to me, "and now in the Philippines he has *millions* of followers, and wherever Filipino people are living, he has millions more. Here in Hong Kong there are many thousands of us, and even though he's up in age—he's almost eighty—and he's kept extremely busy, he manages to visit us regularly."

The following week Isabel invited me to go to church with her and her friend, Laura, Ella's helper and, though I had mixed feelings about charismatics, I didn't want to offend her and so I accepted; but when Sunday came Laura was under the weather and Isabel and I had to leave her at home. In Central we changed from a Number 10 bus to a Number 104 and rode through the harbor tunnel to Kowloon, where we changed to a Number 6, heading into the New Territories. Soon high-rises were giving way to two-story houses, bungalows, lumberyards, garden centers, and truck farms. We drove beside narrow streams that threaded through deep valleys and skirted mountains, starkly desiccated in the dry season; and shortly before ten we reached a harbor teeming with fishing boats and ringed by rustic restaurants full of Chinese families enjoying their weekly dim sum. We got down from the bus and, without even a glance at the excitement in and around the harbor or at the glorious view across to palm-fringed islands in the bay, set off up a steep rise that led to the wide yard of a Catholic school. In her niche above the west door of the neo-Gothic chapel at the far end of the yard, the Virgin Mary, flanked by John the Baptist and Saint Peter, gravely surveyed the scene. At the other end, above a wide platform on which an orchestra was playing Christian pop music, hung a huge banner. YAHWEH EL SHADDAI, it read in three-foot-high letters. Aside from the orchestra—guitarists, saxophonists, drummers, trumpet players, and two youths on keyboards, sharply dressed in white overshirts and white sharkskin pants—whose members worked during the week as drivers for wealthy Chinese businessmen, all of those crowding into the schoolyard in their Sunday best were female Filipina domestic helpers aged twenty to forty-five.

"What does 'Yahweh El Shaddai' mean?" I asked Isabel.

"That's Hebrew."

"Yes, but what does it *mean*?"

"God Almighty who is more than enough," Isabel replied and flashed me a beatific smile.

As we made our way through the crowd, she stopped here and there to introduce me to her friends. "Cruz, this is my new employer," she said, whispering to me, "Cruz is a dentist." After I'd met a high school teacher, a lab technician, and a pediatric nurse, she introduced me to Reynalda, a statuesque woman in green linen. Reynalda, Isabel whispered, was a vet. Back home in the Philippines, not one of the women I met that morning had ever worked as a maid.

We reached a spot shaded by a tall acacia tree beside the playground's chain-link fence. "This is where Laura and I sit every Sunday," said Isabel, taking two folding canvas stools, one green, one yellow, and two embroidered handkerchiefs out of her shopping bag. "Since Laura wasn't coming I was able to borrow her stool and her handkerchief. Out of respect, we cover our heads," she added as the orchestra struck up, the choir, twenty women in white floor-length gowns, launched into "I Never Need to Struggle Because I'm Living with the Lord" and several thousand women, arms raised in praise and exaltation, began clapping and swaying to the erotic beat. As directed, I covered my head and clapped; but since I didn't know the words, I couldn't sing the song and I couldn't quite bring myself to sway.

After the opening set, a radiant young woman in traditional broad-sleeved Filipina dress swept onto the platform to thunderous applause. "That's Cristina," Isabel whispered. "She's our evangelist. Only twenty-six years old when she got breast cancer. The doctors said it had spread to her stomach, she was finished. But she prayed for a miracle and God heard her. The next time they x-rayed her, the tumors weren't there!"

Cristina unhooked the microphone from its stand. "Welcome, sisters!" she cried. "I bring greetings from Brother Mike. He loves us, he believes in us, and he tells us never to forget his message. And what is his message?"

"Whatever we give to God, he'll give back to us a hundred times!" the crowd roared.

"Does God like to see us suffer?"

"He wants us to be happy!"

"Does He like to see us poor?"

"He wants us to be wealthy!"

"Does He like to see us sick?"

"He wants us to be healthy!"

"Does God hear our prayers?"

"He hears them, Alleluia!"

When she switched to Filipino, Cristina lost me but it was obvious that, with her confidence and forcefulness, her glamor and dazzle, she was sweeping the congregation along. "Praise God, Alleluia, Glory to God!" they shouted. I couldn't understand a word Cristina was saying but the atmosphere she generated was *electric*. She swept me along as well.

I suddenly remembered that once, long ago in Cuernavaca,

Mexico, my landlady Ana María and I had driven by a normally serene colonial-era church which, on this Wednesday evening, was being shaken to its foundations by amplified pop music. "Charismatics," Ana María had said, making a sour face. "They rent it on Wednesdays." Who exactly were they? She'd shrugged. "They jump about and make a great deal of noise."

"Are they Baptists?"

"Unfortunately they are *Catholics*...a new breed."

Now Cristina was inviting all those wishing to testify to join her on the platform. Over the next hour or so at least two dozen women took the microphone to speak with joy and sometimes biting humor in a pastiche of languages about the transformations El Shaddai had wrought: sobriety (for themselves or— more frequently—for sons and husbands), health after long bouts of sickness (for themselves, for family members), spousal reconciliation, better jobs, new friendships, fine houses built at home in preparation for their own eventual return and meanwhile for parents and children to live in, peace of mind after years of mental torment, and steadily rising savings accounts.

Isabel had never testified. "I'm not ready yet," she explained during the pause after the last testifier had finished. Though Yahweh El Shaddai had performed miracles for her—Mam Ella taking her in off the street being the most recent—she was waiting for one in particular. When her son Ernesto finished his schooling and got a job that brought in enough to support the two of them so that, instead of signing another contract, she could go home—"When God grants me *that* miracle, I'll go up there and tell everyone about it!" But Ernesto was a fifteen-year-old high school freshman.

During the bout of hymn singing that followed the testimonies, women wearing white skirts and green blouses, indicating officer status, and carrying collection boxes fanned out across the yard. Isabel felt around in her shopping bag and pulled out a sealed brown envelope, and when one of the women came down our row, she slid it through the slot of her box. After the singing ended in a final ecstatic chorus and the band was taking a break, she remarked, "We received our January salaries on Thursday, the last day of the month. So today we handed in our tithes along with our prayer requests."

Tithes? Did that mean these unfortunate women were required to give 10 percent of their earnings to the church? I supposed so.

"Mostly I request the same thing—please God, make Ernesto focus on his schoolwork instead of soccer! When I was his age I studied so hard, especially English. I loved reading—magazines, romances, anything I could lay my hands on. But these days, teenagers aren't interested in reading," she said glumly, "at least, not the boys. About all I can do from this distance is pray and ask our officers to pray with me..." She brightened. "On my way back to the flat I'll stop off in Central to send the money order and then I'll go shopping." She stretched out her feet to show me her red canvas sandals. "See, the left buckle's broken and the shoe mender told me it couldn't be fixed. I saw some sandals I liked last Sunday. I didn't have the money then but you gave me my salary on Thursday... You must be feeling hungry, Mam" she added. "After mass we'll eat the sandwiches I brought."

"There's going to be a mass now?" With so much clapping and swaying, I'd forgotten El Shaddai was a Catholic church. "Outside in this yard?"

"Brother Mike *prefers* the open air, Mam. This way we're closer to God," said Isabel matter-of-factly. "We started meeting here four or five years ago. Though it's a long way for most of us to travel, it's good because the priest here doesn't charge us anything so long as we clean up afterwards."

Four white-clad musicians appeared with a long table that they set down in front of the stage and Cristina ran up to cover it with a starched cloth and line up four brass candlesticks and a crucifix.

A priest in surplice and embroidered vestments emerged from the school chapel. "That's Father John," said Isabel. She was vague about where he was from. "One of those European countries..." Beside Cristina in her vigorous youth and beauty, balding Father John looked unappetizingly wan.

It was one o'clock and time for me to go back to the city. "I have to go home now. My husband's expecting me," I told Isabel. "I'm sorry to miss the mass."

"Because you are a Protestant, is that why you're leaving?"

"Not at all, that's got nothing to do with it." Of all the rituals I'd ever witnessed, the Eucharist was the most compelling. "Take, eat... This is my body... Drink ye all of this... This is my blood... which is shed for you and many for the remission of sins... Do this in remembrance of me." The promise of redemption might be only a beguiling myth; but by complying with the command to eat and drink and remember, I admitted to sorrow and to the need for solace. And I was always glad to keep company with people who felt the same way. "I really do have to go home."

Isabel looked stricken. "But you'll also miss the healing!"

"Healing?"

"That's what we come for, Mam. It helps us. It would help you too. Next time you must stay for it."

As I walked down to the bus stop, I wasn't sure there'd be a next time. I'd found seeing three or four thousand women singing their hearts out simply too sad.

My husband spent his days at the university teaching his classes, seeing students, and attending faculty meetings—in fact, not so differently from how he spent his days in America. Having no formal affiliation with the university, in theory I was fancy free. But in reality I was under a jail sentence. On my computer was a manuscript with which I had a long-standing love–hate relationship and before I started exploring some of the 230-odd islands that, according to my Lonely Planet guide, make up Hong Kong, or studying Chinese porcelain, let alone taking a crack at Mandarin 101, I had to finish it; and to get my sentence over as quickly as possible, it was essential to keep distractions to a minimum. So instead of working in a room that overlooked the narrow channel leading into Hong Kong Harbor with its enthralling parade of fishing boats and ferries, freighters, container ships, and tankers flying the flags of a dozen different nations, and the occasional American aircraft carrier, I chose

one that faced in the opposite direction. Its windows looked out
at a densely forested hillside on which, apart from leaves in the
wind, the occasional bird, and the odd feral cat, nothing moved.
I'd sit down at eight in the morning and work till five, when I
went for a jog beside the reservoir. Every couple of hours Isabel,
in flowered blouse and black cotton trousers, curly hair in a
ponytail, would bring me a pot of tea and a cup on the bamboo
tray she'd had me buy at Ikea. At noon, she'd appear in the
doorway to ask if I wanted a sandwich or noodles with salad for
lunch. Thirty minutes later, she'd summon me to the dining
room.

Sometimes, while I ate, she'd stand facing me at the other end
of the long table, hands gripping the back of a chair—I could
never persuade her to sit down—and we'd talk about life in
America, which, to my surprise, she'd visited once with her
"previous employers." It turned out that both husband and wife
had been gamblers. In the early years that Isabel worked for
them they'd gambled just an hour's ferry ride away in Macao.
But, increasingly prosperous, they'd started going to Las Vegas
over Chinese New Year, and on one such trip they'd taken their
children and Isabel along. Unfortunately Isabel's U.S. experience, blurred by jet lag, had been restricted to Los Angeles airport (so many fat people!), Caesar's Palace (she'd won
eighty-one U.S. dollars in a slot machine, and lost it all at
roulette), and a drive through the Nevada desert. (She'd hoped
to see cowboys but aside from tumbleweed, she'd only seen two
hares and one coyote.) Still, she'd had a "taste" of America and
she hungered for more. Because I hadn't been a child in America and therefore hadn't been exposed to the propaganda of middle school civics and, since my arrival on American shores in
early adulthood, had lived pretty much in an ivory tower, she
found me a less than satisfactory source of information on the
world she'd seen in exported TV soap operas.

So mostly we talked about life Before and After—that is, before and after she came to Hong Kong. The eldest of six, Isabel
had grown up in a village two hundred kilometers north of
Manila. Her father, a cattle farmer, and her mother, who had a

dressmaking business, were just well enough off to send her to college in the capital of their province. In her first year, she fell in love with a young man named Eddy. Eddy had grown up in a village just like she had; only his father had drowned in a fish pond when he was eight, his mother had died not long afterwards and then he'd gone to live with a man whom he called uncle but in fact was a distant cousin of his mother's who'd resented having to take the boy in. When, at fifteen, Eddy had lit out for the city, his "uncle" been only too happy to see his back. After mass on the third Sunday morning of her first semester in college, Isabel was outside a movie theater gazing at stills of coming attractions when Eddy, who'd already been living in the city for a number of years, spotted her. In her heart-shaped face and cautious smile he glimpsed traces of a long-vanished Eden, while to Isabel, fresh from the village, the combination of polo shirt plus logo, stylish haircut, and high-topped sneakers had made Eddy look like an urban sophisticate. When he asked her to go for a Coke, she accepted shyly. She'd never spoken to a real city boy before.

Eddy drove a truck for a construction company and earned enough to support a wife, he assured Isabel's father, and after Isabel's second year in college, they got married. They planned for her to continue her studies but six months after their wedding Eddy lost his job and by then Isabel was five months pregnant. Isabel took a leave and went home to her parents and Eddy went looking for work. "I'll send for you just as soon as I find something," he promised as he put her on the bus back to her village. She heard nothing more from or about her husband until, after their son was born, her brother Paul went to the city to find Eddy and discovered that the street address he'd given Isabel was fictitious. Paul went to Eddy's village, where he learned from Eddy's foster father that Eddy had gone to sea on a freighter a couple of months back. When baby Ernesto's first birthday came and went and still Isabel had had no word from her husband, her father told her that he could no longer afford to support her. Paul had another year's training for the merchant marine and Tommie would soon be going to college; and that left Carla, Be-

nigno, and Concepción, the baby of the family, still to be educated. Isabel would have to go to work to help not only her small
son but her brothers and sisters as well.

What had her fourteen years of education prepared her for?
She might be able to find work in a shop, but shop girls got paid
very little and, if she was lucky enough to get it, the same would
be true of factory work. But in Hong Kong, where Chinese
women willing to do domestic work were becoming rarer and
rarer, Filipinas were pouring in to fill the gap. A lot of Hong
Kong people really preferred them to locals because young Filipinas were generally more docile and easier to deal with than
middle-aged cantankerous Cantonese amahs, who tended to be
deeply resistant to taking orders from employers often many
years their junior. Another great advantage to Filipinas was that
they spoke English, which upwardly mobile Hong Kong parents
desperately wanted their children to learn. When they got home
after long days working in banks and managing factories, even
parents who knew the language hardly had the energy to speak
it. And anyway, after 130-odd years of British rule, most of them
didn't speak it. Increasingly, they were looking to Filipina maids,
who'd been educated in English medium schools, as the solution. Hadn't Isabel always come out at the top or close to the top
of her class in English? Being the eldest of six, didn't she have a
great deal of experience with young children?

Help was solicited from Cousin Elsie's Gloria, who'd already
been working in Hong Kong for seventeen months and sending
home two-thirds of her wages; and by great good fortune Gloria's Mam had a friend who was looking for a helper. Five weeks
later Gloria's Mam's friend had signed the necessary sponsor-
ship papers, Isabel had weaned little Ernesto, who'd just started
walking, and for the first time in her life taken a bus right
through to Manila. The flight to Hong Kong took ninety minutes, no longer than the bus ride from her village to the city
where she'd gone to college and fallen in love and been deserted.
When her plane, the first she'd ever taken, rose from the runway,
her milk came down and, as two dark patches spread across the
front of her blouse, her heart cracked and splintered.

She arrived in Hong Kong on a Tuesday at the beginning of the monsoon season. Cousin Gloria wasn't at the airport to meet her because this was the first Tuesday in the month and she'd had to take her Mam's poodle to be clipped. When Isabel emerged from baggage claim with her bulging cardboard suitcase, she saw a man holding up a sign with her name on it and underneath, in same-size letters, Mr. Charles Hsiao Chiang: her new "Sir." Beside him, in a black sheath dress and patent pumps, stood his wife: Mrs. June Piu Chiang, Isabel's new Mam.

The Chiangs lived on the eighteenth floor of a high-rise in the pricey Mid-Levels area of Hong Kong. When the southwesterlies were blowing, the view from their floor-to-ceiling plate-glass living room windows reached clear over to Macao. (The window of the maid's room, where the sun never entered, looked directly across a narrow chasm into another maid's room.) Charles Chiang was a lawyer; June Chiang sold dresses, trouser suits, and jackets of her own design in her shop, Eleganza, on Stanley Road. Eleganza was doing so well that Mrs. Chiang was about to open Eleganza II in Tsim Sha Tsu. But bossy Lim Hong, the amah, or housemaid, who'd been taking care of seven-year-old James and four-year-old Betty, was getting on; and since she spoke not one word of English, she couldn't help them with the homework they brought back each afternoon from their exclusive private school. Mrs. Chiang hoped Isabel da Costa, hired sight unseen, would be a major improvement over Lim Hong, whom she planned to send back to her village in Guangdong just as soon as she'd shown "the new Filipina" the bus route to the children's school in Happy Valley, and how to starch Charles's shirts, defrost the refrigerator, manipulate the Electrolux and its attachments, and where—and where *never*—to shop.

By the time Isabel had mastered these assignments and Lim Hong had been dispatched to her son in the Pearl River Delta, the schools had closed for the long holiday, typhoons were storming in, and James and Betty, imprisoned in the flat while rain slashed against the windows and air conditioners hummed and dripped, were at each other's throats perpetually. They rejected everything Isabel offered except noodles and papaya; they refused to speak English and showed few signs of understanding it either; and when Isabel, terrified they were about to kill each other, managed to wrench them apart, they kicked and cursed her in Cantonese.

Every night she dreamed about Ernesto and every morning she awoke, grief- stricken, to face another endless day. Apart from cousin Gloria, who'd telephoned only once and promised to met her in Central "one of these Sundays" but hadn't actually made a date to do so, she knew nobody. She survived those early months in Hong Kong because survival was essential. Without her money orders, how would her parents afford to feed Ernesto, let alone keep Paul in the merchant marine academy and pay Tommie's college fees?

When September came, the wind died, the torrential downpours ended, the children, who'd become a mite more malleable, returned to school, and she made friends with Filomena, whom she encountered several times each day in the lift. Filomena, who worked for the Lees on the fifteenth floor, had left her husband, Johnnie, who was failing to make ends meets as a TV repairman, and two little daughters in Bandong Sinag. Back home between contracts the previous Christmas, she'd discovered that Johnnie had taken up with another woman.

It was the younger girl who'd spilled the beans. "Maria's visiting her auntie," the six-year-old had told Filomena mournfully. "Who's Maria?" "Papa's Maria. She paints her toenails red and silver. She's nice. She makes macaroni and cheese whenever we ask." Confronted, Johnnie had blustered and denied Maria's existence and Maria had had the wit not to show up while Filomena was around. But Filomena had no doubt that the moment she'd left for Hong Kong, Maria had returned to share the marital bed and to cook on the four-burner propane stove, both of which she, Filomena, had bought with her savings.

"You're lucky, you were *deserted*," she told Isabel when they were exchanging introductory stories over *adobo* after mass the first Sunday they went downtown together.

"That makes me *lucky*?"

"Better not to *know* where your husband is or what he's up

to. How would *you* like to be supporting not just Eddy and Ernesto but Eddy's *girlfriend* as well?"

"Eddy hasn't been gone two years yet, and you know how it is with ships—from time to time they need refitting. Maybe his ship's getting refitted somewhere and it's taking longer than it should. Eddy will come back, I'm sure of it," Isabel added, even though with each passing day she believed less in the possibility.

"At least you know your *mother's* cooking your kid's food, bathing him, washing his shirts..." Filomena paused. "Does your kid love your mother?"

"Of course! She's the one taking care of him."

"Well, Maria's the one taking care of *my* kids," Filomena said bitterly. "Already they love her more than they love me."

Isabel and Filomena hung each other's laundry out to dry on the roof of the apartment building and brought it in when it looked like rain; they went to the shops and the markets together and, after mass at St. Joseph's and now and then at St. John's, they idled away their Sundays under the frangipanis in Chater Garden. One Chinese New Year they took the tram up the Peak to see the view across the harbor to the Mainland, ate ice cream and popcorn, and walked all the way back down. Another year they rode the ferry to Macao, where they marveled at the shell of the cathedral, the great walls of the fortress, and the ornate squares of the old Portuguese city.

Filomena persuaded Isabel that, for all that they were married with children, they had a perfect right to go dancing and they started going to clubs in Wan Chai that westerners frequented. Even though their evenings on the town were cut short because they had to get back before eleven o'clock, when Mrs. Chiang and Mrs. Lee double-locked their front doors, they had adventures. Isabel acquired a serious admirer, a Canadian named Nick who was working on the Lantau landfill.

"He bought me a gold watch and a pearl necklace," she told me. "I left them behind in the rush when I shifted to Mam Ella's."

Nick asked her to quit her job and move in with him. "He had a flat near the Mong Kok metro station—decent furniture, carpets, hi-fi, everything. But the first time I went up there I saw a photo of two kids stuck in the edge of the bureau mirror, so I asked about them and he said they were his and they were living back in Canada. He swore he'd never married their mother. He called her his common-law wife, and anyway, they'd split up before he'd come to Hong Kong. But *I* was married. Though I hadn't seen or heard from Eddy in four years, all the same, it didn't seem right to move in with another man."

And besides, when Nick had a lot to drink he could be nasty. He'd get into fights. Mostly in clubs, but not necessarily. One Sunday when he was drinking in his flat, he'd flown into a rage and punched her because the steak she'd cooked was overdone. Next morning, she got out of bed with a splitting headache and a black and green right eye. She did what she could with pancake makeup and her employers were too busy getting ready for work to notice. But while she was serving breakfast, the children did.

" 'Whatever happened to *you?*' James said. I said I'd tripped on the curb outside the post office in Central. 'Oh, Isa, that must *hurt,*' said Betty. 'You've got to put ice on it.' She ran to get ice cubes out of the freezer and wrap them in a kitchen towel and then she stood, hand gripping my shoulder, while I pressed them against my eye. She wanted to stay home from school to take care of me. 'What if your eye pops out?' she asked me. 'You'll need someone to take you to hospital. You shouldn't go by yourself.' "

Not long afterwards Nick got transferred to Saudi Arabia. For a while he sent postcards of Arab dhows and camels. On the last one Isabel received he'd written, "Coming to get you." But he never showed up.

By the late 1980s a lot of people were getting scared of what might happen when Hong Kong, a proto-capitalist enclave, reverted to China and the territory came under Communist rule. Those who could muster the necessary contacts and resources started looking for havens. Britain, the colonial master, wouldn't take in many; but Canada, Australia, and New Zealand were easier to get into, and New Zealand was where

Mr. and Mrs. Lee went, taking Filomena with them. Meanwhile Hong Kong was booming and Mr. Chiang, who specialized in real estate transfers, had almost more work than he could handle, and Eleganza I and Eleganza II were doing great business also. Mrs. Chiang's brother Bill had moved to Vancouver and was making a go of it, and the Chiangs figured, if things got really bad after '97, Bill would help get them into Canada; but they were digging in for the time being, which meant that Isabel dug in too.

Because Filomena had been right there in the same building, only three floors down, Isabel hadn't tried that hard to make other friends. "I'd meet up with my cousin Gloria occasionally, but she's different. She's never been interested in getting married or having a family, if you know what I mean. She likes Hong Kong much better than the Philippines. She says she can be a lot freer here and she's planning to stay for good if she can." A few years ago Gloria had gone to work for a European couple who admired her for what they called her "spunk." In fact she gave them only a few hours a week and the rest of the time she worked freelance and got paid by the hour, making at least twice as much for half as much work as an ordinary live-in. On Sundays she never went to church and she didn't sit around in Chater Garden either.

"She's *political*," said Isabel and there was a note of awe in her voice. "She says the system's unjust and she has to *fight* it." At the weekend, she'd either be holed up in a tiny office without an air conditioner in Kennedy Town organizing the campaign for domestic helpers' rights or else she'd be down in Central, handing out flyers. She had no time for Isabel, whom she considered hopelessly docile.

With Filomena gone for good, instead of looking forward to Sundays, Isabel found herself dreading them. After mass she would gaze at shoes—she was particularly fascinated by shoes— that would have cost her two months' salary in shop windows on Peddar Street and get herself some takeout, which she'd eat by herself in Chater Garden while all around her other Filipinas were relaxing and enjoying themselves.

"One evening I was thinking to myself, though it's only six o'clock, what's the point of staying out longer, I might as well go back to James and Betty, when a lady sat down on the grass next me. She said she'd often seen me there with my friend and we'd always seemed to be having such a good time together. 'Is she sick or something?' she asked me. 'She's not sick. I wish she were, because then she'd still be here,' I said, and the tears that had been behind my eyelids ever since morning came rolling down. I told her everything—about Eddy going off, and Ernesto calling me auntie when I went back home on holiday, and my dad having a heart attack with me far away and unable to go to his funeral. I told her about Filomena and me bearing our burdens together and with her gone, my not knowing what to do with myself.

"By and by the lady told me her own story, which also included many disappointments. And then she started talking about her church that she'd just come from. It didn't sound like any church I knew. For one thing, there wasn't any *building,* and when it rained they just put up their umbrellas. She said if I wanted, she'd take me along. In those days they were meeting in a corner of Victoria Park."

Isabel was looking over my head to the forested hillside beyond the dining room window. "Her sitting down like that and talking to me, a complete stranger, was my first miracle," she said softly. "Not long after, I accepted Jesus, and though I've had plenty of problems since... Well," she finished, "I'm alive, and my son's still studying, he hasn't flunked out of school or quit."

When Chinese New Year, the Year of the Horse, began at two a.m. on Tuesday, February 12, the cavalcade of ships passing between Lamma and Hong Kong Islands halted. Waking a few hours later, my husband and I saw that, aside from the odd sailboat and a few ferries, the channel was empty. Ten thousand unregulated Mainland factories had stopped belching smoke and closed down for the holiday, and the pollution which, from October through April, blanketed the landscape had been driven south by the prevailing wind so that, for the first time since our arrival in Hong Kong, we could see the harsh mountains of the New Territories in their full majesty. For the next five days the locals would be busy visiting and entertaining their relatives; but we foreigners, far from home and family, had time on our hands.

On Wednesday, the second day of the New Year holiday, which was a holiday for domestic helpers as well as for everyone else, Brother Mike would be making a flying visit, and for a rally of the faithful, El Shaddai had the City's permission to close off three blocks of Chater Road.

"We're expecting eight thousand," Isabel informed me, "so we'll have to get down in good time." I was about to say I'd have to miss the rally because I needed to work on my book. But to use the book excuse would have been churlish. The truth was that, due to Isabel's taking total charge of the household, I was making quite good progress. I could afford to take a day off. Besides, I was curious to see Brother Mike.

The rally was scheduled for eleven, and Isabel and I and Ella's Laura, a small, efficient person who, for this auspicious event, had exchanged the neat gold studs she habitually wore for dangling earrings that almost touched her shoulders, were down in Central before ten with umbrellas to shield ourselves from the sun, which, with the short Hong Kong winter over, was steadily gaining strength. The sidewalks of Des Voeux Street were wall to wall Filipinas, and as we picked our way between and around them I managed, with great effort, to keep my eyes away from the delights in the windows of Armani, Gucci, and Calvin Klein. A froth of pink in Chanel's window deserved close attention but I didn't dare slow down for fear of losing Laura and Isabel.

As we were rounding the corner into Chater Road, Isabel stopped abruptly. Pacing up and down in front of the old law court, just a hundred feet from us, were five stocky Filipinas carrying placards that read "Domestic Helpers Demand Pay Hike" on the front and "End Exploitation Solidarity for Ever" on the back. In red shirts and black jeans and with hair cut very short, they looked a lot more like nightclub bouncers than domestic helpers. The one in the middle, Isabel whispered to me, was her cousin Gloria. When I said I'd like to meet her, Isabel shook her head urgently. "Oh no, Mam, she wouldn't like that."

"Why not?"

"Because of my being here with you..."

"You mean, because I'm your employer?"

"She says helpers and employers should have nothing to do with each other away from the workplace."

"Do you agree?"

"Being friendly can get you into trouble, is what she says."

"Trouble? Like what, for instance?" But Isabel didn't elaborate. Face averted from the demonstrators, she hurried on.

At the far end of the blocked-off section of the street a stage, swathed in dark-blue, light-blue, and red fabric, the national colors of the Philippines, and edged with pots of yellow chrysanthemums and miniature orange bushes heralding the New Year, had been erected. The street itself was already packed with Filipinas greeting one another, hugging, chattering like birds. Mingled with them were men and women sporting press badges. Some were talking to church members and taking notes; others were smoking cigarettes and looking bored. On platforms high above them, TV crewmen were adjusting cameras.

"That's Filipino cable," Isabel said happily. "Wherever Brother Mike goes, they go too."

Isabel's friend Reynalda had arrived ahead of us and had saved space for our stools three rows back from the stage. Resplendent in pink polyester, Reynalda deposited herself between me and Isabel and within moments it became clear that she had an agenda: she wanted to apply for a U.S. visa and she wanted my help. She claimed to have been to vet school in Cebu, and, though I'd never met a vet who looked anything like her, I had to take her word for it. She said she and her husband had been in practice together but they hadn't made enough money inoculating goats and buffalo to educate their two daughters and a son, and so ten years ago they decided she would have to leave the family and go overseas. Given her training, she'd hoped to work as a veterinary assistant but the job she'd thought she had fell through. To avoid being deported, she'd signed a contract to take care of an elderly Chinese woman, Mrs. Lu, who lived with her unmarried daughter, Mabel, in Aberdeen. But the old lady had died the previous Christmas and now that she'd done her duty as a daughter, Mabel was planning to resign her position and move to Boston, where she had a brother. The brother said that out of gratitude for the devotion Reynalda had showed his mother, he would be willing to have her stay in his house while she looked for a job as a housekeeper. Only he wasn't willing to sponsor her for a visa. He drew the line at that because he had enough to do sponsoring his sister.

Since the orchestra was playing at an ear-splitting pitch a dozen yards from where we were sitting and Reynalda's English wasn't as good as Isabel's, I had difficulty understanding what she was telling me; but I understood her main point perfectly: having miraculously appeared from Boston, my *destiny* was to be her sponsor. "There will be some forms to sign and after that I'll be no bother to you, Mam," she assured me. As I was thinking about how best to respond (firmly in the negative but as gently as possible), some elegant Chinese women in the front row to the right of the stage caught my eye. They looked as if they'd just walked out of the Calvin Klein store we'd hurried by moments earlier. Beside each of them sat a Filipina. Clearly, I wasn't the only employer intrigued by Brother Mike.

To a drumroll, Cristina, sheathed in purple satin, mounted the stage, arms in a wide embrace for the church members, who stretched back all the way to the dung-colored slab of the Mandarin Oriental Hotel. Her task, with the help of the orchestra, a male singing group in black suits headed by a pompadoured Elvis Presley look-alike, a troop of dancers in purple skirts and yellow charmeuse blouses, a children's choir composed of eight heavily made up purple-kilted preadolescent girls, and an hour's worth of exceptionally dramatic testimonies, was to hold the crowd's attention for as long as necessary. Though Brother Mike was slated to arrive at three o'clock, he might be early or, more likely, late.

Today was both the second day of the Chinese New Year holiday and Ash Wednesday, the first day of Lent, hence the preva-
lence of purple.

Mass was conducted by Monsignor Tom, an unusually tall
Filipino in Lenten vestments, who, I understood from Isabel,
was much beloved. His homily on the transformation of flaws,
delivered in English, was optimistic, humorous, and, mercifully,
short. But, given the many thousands wishing to receive it, the
Eucharist took a very long time. Meanwhile the cloud cover
burned off and our little group—Laura, Reynalda, Isabel, and
I—had to wait in line for more than twenty minutes with the sun
beating down on our umbrellas. When, finally, Monsignor had
given the benediction and retired, the children's choir raced onto
the stage and, led by a six-year-old boy wearing a black vest with
gold buttons over a purple turtleneck, belted out "Shout to the
Lord!"

Roused to a fevered pitch of expectation, we finally received
our reward. Brother Mike, a small man wearing thick makeup,
a blue three-buttoned blazer, bright white shirt, white trousers,
white loafers, and a scarlet bow tie, came bounding onto the
stage and, with a roar of adulation, eight thousand women rose
from their stools. As he bade them let go of the past with its bit-
terness and disappointments and look to a future in which Yahweh would grant their hearts' desires, Brother Mike's smile was
radiant.

For more than two hours he wooed the children of El Shaddai, flirted with them, enticed them, sought eye contact, held
their gaze. They laughed at his jokes, yelped gleefully at his sug-
gestive hip movements, and quivered, just as he did, with the
power of the Holy Spirit. When he plucked chrysanthemums
and miniature oranges from the potted plants ringing the stage
and tossed them, his love offerings, into the crowd, they dove
to retrieve them and toss them back again; and when he told
the story of his own conversion, though surely they'd heard it
innumerable times, they listened in wide-eyed enchantment.
At first, I found this septuagenarian's antics deeply distasteful;
but his delight in life and his conviction that no human being

could resist him won me over. I became his devotee—for the afternoon.

The "parachute" visit—Brother Mike had flown in at midday and would return to Manila that night—concluded with a healing. I'd expected that the halt and the lame would be invited to the stage, where he would pray for them; but it wasn't like that at all. His purpose was to heal *souls,* to help us slough off the burden of self-doubt so that, instead of cowering before life's obstacles, we'd have strength and confidence to overcome them. He told the Bible story of Christ casting out demons, demons of self-hatred and despair. He urged us to put behind us the slights and abuse we'd suffered at the hands of employers, relatives, and strangers. He invited us to live righteously, with joy.

"Stand up, everyone, and take a partner," he yelled and Reynalda seized my hand. "Are you ready to throw away your worries?"

"Ready!" we yelled back.

"Then tell me your good news! One, two, three..."

"Jesus is in me!"

"One, two, three..."

"Jesus loves me!"

"One, two three..."

"Jesus knows I'm priceless!"

Like children at a birthday party, we danced and clapped and sang our hearts out and chased our worries away.

"Close your eyes," Brother Mike instructed. "Imagine you're holding *Jesus's* hand. Now, tell him you love him!"

As cries of "Lord, I love you!" swept Chater Road, Brother Mike blew us farewell kisses, stepped down into his white limousine, and headed for the airport, leaving us healed—for the moment, at least.

Next morning, the *South China Morning Post* didn't mention the rally. Though I didn't know about the Chinese language papers, I was willing to bet they didn't either. But Isabel's little sister, Concepción, wrote from Bandong to say she'd seen it on the evening news. Concepción was in her final months of nurse's training, financed in part by brother Tommie, who was working as a driver in Milano, and in part by Isabel. When she graduated, she planned to emigrate to Toronto, where nurses were needed desperately.

Aside from short trips with my husband to a meeting in Beijing and a wedding in Taipei, and two weeks on my own in Kathmandu, I spent the next few months in my study grinding out my book. As spring advanced toward summer, the humidity level rose steadily. Our parquet floors, swollen with moisture, grew increasingly uneven and, despite six air conditioners cranking away, the flat smelled depressingly of damp.

"This climate's disgusting," our benefactress Ella said cheerfully when I encountered her in the driveway one May evening. "Yesterday I found mold growing in my best Italian shoes, and that's only the beginning... By the way, shall we go out somewhere delicious for dinner on Sunday? Surely we owe it to ourselves to observe Mother's Day."

I'd forgotten about Mother's Day, but Isabel hadn't. El Shaddai was having a celebration and she was counting on me to attend it with her, she told me when she saw me writing "dinner out with Ella" on the kitchen calendar. "Being a mother, it's something you shouldn't miss, Mam. You'll be home before dinnertime."

On the journey out with Laura and Isabel that Sunday, I remembered Mother's Days when my son and daughter were young: the huge effort they'd put into assembling hand-squeezed orange juice, scrambled eggs, buttered toast, and raspberry jam and bringing this feast to me in bed at seven o'clock in the morning. How, as they got older and slept later, Mother's Day breakfast got pushed back to brunch—lox, cream cheese, bagels, onion rings, and capers—in the kitchen; and finally, when they were high school age and were never awake before noon, to quiche and fruit salad around two p.m. in the garden. But they were both grown up now and lived thousands of miles away in New York and Berlin and, given their distant time zones, mightn't remember Mother's Day until the day after. Isabel had told me everyone would be bringing photos of their children and I should too, and so in my purse was a photo I'd taken of them with our Labrador Nellie on the living room sofa at Christmas the year before last.

Again, the schoolyard was packed and the day's events were ordered identically. The only difference was that the women who were mothers—the large majority—had brought photos of their children that they passed around among their friends during the breaks and held to their breasts during the hymn singing. Laura had brought a colored photo of her daughter, Amelia, aged nine, and Isabel had brought two photos. One was of her son, Ernesto, which she passed around for her friends' inspection; but the other, of a teenage girl, she kept with her. "Is that your little sister?" I asked while we were waiting for the mass to begin.

Isabel shook her head. "Oh no, Mam. Our Concepción is already twenty-three. This girl is Betty, my previous employers' daughter." She spoke so quietly that I could barely hear what she said.

"Is she in Hong Kong?"

Isabel gave me a grief-stricken look and, as the orchestra struck up and Father John, followed by a column of El Shaddai officers, emerged from the school chapel, she turned away.

At the end of the mass rain, which had been threatening since morning, swept in, pounding hastily opened umbrellas. But within moments it had passed on and bright sunlight flooded the schoolyard. As we were closing our umbrellas, a twelve-year-old girl dressed in a pink tutu mounted the platform and took the microphone.

"My name is Elena and I live in Shau Kei Wan," she announced. "My dad's a driver and my mom works in an office. I'm lucky because when I wake up in the morning my mom's the first person I see and she's the last person I see before I go to sleep at night. I'm going to sing a song for all those kids who aren't as lucky as I am because they're living in the Philippines and they only see their moms for a week or two every other year."

Throwing back her head, Elena threw her heart and soul into a song in Filipino, and every woman in the schoolyard wept.

At the end of the afternoon Laura said she had to hurry back but Isabel wanted to show me the harbor. After helping clean up the detritus in the schoolyard, we walked down into the town for sodas, which we drank on a bench on the quay looking out to boats with blue-and-white-striped sails skimming between islands newly verdant in the early summer rains.

"Will you tell me about Betty?"

For a long moment Isabel gazed into her Sprite. "Last year on Mother's Day as I was getting ready for church she came to my room to give me this," she said finally, and she touched the crucifix at her neck. "She'd wrapped it in pink tissue and tied it with silver ribbon, and there was a card she'd made herself as well. 'For my Isa. Please wear it always.' Like that little girl said, I was the first person she saw in the morning and the last person she saw at night...

"But that night she didn't see me..." Her voice trailed off.

"What happened?"

Bemused, Isabel shook her head. After some moments, she took a deep breath and in a steady voice remarked, "Chinese parents always favor sons over daughters, but the Chiangs really overdid it." Their son, James, was the sun in their firmament. Not that he was anything special to look at. His ears stuck out, he was stringy and nearsighted. He couldn't kick a ball straight and he never learned to crawl properly, for all the swimming lessons his parents paid for; and he hardly ever said thank you, whatever you did for him. But to his parents, looks and sports and being an agreeable person weren't important. What counted was school performance and to their immense pride and gratification James was always at the top of his class in every subject except English. To call him arrogant would have been a serious understatement.

"I was only 'the Filipina,' " said Isabel. "The fact that I spoke English better than he did never impressed him. But then, nothing I did impressed him. He knew better than I did about everything. He had the habit of leaning up against the kitchen counter while I was preparing supper. He'd watch me like he was the guard and I was the prisoner. 'You should add more ginger,' he'd snap. Or 'you should use sesame oil, not sunflower oil.' 'How do you know that?' I'd ask nicely. 'Lim Hong never used sunflower oil,' he'd say, even though Lim Hong, their old amah, had been a really bad cook. Mrs. Chiang used to complain about her to Filomena's Mam.'"

When he got older and started demanding pizza, the home section of the *South China Morning Post* became his bible.

" 'Your crust's *mushy*,' he'd tell me and from the look on his face you'd think I was trying to poison him. 'You've got to let the dough rise *twice*, first time in the fridge, second time on the counter.' 'Since you're the expert, *you* make it,' I'd tell him. 'Why should I? I'm just giving you a tip so you can do better at the job my parents are paying you to do.' "

Betty, lithe and perfectly coordinated, had mapped out her future. She planned to be a film star when she grew up; in the meantime she loved to dance and sing and act out stories. These shows required an audience that her parents, who weren't often at home in the evenings and in any event had already decided she was to be a lawyer like her father, weren't about to provide. As for her brother, whatever its theme, he pronounced her performance stupid.

After their first adversarial summer together, Betty realized Isabel was a huge improvement over Lim Hong. When Betty said she wanted to be an eagle, Isabel knew just what an eagle should look like and, being a seamstress's daughter and expert with scissors and sewing machine, was adept at conjuring one up. She had an endless store of tales about demons and angels and sea monsters that just cried out for dramatization. Most important, deprived of her own child, she was in dire need of Betty as an object and source of affection; and Betty, a sideshow to her insufferable prince of a brother, Einstein in the making, according to their parents, welcomed her attention like a seedling welcomes the sun.

One of Isabel's duties was to escort the children to and from school on the Number 28 bus. One small woman (four foot ten) and two young children could easily have occupied a single seat; but James insisted on sitting separately. "You two talk such rubbish," he'd say, and take himself off to play Nintendo in the back of the bus, leaving his sister and domestic helper to talk rubbish undisturbed.

A fair-skinned Chinese girl, black hair hanging straight to her shoulders; a curly haired Filipina with an amber-colored heart-shaped face. No one who saw them holding hands on the bus could ever have taken them for mother and daughter. For all the world to see, they were a mother who longed for a child and a child who needed a mother.

Betty, who had lived the whole of her young life in a high-rise in one of the densest urban areas on earth, had an unquenchable appetite for news about Isabel's brothers and sisters in their village on the other side of the South China Sea. Whenever a letter arrived from the Philippines, she'd demand to be told the latest about Paul and Tommie and all the others, not forgetting the goats, buffalo, dogs, and kittens whose births were regularly noted; and she developed a special long-distance attachment to an elderly donkey named Dolly. When Ernesto was still a toddler, she would pepper Isabel with questions about him as well; but as he grew older her interest in him faltered. By the time he entered school she'd stopped asking about him altogether, not wanting to be reminded that Isabel had a child of her own.

By and by, the prospering Chiangs exchanged their Mid-Levels flat for a faux-Moghul townhouse higher up the Peak. It had an even more spectacular view than their old flat had, though they weren't home too much to enjoy it. They entertained often, but only in restaurants or on the motorboat they moored at Aberdeen, events that rarely included their children. Secure in the knowledge that their home life was in Isabel's competent hands, they had only fleeting regret over the fact that their professional lives were taking ever more of their time. They congratulated themselves on their sagacious choice of helper, whom they rewarded with small annual salary increases and, at New Year, a thousand Hong Kong dollars in a scarlet envelope.

When Betty was eleven, the Chiangs removed her from the Happy Valley school that both children had attended since kindergarten. Though myopic Einsteins-in-the-making like James thrived there, Betty was not of that tribe and she was shifted to a girls' school in Kowloon, not far from Eleganza II, that emphasized the arts. James was certainly old enough to travel back and forth to school on his own, but Betty still needed an escort. Mrs. Chiang, who drove herself to work in her midnight-blue BMW convertible, dropped off her daughter in the morning and Isabel fetched her in the afternoon. The journey home included an eight-minute ride on the Star Ferry, an experience of which Isabel and Betty never tired: the impatient wait, with hundreds of others heading home at the end of the day, for iron gates to swing open; the rush down the concrete quay; the dash to the bows for an unimpeded view of glass, steel, and concrete stalagmites reaching further up the Peak each year; the clangs and whistles and surge of dark water as the ferry drew away from the quay. As it ploughed across the harbor, the wind would cut across the deck, salt lips, catch at hair, and lighten the heart.

Betty met the Sindi boy on the ferry two months before she turned sixteen. Though they'd been eyeing each other since Christmas, they didn't speak until one April evening when the boy edged his way over to Betty and Isabel in the queue behind the gates. He nodded gravely to the helper and addressed her charge. "My name is Rahul. I would like to get to know you." Over the next few weeks, get to know each other they did, in closely chaperoned eight-minute snatches in the bow of the ferry and occasional phone calls when the coast was clear. A Chinese girl whose father was a lawyer trained at the Inns of Court in London and whose mother had studied at St. Martins School of Art didn't socialize with an Indian boy, even though the combined worth of his grandfather, father, and uncle, who sold ornate gold jewelry to South Asians and Arabs on Nathan Road, was greater than the Chiangs'. (A Sindi boy was *expected* to have adventures so long as in the fullness of time he married the Sindi girl his wise parents had picked out for him.) So the romance had to be kept secret not only from Mr. and Mrs. Chiang but also from James, who, had he got wind of it, would surely have squealed to his parents; and then the fat would have been in the fire.

Isabel, the confidant, was perfectly aware that she should be trying to stop the friendship; but she also knew that if she did so, a gulf would open between her and Betty, a prospect she dreaded. Besides, she liked Rahul. He was courteous and billboard handsome, and he made her laugh, in contrast with James, who irritated her most of the time.

The Handover from Britain to China was scheduled for July 1, 1997 and at the end of August both Chiang children would be leaving Hong Kong for the States, James for MIT in Cambridge, Massachusetts, and Betty for a nearby boarding school. Though in Charles and June Chiang's youth, the local elite had kept their children home or, in the case of the wealthy, sent them to Britain, nowadays educating one's children in America had become the status marker par excellence. James couldn't wait to go, but Betty had been indifferent to the whole application process; and when, in March, she heard she'd been admitted to the school of her parents' choice, she shrugged and said, "I suppose I'd better go, right?"

"Right," said her father.

But that was before Betty met Rahul and before the Asian economic downturn started. The week after the Handover she told her parents she'd changed her mind, she didn't want to go school in America. At first the Chiangs, aghast at early intimations of the downturn, were too preoccupied to hear her; but as the enormity of Charles Chiang's real-estate losses was brought home to them, they did hear her and, realizing how much cheaper it would be to keep their daughter at home, they agreed to her finishing secondary school in Hong Kong.

With spying James's departure and the acquisition of mobile phones that both Betty and Rahul requested and received as birthday presents, communication became a whole lot easier. Provided her parents weren't at home, Betty would punctuate long homework evenings with phone calls to Rahul; and soon they were seeing each other not only on the ferry but on unchaperoned weekend afternoons as well. Betty would tell her mother she was going window-shopping in Central with her best friend, Heather; or else she was taking the bus out to Stanley Market with her second-best friend, Linden.

"You've got your mobile," her mother would remind her. "Phone if you need anything."

In order to maintain the fiction, Betty did occasionally phone her mother with reports of jeans or sweaters spotted in shop windows and urgently desired. Meanwhile more and more often, instead of shopping with Heather and Linden, she was meeting Rahul in places where their parents, relatives, and family friends were unlikely ever to go: McDonald's in Kwun Tong and Heng Fa Chen (Rahul's circle, being Hindus, didn't eat beef; and Betty's, being sophisticates, would sooner drop dead than set foot in McDonald's) or action movies in hole-in-the-wall theaters in which, while Jackie Chan took on the bad guys or the good guys and sometimes both together, they were locked in each other's arms.

In the first year of her romance, Betty made a point of telling Isabel where she was going; but increasingly, as time went on, she'd forget to do so or chose not to do so, though usually she'd say where she'd been when she got home. Once Rahul got his driver's license and access to a family car, a five-year-old Mercedes, they started driving out to a remote park in the New Territories where the only people they were likely to encounter were a few serious hikers with heavy boots and compasses and former Gurkha soldiers in training for the Marathon. Because he'd often camped there with his Boy Scout troop as a kid, Rahul knew the park pretty well.

But he and Betty didn't go out there to take exercise. They went out there to make love high on a mountainside.

"We climbed up to see the view. It was a stiff climb but it was worth it," Betty told Isabel after that first afternoon. She said they could see the whole gleaming sweep of sea from Macao to Lantau. She didn't say they'd made love; but the girl's new distracted softness told Isabel this was so.

"What was I supposed to do? Warn her about getting pregnant or about getting her heart broken? She'd say, 'I love him,

Isa,' but she never said a word about *making* love with him. And so I never spoke about it either." Afraid that if she intruded, if she stepped in where she wasn't welcome, Betty would close her out, Isabel kept her mouth shut.

"A few more months and she'd be leaving for college in America," she said to me. "As soon as she was on that plane, I'd have lost her. But for the time being, I was still waking her up in the morning and looking in on her last thing at night."

On Mother's Day Isabel got home about ten o'clock in the evening after eating Thai takeout with Laura, Reynalda, and Cruz; she found the house in darkness and Mrs. Chiang's BMW gone from the garage. Her employers might be out six nights running but the seventh invariably found them at home preparing for the work week ahead while, up in her room, Betty struggled with the history essay due first period on Monday morning.

"I knew something terrible had happened. I didn't turn on any lights. I just sat in the front hall, waiting," Isabel concluded and fell silent.

"Had Betty eloped with the Sindi boy?"

Her face heavy with sorrow, Isabel stared blankly at the sailboats tacking across the bay in the early evening breeze. "*Was* I to blame, Mam? What do you think?"

"To blame for what, Isabel?"

"Maybe the parents were right—it *was* my fault, I *could* have stopped her."

After a long silence, she added, "But I'm not so sure. Teenagers have their own ideas. They are full of desire. We don't have much control, do we?" She turned to me and smiled sadly. "You should hurry back now. You don't want to keep Sir and Mam Ella waiting. Though you're a long way away from your children, it's good to celebrate Mother's Day."

I don't believe Betty eloped with the Sindi boy. I think something very much worse happened—that the Sindi boy lost control of his Mercedes on a sharp bend on a deserted road in Tai Mo Shan Country Park and crashed into the cliff face. Perhaps the boy was killed; or perhaps, miraculously, he was thrown clear, walked away without a scratch, and went on with his life as planned. So far, I haven't made up my mind. But this is what I think happened to Betty: that a park warden found her, chest crushed, neck broken; and that he summoned the police on his mobile to take her still warm body to the morgue.

Finding her parents was easy: her school ID was in her purse.

The Chiangs got back from the morgue when the clock on the front-hall table in their faux-Moghul house was striking eleven. Mr. Chiang was first through the door, followed by his brother and sister-in-law. "Whiskey," he told Isabel who'd been sitting in the front hall in the dark for only an hour, though it had seemed like an eternity, "bring five whiskey-sodas." Mrs. Chiang and her sister, Mrs. Wong, drove up a few minutes later. Mrs. Wong was the one who told Isabel about the accident, following her into the kitchen, where she was getting ice cubes out of the fridge. After thirty-five minutes the visitors drank up their drinks and left and the Chiangs went to their suite with its mirrored walls and antique Chinese screens.

Neither of them had said one word to Isabel about Betty.

Lying on her cot in the darkness, Isabel felt as if her chest, too, had been crushed.

When it began to get light, Mrs. Chiang burst into her room. Her eyes were red and her habitually sleek black hair hung lank and lifeless. She hadn't washed off yesterday's makeup, mascara was smudged on her cheeks. "We trusted you with our daughter and you betrayed us!" she screamed at Isabel. "We paid you better than anyone else paid their helpers, we took you to Singapore, Taipei, Las Vegas, and this is what we get for it!" She started slapping and scratching Isabel, and then Mr. Chiang ran in and set on her as well. "You knew what she was doing with that boy and you just kept quiet about it! Now she's gone and it's all your fault! You're the one to blame!"

They tired themselves out eventually and, dumping Isabel back on her cot, went off to get ready for their day. Later, Isabel heard them leave and a little after that the front doorbell rang. It had to be the man coming to wash the windows, as he did alternate Mondays. But when nobody answered the door he left, the house became silent as death, and Isabel knew she had to get going. So she stuffed a few treasured possessions into one small zippered bag, took the Number 10 bus to her friend Laura's, and threw herself on the beneficence of Mam Ella.

By the time she came to work for me and my husband, she was beginning to recover from the fall-out; and by the time we left Hong Kong eighteen months later, judging by the way she'd sing along with the hymns on station DWXI, it seemed that the blame for the part she'd played in it, whatever it might be, no longer lay so heavily upon her.

But I doubt I'll ever know how the fall-out actually happened.

JUST SITTING

Zen in America

One afternoon when I was browsing in Pilgrim Books, two streets over from Guruma's nunnery in Kathmandu, I picked up a book about how Buddhism came to America. At the time, I wasn't all that interested in how Buddhism had come to America, or in how, after it arrived, it had fared; but as I flipped through a chapter on Zen a short passage jumped out at me: "After studying for many years in Japan, Simon Peters received dharma transmission as the first American Zen master. Returning to the United States, he bought a New England farm on which he established a Buddhist community."

Two years earlier while we were hiking a modest section of the Appalachian Trail, my husband and I had had our enthusiasm dampened by hail and driving rain. Tired of bemoaning our fate as we huddled over the woodstove in our rented cabin, we'd started looking at real estate ads, and before the week was out we'd signed a purchase and sale agreement on a house (which, though it had three bedrooms, two bathrooms, and three heating systems, was called a *camp*) on a lake (which, though ten miles long, was called Whiskey *Pond*) in a town we'd never heard of, in a state we knew little about. A month later I left for Kathmandu and, though my husband went up from time to time, for me our camp remained a fantasy until, back from Nepal, I spent the tail end of a summer there.

While we were drinking coffee on the deck on my first morning, our caretaker, Dana Cunningham, gave us a history of Haddon—"our" town—in which his family had lived since 1803. He said that if we went to the cemetery and looked at the gravestones we'd see no more than eight or ten last names, the names of the original settler families, his own included. Aside from logging and farming, there were never too many ways to make a living in Haddon. Once they were grown, young people headed west to Ohio and Indiana, where much better land was opening up, land that could grow wheat, sorghum, and barley, not just rocks. Later on they headed south looking for factory work, and mostly they didn't come back. In the early nineteen hundreds city people started coming to the lake in summer. They needed their camps built and taken care of when they were gone, which was most of the year; and that meant a bit more work for the locals. Even so, the young kept on leaving. The flow only started to reverse in the 1960s, when people from "away" began moving in.

"They were artists and writers wanting peace and quiet, I guess," said Dana, "and retirees who didn't fancy Florida. A few tried farming. In 1966 my uncle Darius *quit* farming. Sold off his cows and opened a gas station at the corner of 136 and South Bend Road, just when those New York City folks started settling in to grow potatoes. Back then you could buy land on the water for forty bucks an acre. One acre with no more than a water *view* goes for ten *thousand* bucks today . . . Anyways, for some, the rocks got too much and they went back where they came from. But a few stuck it out."

This reminded me of the American Zen master turned New England farmer I'd read about in Kathmandu, so I mentioned him to Dana.

"I wonder where he settled," I said.

"Back of my house," said Dana matter-of-factly.

"Simon Peters is your *neighbor?*"

"Has been for thirty years."

To start with, it had been just him in the old farmhouse he bought from the Carter family. The Carters had been in Haddon longer even than the Cunninghams. The story went that the first of them received a hundred acres from George Washington him-self, instead of pay for fighting in the Continental Army.

"When old man Joel Carter died his wife couldn't manage on her own and their son was down in Connecticut and had no plans to come back, which was why she sold the place to Peters. First couple of years he had a garden, corn, potatoes, half a dozen sheep. Over the winter I guess he painted pictures. Then some youngsters, hippie types, started showing up."

But not all of them were hippies and several weren't even young. Peters had a couple of ladies that would never see sixty again living in his woodshed. Like everyone else they lugged buckets of water in from an outside tap.

"Once Uncle Darius asked a kid with a beard and a ponytail who was gassing up his truck, 'What are you doing here?' and the kid says, 'I've come to study with my teacher, Simon Peters.' 'Are you a painter?' my uncle says, 'No,' says the kid. 'I couldn't paint a man or a dog or a view to save my bacon. I've come to study Buddhism.'" Dana shrugged. "At that time there weren't many in Haddon that knew what Buddhism was. Some said it was a religion but some said it was politics—*Communism*, maybe...Anyways, those youngsters—and the older ladies too —herded sheep, cut hay, fixed roofs, dug potatoes. And Peters brought in some cows as well. Just four to begin with, but then he expanded...Built a new cow shed...At one time his students —that's what he called them—were milking twenty cows. What-ever there was to do, they did it. They were from the city, didn't know a cow from a sheep or an awl from a hammer. But it turned out Peters was real handy, so I guess he taught them a lot besides Buddhism."

Dana took a swig of coffee. "When it was zero out and three foot of snow on the ground, Peters would clap a big old wooden clapper that he'd hung from the rafters at the back of the barn where they did their meditation. It was just two blocks of wood being knocked together but if there was no wind you could hear it a mile away. My wife, she didn't like being woke at four in the morning, and she wasn't the only one who complained...In the dark they'd be coming from their cabins to sit on their backsides

in a big barn they put up. Hour after hour, in silence, no heat
... You had to wonder ..."

By and by the locals got used to the clapper, the ponytails and
the beards. "But Peters?" Dana pushed back his forest-green
cap. "He's a character, that's for sure. I don't know as we've ever
gotten used to *him*."

"Where will I find him?" I said.

"Go past my place, take the first turn to the left, go on a ways
up the hill with a row of little houses on your right and you'll
see his mailbox on the corner. The Carters' old farmhouse
burned down a while ago—nothing left now but the foundation.
So he lives back from the road in the old dairy. Mornings, he's
usually around splitting wood, replacing shingles, fixing gutters,
getting ready for winter."

Pulling his cap on straight, Dana stood up. "Thanks for the
coffee. I'll be heading out."

According to the 1990 census, Haddon had 981 inhabitants.
Outside the town center, where the Methodist church, the town
hall, the historical society, the Yale Gimble Elementary School,
Willard's Market, Cunningham's Gas Station, and a few dozen
clapboard houses jostled one another along Route 136, the population was scattered over thirty-four square miles. Our camp
was eight miles from Simon Peters' farm and the drive over took
me thirteen minutes.

In front of a shingled barn a man with a shock of white hair
was pushing a battered lawnmower. Over the barn door a
crooked wooden sign read "Three Jewels Gallery."

"Excuse me, are you Simon Peters?" I said.

"I am, and who are you?" He didn't look like any Buddhist
master I'd seen before. He was tanned and fit and his eyes, above
ruddy cheeks, were the sharpest speedwell blue; and instead of
a long dark robe he wore a red and green plaid shirt, frayed at
the cuffs and collar, tucked into washed-out jeans, and work
boots. He didn't seem surprised to hear I'd read about him in a
bookshop in Kathmandu. "People write all kinds of nonsense,"

he said with a shrug. "We're having an opening at four-thirty and I've got to tidy up," he went on. "We've had too much rain, the grass got away from me, and this machine's 'bout ready for the trash. Can you come back another time?"

"You're a painter?"

"That's right. I work in oils but I also do lithographs. Landscapes, mostly. Portraits when they're called for." His blue eyes twinkled. "I could paint *you* if you like."

At five o'clock that afternoon several dozen rather elderly men and women were milling around on the newly mown grass. With their pearl necklaces and crisp linens, bow ties and seersucker suits, they looked like prosperous summer people; it was hard to imagine them treading the Buddhist Path or at least trying to, even in their youth. Simon, who'd exchanged his plaid shirt for a black-and-red silk tunic of vaguely oriental design, was working the crowd, and up against the barn wall a woman behind a trestle table dispensed cookies and cups of tea from a gleaming electric samovar. A Three Jewels Gallery opening wasn't a wine-and-cheese event.

Simon spotted me and came bounding over. "So you came back!" He seemed genuinely pleased. "Get yourself a cup and I'll show you the show."

He introduced the woman pouring tea as his sister Louisa. Like Simon, Louisa was tanned and fit but her white hair was tamed into a pageboy and thick lenses tempered the brilliant blue of her eyes.

"Are you twins?" I asked her.

"Heavens no! I *raised* him. With nine of us, Momma didn't have the time so she handed him over to me pretty quick. Here, have a cookie."

"Chocolate chip. She baked them herself. Twelve dozen straight from the oven," said Simon proudly. "Chocolate's still soft."

I followed him into the barn, where oil paintings and Japanese-style lithographs, framed in pale wood and illuminated by a Rube Goldberg arrangement of trailing wires, hung on bare plank walls. By far the largest work was a portrait of a very old lady with a gray topknot and narrowed eyes. I recognized Simon and Louisa's chin.

"That must be your mother."

Simon bowed to the image. "Momma died right here in Haddon last December, one month after her hundred and first birthday, with me holding her left hand and Louisa her right."

"I'm sorry. You must miss her."

"She lived a full life as well as a long one," Simon replied, gazing up at the portrait. "She came as a child of nine to Brooklyn Heights from a place called Landsbro in Sweden and they put her in first grade. By age thirteen she was a foot taller as well as four years older than the other kids in her fourth grade class so she quit and went to work in a sweatshop making ladies' nightgowns. At fifteen she married my dad, who was a just a few years over from the Old Country as well."

"So Peters is Swedish?"

"Right. My dad was born Arne Gustafson but he came over with his uncle Ulf Petersson—with two *s*'s—and at Ellis Island they registered the both of them as "Peters." Uncle Ulf wasn't about to argue, and Dad wasn't about to either. He was scared to death they'd send him back. His parents were dead and though he'd left a bunch of relatives back in Kalmar, Sweden, he was done with Old World. Let it take care of itself, is what he figured. At least, before she quit school, Momma had learned to speak English but my dad never got that good. Didn't stop him from chasing the American Dream though.

"He borrowed the money to buy fifty acres out on Long Island. By then he had four kids and he wanted them out of the city. He knew everybody in New York—except maybe Chinamen—ate potatoes, and he figured they couldn't be that hard to grow. So on his fifty acres that's what he grew. Then he bought another fifty acres, and another couple hundred . . . He ended up with seven hundred–odd."

Simon was number eight in the family and the fourth of four sons. "After me came my sister Signe, and then Momma was done. Every noon and every evening she'd cook for my dad, us kids, and the hired help. During harvest season we'd have ten guys, Swedes mostly, and the odd Norwegian...Dad took care of the farm, but the business side he left to Momma since she knew English so much better than he did...You should have seen her in the fox-fur stole my dad gave her one year for Christmas. We kids called it her Going-to-See-the-Bank-Manager-to Get-Another-Loan costume...

"They did okay, my parents. Chased the American Dream and caught it. After World War II their seven hundred acres turned into prime real estate. In his sixties, Dad got to be chairman of a bank. I finished Momma's portrait just last week," Simon added. "It's a birthday gift for Louisa."

"Your mother looks like a pretty determined lady," I said politely.

"With nine kids, she had to be."

A mountainous woman in black slacks and a purple overblouse was gushing into Simon's other ear about how much she *adored* his lake scenes. "I'd like an oil for my daughter. Gail spent so many happy childhood summers on the pond, but now the poor girl's working like a dog in Silicon Valley. Makes a ton of money but hasn't been up here in four years. Which one would she like, though? They're all stunning! You're going to have to help me decide."

Views of Whiskey Pond appeared to be Simon's specialty and, judging by the number of "sold" stickers on the frames, they were being favorably received.

By the time I went outside again, the cookies had all been eaten, the samovar had been detached from its extension cord, people were getting into cars and driving away, and Louisa was depositing discarded paper cups in a black garbage bag. "Well, that's over till the next time," she remarked.

"When will that be?"

"Simon loves his get-togethers. Any excuse is better than none. 'Louisa,' he'll say, 'Midsummer Day's coming up,' or Botticelli's birthday. 'Botticelli? How in the hell do you know which day he was born?' I'll say. And he'll say, 'Never mind, let's call in the folks.' Because I'm the one with the computer, I send e-mails to those on the list that have e-mail and he phones up the rest. Then he starts practicing the piano and I get out my recipe book and turn on the oven."

"Simon plays the piano?"

"You bet he does! You didn't see the upright in the barn? He also plays fiddle, accordion, and banjo. When we were kids, he'd put on shows for the family, the neighbors, anybody he could drag into our living room. Even the neighborhood *dogs*. After he'd done his star turn he'd get the rest of us singing. Still does. You should come to our next get-together. They're a lot of fun. If you write your e-mail address for me, I'll be sure and invite you."

I nodded toward outbuildings that were scattered across the pasture in back of the barn. "Which one do you live in?"

"None of 'em. Simon *loves* his old outhouse. No hot water? That doesn't bother *him*! Anyway, bathing's never been his top priority. If I were you, I wouldn't get too close in warm weather ...No, I wouldn't live in this dump for a second!" She lived a mile down the road in a house she'd built herself.

"You must be pretty handy."

"Runs in the family. Though to be honest, my sons put on the roof and Simon did most of the wiring. I couldn't quite figure it out."

"Are you an artist too?"

"There isn't an artistic neuron in my body. I'm a high school chemistry teacher, retired. I'll be seventy-seven in November, and my little brother's rising seventy-two."

"Neither of you looks a day over sixty."

"Trying to flatter me, are you?" Louisa grinned. "Well, I guess we have good genes. Survival of the fittest—that's how it was back in Sweden. Momma's done the best in the family so far—she made the century. But my dad was eighty-eight and all of us kids are still in the land of the living, and all but one's within five miles of this place.

"Momma and Dad bought the farm for Simon to get him back from Japan," she continued. "As a kid, several summers, he'd been to Boy Scout camp down the far end of the pond and kind of fallen in love with the area. Anyway, Momma and Dad bought this place as an enticement—he'd been fifteen years over there so they wanted him back pretty bad and he'd been dragging his feet. He was the first in the family to settle in Haddon, then me, and then the others followed. The only one who didn't come is my baby sister Signe. We've twisted her arm but she won't leave Betsy and the grandkids in Corona del Mar, California."

"It sounds like you're a pretty close family."

"We fight like cats and dogs, actually. We *thrive* on fighting. That's maybe why we live so long."

As I drove away from Three Jewels Gallery I noticed a carved stone sign jutting up above goldenrod and wild blue asters: THREE JEWELS ZENDO. It was only then that I remembered I'd forgotten to ask Simon Peters about his Buddhist community. Behind the sign was a graveled parking area surrounded on three sides by tall trees. I parked and, feeling somewhat apprehensive, got out of the car. I knew a certain amount about Theravada Buddhism, which, to me, seemed straightforward and logical, but almost nothing about Zen.

Apart from having read a few confusing books, my only exposure had been a lecture by Japanese master S. that I'd attended in New York. Before the lecture, which was sponsored by a learned society, I'd been invited to a supper party. Since the black-robed guest of honor had taken a vow not to eat after midday, he was seated, pale hands folded, on a sofa, genially watching the rest of us tuck into the lavish buffet. To the guests who approached him he was courteous, smiling. He told me he'd learned his English, which though heavily accented, was colloquial, as a boy in Vancouver, British Columbia, where he'd lived for three years with his mother's cousin, the proprietor of a fish restaurant. It was his experience in the fish market—"It was like *war*," he said, "people were ready to commit murder over tuna" —that made him decide to become a Zen priest. I'd been about to ask him more about his decision when the president of the learned society rang a bell. The auditorium was packed—three hundred people were waiting, he told us. Time for the lecture to begin.

A few moments later genial Master S. had metamorphosed into a tin-pot tyrant who glowered, barked, and spluttered, and slashed the air with a thick stick. When, after an hour of verbally assaulting his audience, he announced he was open for questions, he became even more belligerent. Like some Mafia kingpin bullying his acolytes, he humiliated his interlocutors, mocked, excoriated, and cut them to pieces. As we were leaving, a Chinese friend to whom I confessed my distaste, said patiently, "Master S.'s objective was to shock us, and at least in your case he may have succeeded."

"What's the point of shocking us?"

"To rattle some cherished beliefs. For example, we think there's an objective reality, that things have permanent form. He was telling us that *nothing* is permanent."

"That I know," I said.

"Ah, but he was going beyond impermanence to emptiness. He was trying to convey the central idea of Mahayana teaching—emptiness is form and form is emptiness." Noting my puzzled expression, he added, "And that isn't easy to comprehend."

A rain-streaked schedule on the notice board nailed to a tree announced: "Sunday, 8–10 am, meditation & dharma talk; 10–11 am, tea & discussion. Wednesday, 7–8 pm, meditation; First Sunday in the month, Work Day; please bring rakes." A white arrow painted on another tree pointed to a path winding down through woods that had been cleared of brush and undergrowth. Shading from deep velvety green through gray to silver, moss grew over the roots of oak and maple; chattering squirrels, eyes darting, scuttled across it, scooped up acorns, leapt up tree trunks, flew from branch to branch. On a rise a stone Buddha sat in dappled sunlight; his eyelids were lowered, his right hand touched the earth; and then on the far side of a humped bridge over a narrow stream, eyes wide and gently smiling, the Bodhisattva of Compassion, known to Japanese Buddhists as Kannon, seemed to welcome me. Beyond her the trees thinned out into a meadow that sloped to a small pond bristling with cattails. Beside the pond a long low building lay like an exotic vessel becalmed on a sea of dark-gray stones. The tiled roof ended in the curved finials of a Japanese temple; opaque rice-paper panels were drawn across the windows and the great east door was secured with a massive wooden bolt. To the right, framed by two sculpted pines, was a more prosaic shingled building whose south-facing porch was lined with wooden planters in which white cosmos grew. A deep-blue sky streaked with pink and orange backed a tall brick chimney; a weather-stained door stood slightly ajar. Aside from swifts skimming the evening pond, this enchanted spot was deserted.

When I pushed the door, it swung open to reveal a raftered book-lined room and, at the far end, a man with a gray-flecked beard holding an electric drill. He looked at me expectantly over wire-framed granny glasses. "Hello, what can I do for you?" He sounded friendly.

"I'm sorry. I shouldn't have barged in without knocking. I didn't think anyone was here."

"There *isn't* anyone here except me, and I'm about done for the day."

"I saw the sign up on the road and I was curious. I'm not a Zen Buddhist," I added hastily. "You could say I'm a Theravadin. At least, in Nepal I was going to a *vipassana* meditation center. I just got back."

"From so far away? In that case, you must be thirsty. Would you like a cup of tea? I'm going to have one."

"I had a cup at the gallery, actually."

"Ah, yes, the opening. How did you like the show?" Before I had a chance to give him my considered opinion, he added, "Never mind, you don't have to tell me. Simon's pond scenes aren't for everyone. Anyway, *I* need a cup, so come in the kitchen and we can talk about Asia while the kettle boils." He said his name was Ned Donnelly and he took care of the *zendo*, the meditation hall. "I guess you could call me the super," he added, with a self-deprecating grin.

The kitchen was lined with broad shelves on which enough

crockery and cooking pots were stacked to equip a small army. "It looks like a lot of people eat here," I observed.

"During retreats we often have forty sleeping in the meditation hall and in cabins in the woods. But everyone eats in here."

"Are you also the cook?"

"Only of last resort." He turned on the burner under the kettle and from a large box of tea bags he selected Beach Plum.

"Have you been here a long time?"

"I got back from Vietnam pretty crazy and came here soon after."

"You actually went to Vietnam?"

"I did my damnedest not to, but yes, I actually went." He'd dropped out of college, for which he'd had a military deferment, to work for the antiwar movement in D.C. and it was only a matter of months before he got drafted. "I told my draft board, Okay, instead of training me to *kill* people, at least train me to *save* a few." Four months after induction he was sent as a medic to a post in the jungle a couple of miles off the Ho Chi Minh Trail. "They'd bring the wounded in and if they didn't die before the helicopter came to get them, they'd be airlifted out to a military hospital. But mostly they did die and they got taken out in body bags."

Aside from two in-country leaves, he stayed in the jungle for fifteen months straight. There was a chronic shortage of doctors and toward the end of his assignment there was no doctor at all, which meant that, aged twenty-two going on fifty, he found himself in charge. "To get through, you had to smoke dope," he went on cheerfully, "and I smoked plenty. In fact I was high every waking moment, and by the time I got home I was pretty much out of my mind."

On one of his leaves, he was hitching up the coast and at nightfall the only place he could find to stay that wasn't a brothel or a military encampment was a Buddhist temple. He had no particular interest in Buddhism. He'd been raised a pretty serious Catholic, as a matter of fact. But in the temple he talked to a couple of monks about meditation. They spoke no English, but they did speak French and he still remembered some French from his Jesuit high school.

"In fifteen months, they were just about the only people I ran into who were totally sane, so when I got back to the States I went looking for a meditation teacher. I started in San Diego in an ashram. In L.A. I tried a Hasidic group and for a while I sat with a Tibetan lama in somebody's living room in Los Gatos. After a year I reached San Francisco, where I found a Japanese Zen teacher I liked a lot. By day I worked as an ER medic—one thing I had to thank the U.S. Army for, they'd given me a way to earn a living just about anywhere."

Early mornings and evenings he sat on his cushion, and gradually he felt less crazy and his head began to clear. It wasn't that he'd gone cold turkey on Catholicism. "Sure, I'd stopped going to *mass,* but something stayed with me. I guess it's still with me, as a matter of fact." Ah, I thought, *The Life of the Buddha* (The Movie) hasn't totally erased *The Life of Christ.* In my case, though in my mind's eye I followed Sakyamuni back and forth across the Gangetic Plain, though I paid close attention to his teachings, and was on friendly terms with many of his followers, in particular his stepmother, Mahaprajapati, the first nun he'd ordained, I still stood at the back of the crowd when he preached; whereas when Judas Iscariot and the chief priest's men, armed to the teeth, broke into the Garden of Gethsemane, I was right there, less than ten feet from Jesus, witnessing the sorrow and resolve on his face.

"I was looking for something more from a religious experience, that's all," Ned said, "something that hadn't been imposed ... something I'd chose myself. And I struck it lucky. Despite being old and in poor health, this Zen teacher had a robustness that I found captivating. I helped take care of him until he passed away."

Ned continued, "But I didn't like the approach of the fellow who took over, so I moved to Minnesota to study with another Japanese teacher I'd heard good things about. Only I soon realized I didn't like his approach either. By then I'd heard about

Simon. I had my doubts, his being an American. How genuine could he be? But I thought, shoot, at least I'll go have a look at him. I showed up one morning—walked down through the woods, like you did—when they were framing up the *zendo.* 'Can you use a chainsaw?' Simon asked me. I told him, yes, and he handed me one. That was twenty-seven years ago last August."

"So you liked Simon's approach?"

"Funny guy. Hardly ever reads a book about Buddhism, or anything else for that matter. 'Go ahead, read all you want,' he'd tell us 'but reading won't bring you to enlightenment' All those books out in the dining hall were left here over the years by his students. Not a one by him. 'It's *practice* that'll get you where you want to go,' he'd tell us. '*Zazen.* Just sitting. Concentrate. That's all you need to do.'"

The kettle was boiling and Ned turned off the burner. "Simon radiated an aura of powerful insight into other people. Plus, he had an intensity of focus. I figured if anybody sees things as they really are, it's this guy. He was plenty meddlesome too. Right away, I saw that and I didn't like it. But his intrusiveness was more than balanced by his vitality, which previously I'd only encountered in my San Francisco teacher. So yes, I liked his approach... For me, it was exactly right."

A few days later I ran into Simon in the supermarket in the county seat, seven miles from Haddon Center. He was bouncing past the tomatoes and zucchini, wire basket in hand. Though the air had the nip of fall in it, he wore no jacket.

"I thought you'd be gone by now," he remarked, smiling. "Come Labor Day this place empties out." We talked for a few moments about local politics and I found myself asking him to supper.

"If I say yes, you'll have to come and fetch me."

"You don't drive?"

"Only my tractor."

"Then how do you get to the shops?"

"By presuming on the beneficence of people like you."

The next evening, after putting vegetarian lasagna in the oven and a bottle of sparkling water in the refrigerator, I went to fetch Simon, who was waiting beside his mailbox in clean shirt and pants, hair still wet from the shower. When I drove up he tugged the passenger-side door open, jumped in the car, and sat bright-faced, hands folded in his lap, like an eager child, waiting for the show to start.

"You look well," I observed.

"I *am* well. I haven't seen a doctor in twenty years. Why should I? I'm healthy."

"Even so, every year you ought to have a checkup," I said primly. "Just to be sure."

"Why waste my money?"

"It wouldn't cost you anything, You have Medicare, don't you?"

"Medicare, Shmedicare!"

When we reached our camp he bounded out of the car and up the steps. Pausing on the deck, he remarked, "Nice view. You should let me paint it. I could paint you in the foreground it you like." At that moment Nellie, our Labrador retriever, dashed through the sliding door, tail wagging in anticipation of making a new friend. "I don't like dogs," said Simon abruptly and he raised the hand that Nellie had been about to lick out of range of her pink tongue.

"No dogs at all?" I said.

"No dogs at all."

"But Simon, they're sentient beings. I could have been a dog in a previous life," I reminded him, "and you could have too."

"That doesn't mean I have to like them, any more than I have to like rats."

Simon wasn't a vegetarian, much less a teetotaler. He asked my husband to let him mix his drink himself: half a tumbler of Absolut vodka, a dash of orange juice, no ice. He had two drinks before supper and a refill with the meal, which, though he was polite about it, he found less than satisfactory. Pork, preferably *roast* pork, he liked a lot, and fish—most of all, pickled herring, tuna, and salmon. "Just so that next time you invite me, you'll know."

His taste for pork, pickled herring, and vodka came from growing up in a Swedish family; his taste for tuna and salmon, from living many years in Japan.

"I would never have returned to America if it hadn't been for my teacher," he remarked. "He'd told me that America was where I was needed—which I really didn't want to hear. I traveled back and forth a few times but then he passed away and I thought, okay, time to follow orders. I brought some of his ashes with me and buried them under a big old rock on the farm. But now I figure I've fulfilled my obligation and I can please myself. So when I get old—okay, I'm old already—I mean, *real* old, I'm going back to Japan for good."

As my husband and I told Simon, we'd been to Japan a number of times; but he wasn't interested in hearing about *our* Japanese experiences. He had a story to tell about *his,* one he'd doubtlessly told a hundred times at a hundred dinner tables. But to me it was new and enthralling. Simon was a great raconteur.

As a boy he'd had a piano teacher, a German refugee named Hannah Levensohn. Back in Berlin, Miss Levensohn, an accomplished performer, had lived a fascinating life, from which she'd been ejected into tawdry hard-scrabble America after Kristallnacht in 1938; but for all her scarring losses, her bemused sadness, and her shabby clothes, she'd retained an acute sensibility that enchanted her young student, a farm boy and son of immigrants, whose mother insisted on piano lessons for her children because piano lessons were an important feature of growing up in the New World, not because she cared especially about music.

"I'd started out with the same small-town teacher as Louisa and the others, but by and by that lady convinced Momma that I had talent and should work with somebody better than she was. I don't remember how Momma settled on Miss Levensohn, but I began taking the train to Brooklyn, which is where she lived, on Saturday mornings."

When she fled Hitler's Germany, Miss Levensohn had managed to bring with her a few boxes of books that included a wonderfully illustrated volume about Japanese temple gardens. While he waited for his lesson and sometimes afterwards as well, young Simon would pour over the illustrations. No matter that the text was in German and in a gothic script that he couldn't read. Miss Levensohn gave him the book as a fifteenth-birthday present. "I'll never go to Japan, but one day *you* will, and you'll see these beautiful gardens with your own eyes," she'd written on the card she enclosed with her gift.

"I kept the book in a trunk under my bed and studied the illustrations until I could bring every one of them to mind—number one through number one hundred and eleven. And I'd plan the great garden trip I was going to take just as soon as I was through with high school and could save enough money to pay my passage over. Though I'd change around the rest of my itinerary, Kyoto was always the place I planned to start because the gardens of Kyoto were the loveliest of all."

When news of the attack on Pearl Harbor came over the radio, and the United States declared war on Japan, Simon had a panic attack.

"I felt like a tidal wave had crashed down on me, dragged me out to sea, and smashed me back on the shore in little pieces. I'd never get to see those temple gardens now... But things turned out differently, I'm happy to say."

After graduating high school, he was drafted and shipped to Okinawa to see the war up close.

"By the time we got there, the big battle was over. We were the cleanup crew. They had us form a human chain right across the island and told us to walk north. They taught us a few words of Japanese—"come on out," "hands above your heads," "surrender." But with our horrible American accents, no native could possibly understand what we were yelling. Our orders were to take enemy soldiers prisoner and leave civilians alone. Only most of the guys were eighteen, nineteen, and scared shitless. To get through, they'd get pissed out of their minds, and when not just soldiers but women and children and little old ladies came crawling out of the holes in the ground where they'd been hiding, mostly they shot at them and kept on shooting till the screaming stopped and there was blood and brains all over. It was as close to hell on earth as I've ever been."

After the war ended he spent some months with the army of occupation on the Japanese mainland. "I'd go off base and poke around, so I got to see a few temple gardens that the war hadn't touched... Twisting conifers five hundred years old; rocks that looked like living creatures rising out of perfectly raked white stones. Moss, watercourses...I got to see Tokyo as well. In March 1945, the Americans had fire-bombed it. In a single night one hundred thousand people had perished and a huge swathe of the city had burned to the ground. When I got there the following October, the fires were out but the ruins were still smoldering.

"In 1946 I shipped back to the Land of the Free, back to normalcy, as the government kept telling us, back to art school in New York City. Only I couldn't stop thinking about the people who'd created those gardens. How were they different from us? More important, how were they the *same?* Our government had been telling us the Japanese were demons—just look at the terrible things they'd done in China, the Philippines, Malaya, Indonesia, everywhere they'd been in Asia! The terrible things we Americans had done in Japan—Hiroshima, Nagasaki—were fully justified of course..."

Simon had kept in touch with Miss Levensohn and it was she who introduced him to her friend, a wealthy widow named Rachel Brewer who'd lived in Kyoto in the 1930s. She'd learned some Japanese and studied Buddhism, and during the war she'd been one of very few people who had publicly protested the internment of Japanese-Americans by the U.S. government. "Miss Levensohn said Mrs. Brewer knew a lot about Japanese gardens and the influence Buddhism had on their design. So one evening toward the end of my sophomore year I went to see her on the Upper West Side. It was through talking to her about gardens that I first learned about Zen."

On Tuesday evenings, Mrs. Brewer and a half dozen others

"sat zazen" in her living room and Simon started sitting with them.

"Most of us were youngsters. Mrs. Brewer gave us books to read and discuss with her, but she always said, 'I'm not a teacher. I'm not *qualified* to teach you.' Once in a while a Japanese priest might visit and we'd get to talk to him with Mrs. Brewer translating. But I never quit telling her, 'I don't understand what you're talking about,' till eventually she said, 'Okay, instead of getting frustrated with *me* when I can't answer your questions to your satisfaction, go find yourself a teacher in Japan!'"

Many years earlier she had studied in Kyoto with the abbot of a great temple who spoke some English because as a young priest he'd worked in California in the immigrant community; so she wrote to him and he agreed, as a favor, to take Simon as his student.

"When I told Dad and Momma, Dad went nuts. 'I've worked my fingers to the bone here in America to give you advantages I never dreamed of having back in the Old Country. And now you want to leave your native land and go thousands of miles away to *Asia* to live with our *enemies?*' But Louisa sided with me and Louisa could argue the hind leg off a donkey. She said to Dad, 'Remember, when you were Simon's age, *you* left *your* native land and a whole bunch of relatives and headed west. Now Simon's heading west. You're wondering where he gets his wanderlust? Well, he got it from *you!*' In the end, she convinced him and I went to Japan with his blessing. He even paid my passage over and gave me some extra cash."

Simon arrived in Kyoto with two hundred dollars and a rucksack containing a change of clothes, a sketch pad, and five fine-nibbed pens. Since he couldn't understand a word of Japanese, much less read Japanese street signs, it was with considerable difficulty that he found his way to the house outside the temple gates where his teacher was living in retirement. "When I walked in he looked at me for a minute and then he said, 'I can't teach you anything.' 'Then why did you tell me I could come?' I asked. 'You have to teach *yourself*,' he said.

"I was entranced by Kyoto, by its temples and its gardens,

and by so many people who were generous to me, only five years after the end of that terrible war ... To start with I lodged with a family. The lady of the house was an artist and she spoke English quite well because she'd lived in London. After I'd learned some Japanese I moved to another family in which nobody knew English, and then I got my own little place. Eventually I learned the language so well that people told me, with their eyes closed they wouldn't have known I was a foreigner ... I guess I was young and had a good ear."

He supported himself by giving private English lessons until he found a job in the art department of a women's college. "But often I'd go to my teacher's house at seven o'clock in the morning and stay till evening. He was compassionate, humorous, demanding, and tough as an old boot ... I couldn't tell you what I learned from him—or taught myself, as he would have it. But the day came when he said I was done and told me to go home. He also told me, 'You're an egomaniac, you've got a swollen head, and till that goes down you're not fit to teach anyone the dharma.' 'How long will it take for my head to shrink down to size?' I asked him. 'I'd give it ten years,' he said."

"You didn't wait that long though, did you?" I said.

"I had a couple of years of peace. Spring and summer, I ploughed, sowed, harvested, took care of my sheep and tried to stop the foxes from eating my geese and my chickens. October though April, I took care of my birds and animals, plus I painted. There was a south-facing room in the old house, wonderful light, made a great studio." He smiled ruefully. "But the word got around that I was here and first one kid showed up and then another. Said they were looking for a Zen teacher. Camped on my doorstep, in the fields, out in the woods. Then more showed up and finally, I said, 'Okay, whatever I know I'll teach you— *my* way.' 'Your way's fine,' they said.

"In Japan, a Zen teacher puts the young monks he's training to work in his temple garden. Working with full concentration is a very important part of their training. I didn't have a temple or a garden but I had a *farm,* so I put my students to work on it. Some came and went, depending on the season and whatever else was going on in their lives. But others made the commitment to the full training, however long it might take. We cut timbers and shingles and built a whole bunch of little houses for them. And they settled down, got married, had kids, raised them..." He looked up at the kitchen clock. "My Lord, it's past my bedtime and I need a ride home."

A couple of days after our evening with Simon, we closed up our camp and headed down to Massachusetts for the winter. I didn't expect to hear from him again but in January he called. He'd got our phone number from his neighbor, Dana Cunningham. He said the snow was two feet deep in Haddon and in a week's time he was heading out to Japan.

"It's not that warm over there either, but at least the sun shines most days and in Kyoto it hardly ever snows."

He needed to be met at the bus station, put up for the night, and driven to Logan airport the next morning to catch a six o'-clock plane.

"You're always needing rides, aren't you Simon," I teased. "You should consider exchanging your tractor for a car."

"If you can't fit me in I'll think of someone else who can," he said, sounding hurt.

"We can fit you in, don't worry."

When I arrived at South Station a week later, he was waiting on the icy sidewalk, hatless and gloveless in the bitter wind, holding two canvas bags. The small black one had a broken zipper and clothing peeped out of it; the larger blue one was tied shut with a broad leather belt. "I thought you weren't coming," he said peevishly.

"Am I late?"

"Four minutes."

"I said I'd come, didn't I?"

"You and the professor live such busy lives. You could've forgotten me."

On the drive out of the city my attempts to engage him in conversation proved futile. Though he appeared fully alert and was looking straight ahead at the oncoming traffic, it occurred to me that he must be in deep meditation. Hadn't I'd read somewhere that Zen Buddhists meditated with their eyes open?

When we reached the house he marched, a bag in each hand, up the steps and through the front door. In the hall he stood stock still and stared into the living room until, rousing himself from his liminal state, he spoke for the first time since leaving the bus station. "So you have a piano."

Dropping his bags and still wearing his winter jacket, he strode over to it.

"My great-grandmother bought it in Berlin in 1884," I said. "I had it rebuilt several years ago but now it needs more work."

He leaned down and struck a few chords. "You're certainly right about that! What the hell," he added, "let's give it a go anyway."

He unzipped his jacket, but didn't take it off, and from the stack of music on the piano lid picked up the second volume of Beethoven sonatas and opened it to Opus 110. "I learned to play this with Miss Levensohn. It was one of her favorites," he said and, seating himself on the bench, he went full tilt at the music.

The piano shook, our dog fled to the kitchen, and my husband, lured from his study two floors above us, appeared in the doorway. After the Beethoven, Simon played a Schubert impromptu from memory "to close," as he told us. Slamming the keyboard shut, he rose to his feet and turned to my husband.

"Have I earned myself a drink, Professor?"

At supper, the grilled salmon with a mustard sauce met with his approval but he refused a second helping and dessert as well. "I'm not a big eater, especially not before a long trip." By eight-thirty he was ready for bed. "Will you knock on my door at four? Oh, and by the way, can I call you if I need a bed for the night when I come back through in the spring?"

"When will that be?"

"Louisa will phone me when the first loon returns to Whiskey Pond. Then I'll make my reservations and phone *you*."

"What happens at the *zendo* when you're gone?" I asked.

"Same as usual."

"They can manage without their teacher?"

"They don't have a teacher."

"Aren't *you* their teacher?"

"I was but I quit."

"You *quit*?"

"Before I was a teacher I was a painter." His blue eyes bored into me. "I'd had enough of riding herd on those people. They kept telling me they didn't want to sit zazen at four in the morning, they wanted to shift to seven, eight o'clock. And ten-week training periods were getting to be too much for them. Wouldn't ten *days* be enough, or just a couple of *weekends*? 'The deal was, if you want to study with me, you'll do things *my* way,' I reminded them. 'But now you want to do things *your* way!'

"Momma was alive then and one day she said to me, 'Enough of this pied-piper business! You should go back to painting,' and I thought, she's right, and that's exactly what I did. Handed over the *zendo,* sold off the few cows I still had on the place, rented out a couple of pastures for haying, and let the rest go back to forest. Some of the trees are already more than twenty feet tall."

Simon called from Kyoto in the third week of April. "Loons are back," he told me. "Can I have a bed with you next Thursday? Oh, and I'll be coming in on Northwest at five in the evening. *Flight 672.* Be sure and write down the number."

It happened that my friend Vidya was visiting us from Kathmandu. Vidya was a small, lively man of about fifty whose day job was teaching mathematics in the university; but his passion was the religious art of Tibet, about which he'd recently published a lavishly illustrated book. When I picked up Simon at the airport I mentioned that we had a Nepalese houseguest.

"Is he sleeping in my bed?" he asked.

I thought he was joking but, noting his pained expression, I realized he'd spoken in earnest. "As a matter of fact I did put him in the room you slept in last time," I said, "but our other guest room's larger. I'm sure you'll be comfortable."

At the house we found Vidya by the living room fire reading

the *New York Times.* He jumped up and offered his hand to Simon. "I'm very happy to meet you, sir. I understand you have spent many years in Kyoto. I have a very great friend, Dr. Hide Wagatsama, who teaches at Kyoto University. Like myself, he has an interest in Tibetan art. Two years ago I visited him and then together we traveled to Lhasa. Possibly you know him?" But Simon didn't know Dr. Hide Wagatsama, had never been to Tibet, and, as he said rudely, had no interest in going.

"I like to stay at or close to sea level."

Vodka and orange did nothing to improve his mood. He sat, tumbler in hand, in the living room, staring into the fire. When my husband showed him Vidya's new book, he glanced at the wildly hued Chakrasambhava on the jacket and the blurb on the back and, without opening it, put the book down on the coffee table.

"Took a lot of work, I bet," was all he said.

At supper, Vidya tried repeatedly to draw him into the conversation, but he sat round-shouldered, hardly glancing up from his plate. Aside from complimenting me on my pork roast and apple pie, of which he accepted a hefty slice topped by a scoop of ice cream, he didn't utter a word. I wondered, was he jet-lagged, did he find Vidya's accent so difficult to understand?

Next morning, when he and I, just the two of us, drove to the bus station and he laughed and joked and delighted in the spring sunshine, the blossoming trees in the parks, the seagulls soaring and swooping over the Charles River, I decided his uncouth behavior had been due to having to share the spotlight.

The first Sunday after my husband and I moved up to Whiskey Pond for the summer, I went to Three Jewels Zendo. This was the only meditation center within a hundred miles; so, regardless of tradition, if I wanted to attend one, this would have to be it. I felt some of the same trepidation I'd felt years before in Mexico the first time I'd taken the Eucharist in a Catholic Mass. *I come from a different tradition, I have no business being here, I'm here under false pretenses, they'll find out I don't belong and throw me out!* As it was, when I arrived meditation had already started. A notice in the porch said latecomers should wait to enter the *zendo* until they heard the handbell signaling a break. But what if I didn't hear it through the thick oak door?

A couple came marching out of the woods and over the greensward. They nodded wordlessly to me, removed their boots, and stowed them away on a shelf in the porch. As they appeared to know the ropes, I did likewise. When, by and by, we heard the handbell ringing, the woman pulled back the great bolt and the door swung open.

The long hall, rice-paper screens drawn across the windows, was dim and smelled faintly of incense. The roof was supported by pale pillars fashioned from tree trunks whose bark had been stripped, leaving knots and imperfections. The black slate floor stretched fifty feet to an altar on which a statue of Manjushri, Bodhisattva of Wisdom, holding a broad sword flat against his shoulder was flanked by a bowl of oranges and pink-and-white-striped lilies in a porcelain vase. A dozen people, uniformly dressed in jeans and polar fleece, sat on tatami-covered platforms. I saw a girl with white-blond hair to her waist and a young man with a red beard; but the rest were graying and, to my disappointment, Ned Donnelly wasn't among them. Some sat on black cushions; others on low wooden stools. They stretched stiff limbs, rolled shoulders, or, hands on hips, swayed from side to side; a few, faces impassive, maintained the full lotus; nobody gave us late arrivals a glance.

The couple who had entered with me bowed to the altar and went directly to two vacant cushions on the right, their habitual places, I assumed. The break over, limbs were rearranged in meditation mode. But still I stood there. At the far end I spotted a gap between the blond girl and the bearded youth. I made for it, clambered onto the platform, and got myself seated just as a woman across the hall from me clapped small wooden clappers together with a vigor that set her gray curls bobbing.

After an hour of meditation—in which my attempts to follow my breath were often distracted by the chirping of crickets, the croaking of frogs in the pond, and occasional rumblings in the stomach of the bearded youth on my left—and the reading of a scriptural passage about uncovering the Buddha within, we chanted the Heart Sutra, repeated the four Bodhisattva vows, and took refuge in Buddha, Dharma, and Sangha. Or rather, interloper that I was, I just listened. Three full-length prostrations were the last item on the agenda. Then, having plumped up and replaced our cushions, we bowed to the Bodhisattva Manjushri and circumambulated our way out.

Before going over to the dining hall for tea and discussion, we stood in a circle in the porch and introduced ourselves by first name and place of residence. The woman who had led the session was called Lauren and lived in Haddon, as did everyone else except me and a man who introduced himself as Henry from Wyalusing, Pennsylvania. Like most of the others he was polar-fleeced and in his fifties; he was also strikingly handsome in a fading-blond Gary Cooper way. "It's great to see you back here, Henry," said Lauren smiling warmly. "You've been gone far too long."

Tea there was, but no discussion. I'd just selected my tea bag and discovered that Lauren, who was standing next to me in the line for hot water, was married to Ned Donnelly and taught fourth grade in the Haddon elementary school when Frank, who had unruly hair and a round red face, called out, "Quiet everybody. Ned's visiting his mother, so I'm in charge of Work Day." In his voice there was the trace of the Deep South. "Drink up and we'll be off to the moss garden, which is a foot deep in leaves from the winter. I hope you all brought your rakes."

"I didn't," confessed Henry, the only other out-of-towner.

"Then would you please weed the stones round the back of the *zendo*? Remember, we work not only to keep the place in good order but as an exercise in concentration. So don't talk unless it's essential. We'll meet back here for lunch at noon."

"I don't have a rake either, so can I weed with you?" I asked Henry. We collected buckets from the toolshed and, behind the *zendo*, where the first weeds of the season were already flourishing, we squatted down to work.

"I wish I'd brought gardening gloves," I said, right away forgetting the silence rule. "I gather you haven't been here in a while," I added.

"Sixteen years," Henry replied.

"That *is* a while."

"It's taken me that long to recover."

"You were sick?"

"I guess so... You're new here, aren't you?" I nodded. Henry sat back on his haunches. "Maybe you don't even know Simon Peters."

"I do know him, but not very well."

"Then for Christ's sake," Henry burst out, "don't get to know him any better!" He closed his eyes, took a couple of deep breaths, and went back to weeding.

After a few minutes, he muttered, "He tried to destroy my family. Darned near did as well..."

"I'm sorry, what did you say?"

"He darned near destroyed my family," Henry repeated, voice rising. "One night Emma—that's my wife—told me, 'It's either Simon, or me and the girls. You'd better make up your mind *right now!*' She was burning up with fury but she didn't say another word. Just stood there waiting, biding her time. And finally I told her, 'Okay, *right now* we're getting out!' We packed up the truck, grabbed the kids from their beds, wrapped them in quilts, and headed out. It was three a.m. and it was snowing. I swore I'd never come back."

"Then why did you?"

Henry looked at me, green eyes narrowed, as if he were seeing me from far, far away. "Despite what the Buddha said about women being as capable of attaining enlightenment as men are, Simon didn't actually believe it."

"Excuse me, I don't follow."

"My wife's the most capable woman Simon Peters ever had the good fortune to meet."

He and Emma were in graduate school at UCLA when they first heard about Three Jewels Zendo, Henry told me. Emma was finishing her MA in English, Henry was writing his dissertation for a PhD in philosophy, and they were both in full flight from their Goldwater Republican parents in Laguna Beach, California. "My dad actually gave twenty-five thousand dollars to Goldwater's 1964 presidential campaign," said Henry with a wry smile. "Emma and I were high school sweethearts...We met in Chemistry in the tenth grade and got married after our junior year in college." In graduate school they'd begun sitting zazen with one of Henry's professors who'd studied in Japan with the same old Zen master as Simon Peters. "In fact, he was the person who told us about this place. Working on the farm, pitting oneself against the New England winter, making every moment of every day part of one's practice—it sounded so *right,* so *heroic.* We fell for it. *Totally* fell for it. Without ever laying eyes on Simon, we decided to place ourselves in his hands.

"I was F1 because I had a heart murmur, so dropping out of my program didn't put me in line for Vietnam. A couple of hours after Emma wrote her last exam we started the drive east."

By the time they rolled into Haddon two months later, Emma was having morning sickness. "The pregnancy wasn't planned but we were thrilled to bits anyway. Our baby was going to grow up in a community free of materialistic sludge...In that regard at least, Simon didn't disappoint. He's probably the least materialistic man I've ever met."

The first few weeks they lodged down the road with Madge and Regina, who kept bees and shipped their honey to a fancy grocery store in Boston; and then Simon assigned them a cabin equipped with a sleeping platform. They had just enough time to line the walls and roof with plastic sheeting before the thermometer dipped below thirty-two, heading for zero. "Our daughter India was delivered by a midwife in that cabin and, eighteen months later, so was our daughter Maya. We had no health insurance but even if we'd had it, we'd have done things no differently."

It was just another aspect of the heroic life that they'd fully embraced.

But Emma was almost always too busy taking care of two babies in a cabin without modern conveniences to sit zazen. And since, like her, they were also busy taking care of young children, most of the other women in the community couldn't sit zazen much either. At the end of the intensive training sessions—ten weeks in spring and ten weeks in the fall—Simon would invite his students up to his beautiful old farmhouse to drink vodka and eat his great fish stews and Louisa's pies and bread and cinnamon rolls.

"But almost everyone there was male because almost everyone who attended training sessions was male. Oh sure, Simon accepted female students—he'd accepted Emma as well as me—but most of the women didn't have *time* to be students... Emma never attended a single training session let alone a celebratory feast.

"So there was I, at the center of the inner circle, sitting ten hours a day during fall and spring training, meeting in private sessions with Simon *sensei* to discuss my spiritual progress... fast-tracked to enlightenment. And there was Emma, the way she'd always been, at the bottom of the samsaric heap—at least, that's how she saw it."

In an anguished tone, Henry continued, "But it was a lot more complicated than that. The day we arrived here, when he was showing us around the place, Simon said to me, 'My, you're so *Californian,* like you just came off the beach... water in the desert, manna from heaven...' He spoke low and into the wind so Emma couldn't hear him. And before I knew it he'd stuck her way off in a hut in the woods so he'd have me pretty much to himself."

"He cast his spell, he ensorcelled me... I was delighted to spend sixteen hours a day dealing with his correspondence, paying his bills, doing his grocery shopping, managing his fucking sawmill. And I made a darned good manager," Henry said bitterly. "I was exceptionately well organized. I'd aspired to become a *logical positivist,* for Christ's sake. The thesis I hadn't finished was on *Wittgenstein...*" In an anguished voice he added, "I was more than willing—okay, I was *thrilled*—to do anything Simon Peters fucking well pleased."

At that moment Frank appeared round the corner of the *zendo* and, noting our two small piles of weeds, observed, "I guess you didn't get too much done, did you? But anyway, it's noon and you're to desist from your labors. Lauren's made a great bean soup."

I couldn't stay for lunch because we had houseguests and I had to hurry home, stunned by what Henry had told me. At that time, just about every issue of every American Buddhist publication had an article about some rimpoche or roshi or bhikkhu, whether American or foreign, either sexually abusing his students or squandering *sangha* funds, and sometimes both. Power corrupted and absolute power, which these Buddhist teachers almost always seemed to have, corrupted absolutely. Even so, I had naively hoped that Simon, who, despite—or because of—his eccentricities, intrigued and amused me, and of whom I was growing fond, was an exception. Henry might have been fabricating, he could have been spinning me a tale. In any event, I decided not to repeat it to my husband. If I did, mightn't he, in disgust and indignation, refuse to have anything more to do with Simon? But for my part, having only just begun getting to know him, I wasn't willing to stop.

Over the summer, I saw a good deal of the core members of the *sangha*. Ned had been in Haddon longest. His wife, Lauren, whom he'd met in San Francisco, had come east to join him and together they'd built a cabin down the hill from Simon's house. They'd been living there a couple of years when Simon began putting pressure on them to get married.

"Despite living off the grid, at least figuratively, Simon was an arch-conservative," Lauren told me. "Ned and I weren't the only unmarried couple he got after. I guess he wanted us to get our relationship settled, so we could focus fully on Zen." Children of the sixties, raised in fractious homes, neither Ned nor Lauren believed in marriage; but Simon was so persistent that eventually, like most of the other unmarried couples in the community, they conceded defeat. "And that was just the first step. 'Throw out those birth control pills,' he told us. 'You'll make great parents.'" Both had hated being children and didn't want to inflict the experience on anyone else.

"If Simon was the gatekeeper to the one place in the universe you really wanted to be," Ned continued, "ultimately, you got with his program... Mind you, he wasn't the only attraction. There were the people who'd come from all over to study with him. I found them bright, hard-nosed, humorous, and practical —lots of great characters. I relished their company. And then there was this astoundingly beautiful place—wide swathes of woodland, ancient oaks, white pines a hundred and fifty feet tall, meadows rolling down to the lake, and mountains rising beyond it... A sacred space—and in my view, the *only* one on earth that rated... I'd come back from Vietnam looking, and now that I'd found it, I intended to stay put. As for Simon, maybe you stood up to him to start with, but he was so *powerful*... in the end you did what he told you, or else you got out."

So he and Lauren added an upstairs room to their cabin and an extension out back and had Beth first and then Eliza.

When I met them, Beth had just finished her freshman year in college and Eliza was in eleventh grade. From what I saw of them, Simon had been right. Aside from their obvious intelligence, like their parents, they were gentle and reflective. They listened to what one was saying, they really did seem to hear; and, in my experience, kids their age weren't often that receptive to their parents' friends.

Frank was from an old New Orleans family which, in every generation since the Louisiana Purchase, had sent a son into the Catholic Church. In seminary, he'd begun to read Thomas Merton on Buddhism. In his final year he'd fallen in love with Elizabeth, who'd come to interview him for the local paper; he dropped out of seminary, married, and came to Haddon to study with Simon. He and Elizabeth and their son, Matthew, lived in a cottage with diamond-paned windows that they'd built in a garden full of Michaelmas daisies, bee-balm, mock orange, sweet peas, and rambler roses. Frank had only recently replaced their composting toilet with an ecologically sound flush version set on terra-cotta tiles in a spanking-new bathroom. Relishing the luxury after twenty years of "composting," Elizabeth admitted she was spending too much time in it.

Robert, raised a Quaker on the Philadelphia Main Line, had spent time in Kyoto on his way home from digging tube wells with the Peace Corps in India. He'd intended to become a history professor like his father; but instead of going back to Penn for his doctorate as planned he'd made his way to Haddon. By and by he'd fallen in love with Robyn, raised Jewish in Highland Park, Illinois, who was taking care of Simon's cows. Eventually—with a certain amount of pressure from Simon—they'd got married, bought a ramshackle farmhouse overlooking Whiskey Pond, opened a garden center on Route 136, and had twin sons.

Ned and Lauren, Frank and Elizabeth, Robert and Robyn. They were smart, competent people who could have had conventionally successful careers in the world. But they'd opted out of it. To live with minds as fully concentrated as possible had been their focus for decades.

One Sunday after zazen, a dozen of us were discussing the benefits of practice, the fruits of meditation.

"I control my anger better," said Jason, the young man with the red beard.

"I'm less anxious," said Libby, who'd come to the *zendo* for the first time that morning.

"I'm starting to forgive my parents," said Amanda, the girl with the curtain of white-blond hair.

"Fruits, benefits?" said Robyn. "Which improvements in my character are due to living, growing older, and learning from my mistakes, and which are due to sitting on my cushion morning and evening my whole adult life? I really couldn't tell you."

"Meditation is just what I *do*. Pretty much like eating or bathing or taking a shit," Ned said, and the other old-timers nodded their agreement.

I saw quite a bit of Simon too that summer. When I drove by his farm in good weather, I'd sometimes spot him at his easel in a distant pasture and I'd drive on by; but if he was splitting wood by the barn I'd stop to visit and receive a smacking kiss and a hug. He'd take me into the former shingle factory that he'd converted into a studio and show me whatever he was working on; sometimes he'd play me a J. C. Bach sonata on his upright piano, or a J. S. Bach sonata on his fiddle. And he'd chatter away about days long gone—small-town life on the Long Island of his childhood; Okinawa; Cooper Union, where he'd studied graphic arts in New York City; and, of course, Japan. But he hardly said a word about Buddhism—and about his creation, Three Jewels Zendo, he said nothing at all.

I learned from Frank that when Simon resigned as their teacher he'd signed over the *zendo,* the dining hall, several cabins, and the ten acres on which they stood to the *sangha,* and had never been seen on the place again. It seemed that in his mind the narrow strip of forest between his farm and the *zendo* was as wide as the Atlantic Ocean had been in his father's mind when he left Sweden. Whatever lay behind that wall of trees was no longer of interest.

One morning when I stopped in, he said, "I want to show you something," and he took me to a shingled building that had once housed geese and Muscovy ducks. Against one wall was an altar on which stood a green jade Buddha, ten inches high; on each side hung Japanese scrolls depicting gray-robed monks, curving bamboo, and high-peaked mountains, surrounded by rich silk borders. Black cushions had been set out on new floorboards and light filtered through rice-paper panels covering the only window. "How do you like my *zendo?*" he asked eagerly.

"It's lovely."

"My Buddha was a gift from my teacher and the scrolls were given to me by a lithographer friend in Kyoto. I just finished getting everything together...I've asked one or two people if they'd like to sit with me in the morning." And then he added, "Would *you* like to sit with me, mornings...at seven o'clock?"

"Oh, Simon, I can't." I had it on the tip of my tongue to say, I sit with the others, I'm already *committed.* But instead I said, "That's just the time when I walk Nellie."

"That damn dog!"

❧

Following a continuous stream of houseguests at the camp, my husband announced that he was tired of doing the dishes and, throwing environmental concerns to the winds, we bought a dishwasher. Easy enough, but its installation posed problems. To accommodate it, our kitchen would have to undergo a major reorganization. When I asked Ned Donnelly if he could recommend a carpenter, he replied, "I'll do it," and that fall, for two-thirds of what any other carpenter in the area would have charged us, he renovated our kitchen.

One late fall day when I'd come up from Boston to see how the work was progressing, I told Ned about my conversation with Henry. All summer I'd kept the memory of it under lock and key in the back of my mind.

"He told me he had an affair with Simon," I said.

Ned looked at me over his granny glasses. "Is that what he told you?"

"Not exactly, but that's what he seemed to be telling me. Is Simon gay?"

Ned put down his pliers on the reconstructed counter, took off his glasses, and washed them under the faucet. After he'd dried and replaced them he said, "When I first came up here, Simon was in the prime of life, a compelling presence, an extraordinarily good-looking guy ... *radiant*. Those blue eyes of his—when he looked at you, you felt like he saw into the deepest recesses of your mind, that he knew you better than you knew yourself, and that whatever doubts and confusion you might have, just stick with him and he'd pull you through. I guess that's hard to imagine, given the way he is nowadays—kind of childish. But until the day he wrote a note on a sheet of paper he'd torn out of an exercise book—"I will no longer be your teacher"—and pinned it to the door of the *zendo* for us to see when we went in to sit at four the next morning, he'd given us his full attention. He'd had magnetism, *charisma* ... We all thought—*assumed*—he was enlightened, that he'd had his satori, and that if we did pretty much what he told us, we'd have ours too. *Was* he enlightened? Maybe. But enlightenment doesn't stick, you have to keep working at it. You have that flash of insight, knowledge, whatever you want to call it, and then it's gone...

"Before Simon turned his klieg lights out and the stage darkened, a lot of people doted on him—men and women both. Some of those ladies you saw at his gallery opening, they *threw* themselves at him when they were younger. But *sexually* he had nothing to do with them as far as I know.

"There was Carlos, a Puerto Rican fellow he'd met in his art school days in New York, and even after I came up here—by then he'd been graduated from Cooper Union almost twenty-five years—Carlos would sometimes visit. One time I remember in particular. Carlos happened to be around during training session and he showed up at the feast at the end in drag—décolleté dress, heels, bangles, cute little hat with a feather...He drank a lot of vodka and did a crazy dance...He was a lot of fun, I liked him, everybody did. We heard through the grapevine he became a Jehovah's Witness...Anyway, he hasn't been around here in years."

"Were Simon and Henry lovers?" I persisted.

Ned shrugged. "I disagreed with Simon about a lot of things, and though I believe he kind of enjoyed our arguments, he never let me into his inner circle. So I wasn't in a position to see things he wouldn't have wanted me to see." He paused. "What can I say? Henry and Emma were a great couple, as plucky as they come. Real pioneers...optimistic, nothing seemed to get them down. Their pulling out came as a terrible shock to the rest of us. We missed them—*mourned* them is a better word. They left a big hole in the community.

"But how much can you actually know about people? I guess behind that sturdy golden-boy exterior Henry had another side. Since he left here, I don't believe he's done too much. It's Emma who's been earning the family living. She started some kind of mail-order business...sweaters...real *fancy* sweaters...Out in a small town in Pennsylvania, she's got a whole team of women on knitting machines." Ned paused. "And Henry...the poor guy's been in and out of mental hospitals for years."

I took a few moments to absorb this reality.

"When Simon was your teacher, would you have been shocked if he'd come out of the closet?"

"Would *I*? After all the drugs *I'd* done and God knows what else? No, and no one else here would have been either. So why didn't he come out? Shame? I doubt it. Inhibition? I really doubt *that*. He's the soul of spontaneity . . . As I see it, Simon's all about hierarchy and running the show. Intimacy demands *equality*, and that's not what he's about . . . When he resigned from teaching Zen he was sixty. I guess he figured that so late in the day, and without a partner, it wasn't worth his while to come out."

The renovated kitchen was a great improvement and we hired Ned to do more work over the winter while we were traveling in Asia. Just before we set off in January, Simon passed through Boston on his way to Japan. This time he was our only houseguest. He pressed me to let him paint my portrait. He noted for the first time—and with approval—a lithograph in our living room by a New York School painter, his exact contemporary, whom he'd known in his student days. He played some J. C. Bach, and didn't complain about our piano.

In Nepal later that winter, I visited the Saint of Kathmandu, whom I hadn't seen since before I'd discovered Three Jewels Zendo. I told her how astonished I'd been, after reading about it in the bookshop round the corner from her nunnery, to find it was just a few miles down the road from my house in America.

"It was your karma," Guruma said, and I had to agree. "And who is the abbot of that temple?"

"There is none. The man who founded it resigned."

"He disrobed and became a householder?" She shrugged. "Often our Nepalese monks do that as well."

"He was a layman, not a monk. But anyway he left the temple without appointing a successor. The place is a long way from the city and up till now his students haven't found a replacement."

"So who teaches the dharma?"

"Once in a while a teacher from another temple comes for a day or two."

"In and out, in and out? That's not good enough, is it... I'd come myself during the rainy season retreat if I didn't have so much work here. And besides, I don't know English." Guruma was silent. "But our Khema knows English very well," she said, brightening. "She studied in the university and after that she had a government job and had to write long reports in English. These days she travels from village to village to teach the children. She rides the motorcycle a Taiwanese doctor gave her. Without her, the children would know nothing about Buddhism. She has energy and great equanimity. She's not afraid of Maoist guerrillas or government soldiers when they stop her on the road and point their guns at her head. She's not afraid of wild dogs that run in packs through the countryside either. She's *fearless*. So let me send her to teach you and your friends in America."

I pictured Khema on her motorbike, pink-and-orange dress flying, black helmet tightly strapped under her chin, charging over a rutted road in the western hills—and, in an instant switch, leading a discussion of karma and rebirth in the dining hall in Haddon. "I'll have to ask the committee," I said hastily. "You see, they're Mahayanas. They don't read the Pali Canon, as you do. In fact they read different scriptures entirely..." Head cocked to one side, Guruma listened intently. "They believe that every sentient being is *already* a fully enlightened Buddha and they meditate in order to uncover their true nature... They don't seem to be so interested in getting rid of character flaws like envy, ignorance, and hatred, or in getting along with other people, the way all of you are here."

I explained that Americans were very individualistic, and people had to look out for themselves because, in an extremely competitive society, no one else would.

"Remember, when he was dying the Buddha said to his followers, 'Seek your own enlightenment with diligence.' Well, that's what most interests American Buddhists. It doesn't mean that they aren't generous and ready to help other people. But for them, because they think meditation is what will bring them to enlightenment fastest, meditation is more important than anything else."

Guruma shrugged. "But you just told me your friends have no one to guide their meditation. Khema is an experienced teacher and she's used to foreigners. She teaches the ones who come to our retreats, and sometimes they're quite numerous. Please tell your friends about Khema and hear what they have to say."

One afternoon when I checked my e-mail in a cybercafé in Thamel there was a message from Ned Donnelly: during a freak winter thaw, the snow on our roof had melted and when Ned turned up for work the next morning, water was pouring in, down the stairs, and into the basement. He'd immediately called in a roofer, who'd told him that the tiles were worn out and the whole roof would have to be replaced; but aside from covering it with a tarpaulin, he couldn't fix it till spring.

"Before the temperature goes back down below freezing, I'll see what I can do about the six inches of water in your basement," Ned wrote.

When, two weeks later, I drove up to Haddon, I half expected to find that our roof had caved in; but the place looked no different from the last time I'd been there in December. Ned's red truck was parked at the back door and inside the house was toasty and looked just as usual.

"How did you manage to dry it out?" I asked Ned, who was having a cup of tea in the kitchen.

First he'd brought in a pump and pumped out as much of the water as he could and then, instead of turning on the electric heat, which, in his view, would have cost us too much money, he'd lit the two woodstoves and driven over three times each day for fourteen days to stoke them with logs he'd had to haul in from the shed at the top of our road.

"You're a bodhisattva," I told him, and I meant it. Our caretaker, Dana Cunningham, was in Florida visiting relatives and wouldn't return till late in March. "Without you, we might never have known about the flood until Dana came back and found the place a wreck."

"Take a look at the basement while I make you a cup of tea," Ned said. "Then you'll tell me about your travels."

Later, I asked him what he thought about a Nepalese nun coming to teach Buddhism. For a second he looked startled and then he grinned.

"Well, that would be a change."

"From Simon?"

"Of course."

"For the better?"

"I don't think Simon ever really liked the idea of teaching Buddhism. Landscapes, portraiture, lithography—fine. But Zen?" Ned shook his head. "He went through all those years of training in Japan for his *own* sake . . . He didn't want to have to deal with the young people who came traipsing to his door in the sixties. Even so, he agreed to—first, because however many times he turned them away, physically threw them out on occasion, they kept coming back. And second, out of duty to his teacher. And once he'd agreed, despite being on a New England *farm*, for heaven's sake, instead of in a Japanese monastery, he made a great effort to train them—me included—in the traditional way, the same way his teacher had trained *him*—'Don't explain anything to your students. Just pull and push them into one confusing situation after another and force them to respond . . .'

"He got a perverse joy out of making life difficult for us. But maybe that's true of all effective Zen teachers . . . Perversity is just the Zen way. From the start, I saw Simon was *tricky*. But to be honest, I was tricky myself . . . I kind of knew I was being *handled*," Ned continued, "and—perversely—I kind of enjoyed it. I guess I was able to keep a step ahead of him and never quite get thrashed. And in the long run, I benefited immensely."

"So what are you thinking?"

"That for years I thought, 'I've had enough of being jerked around and tripped up and manipulated. The very last thing I want is another teacher. Simon was more than enough for one lifetime,' is what I used to think. But now?" He smiled faintly.

"I do believe I'm over him... So, yes, I'm up for trying a different approach."

Ned took off his glasses and polished them with his handkerchief. When he'd put them back on his nose, he looked straight at me and grinned. "Shall we ask the others what *they* think about having a Nepalese nun come to teach us Buddhism?"

Printed in the United States
by Baker & Taylor Publisher Services